"Stunningly clear. Tightly focused. Brilliantly insightful. With this book, you can change the world. Without it, you'll be road kill."

—GUY KAWASAKI
FORBES COLUMNIST, CHIEF EVANGELIST OFFICER
OF GARAGE.COM, AND AUTHOR OF *RULES
FOR REVOLUTIONARIES*

"Once again, Terri Lonier tackles her subject with the thoroughness and gusto we've come to expect from her. Sharp entrepreneurs will find an abundance of smart strategies to help their businesses blossom. Keep this one within reach."

—BARBARA J. WINTER
AUTHOR OF *MAKING A LIVING WITHOUT A JOB*

"This book will help keep you from getting overwhelmed when you're ready to grow your business to the next level. Stay focused on one aspect of business at a time with this comprehensive resource guide!"

—TOM HOPKINS
MASTER SALES TRAINER AND AUTHOR OF
SELLING FOR DUMMIES AND *SALES
PROSPECTING FOR DUMMIES*

"If you've been looking for a sure-fire system to organize your continuing business success, it's all here in this book. Terri Lonier takes the mystery out of achieving precision performance. *Smart Strategies* is a big help every step of the way."

—JULIE MORGENSTERN
AUTHOR OF *ORGANIZING FROM THE
INSIDE OUT*

"There's no one smarter, savvier, or more experienced at the fine art of succeeding in the new economy than Terri Lonier. If you're an entrepreneur looking for hands-on advice about growing your business, you need this book: It's a mentor published between two covers."

—ALAN M. WEBBER
FOUNDING EDITOR, *FAST COMPANY* MAGAZINE

SMART STRATEGIES FOR GROWING YOUR BUSINESS

Also by Terri Lonier

Books
*Working Solo**

*Working Solo Sourcebook**

The Frugal Entrepreneur

The Small Business Money Guide (with Lisa M. Aldisert)*

Audio Programs
Working Solo: Getting Started

Working Solo: Getting Customers

* Published by John Wiley & Sons, Inc.

SMART STRATEGIES FOR GROWING YOUR BUSINESS

Terri Lonier

JOHN WILEY & SONS, INC.

New York · Chichester · Weinheim · Brisbane · Singapore · Toronto

Copyright © 1999 by Terri Lonier. All rights reserved.

Published by John Wiley & Sons, Inc.
Published simultaneously in Canada.

This publication is designed to provide accurate and authoritative information in regard to the subject matter covered. It is sold with the understanding that the author and publisher are not engaged in rendering professional services. If professional advice or other expert assistance is required, the services of a competent professional person should be sought.

Working Solo is a registered trademark and The Frugal Entrepreneur is a trademark of Terri Lonier. All other trademarks used in this book are the property of their respective holders.

Library of Congress Cataloging-in-Publication Data:

Lonier, Terri.
    Smart strategies for growing your business / Terri Lonier.
        p.   cm.
    Includes bibliographical references (p.   ) and index.
    ISBN 0-471-24800-2 (pa. : alk. paper)
    1. New business enterprises—Management. I. Title.
  HD62.5.L66   1999
   658.4'012—dc21   98-42280
                                               CIP

Printed in the United States of America.
10 9 8 7 6 5 4 3 2 1

Photo of author: Arthur L. Cohen

To David, Elaine, Harold, and Roxanne—

my virtual brain trust

(see Chapter 10)

Contents

Acknowledgments

A s experienced solo entrepreneurs know, one of the smartest strategies for business success is to build a team of exceptional colleagues. In writing this book, I have been fortunate to work with an outstanding group of individuals. Each played an important part in this project, and it's my pleasure to acknowledge them here.

First, thanks to editor and solo colleague Janice Borzendowski for sharing her talents and ideas and for asking the probing questions that helped to clarify my thinking. Special appreciation goes to Anne Allen, my managing associate, for her insights and personal entrepreneurial spark, and for keeping Working Solo, Inc. running smoothly as this project developed.

I am also indebted to other business colleagues who shared their ideas, experience, and encouragement along the way: David Garfinkel, Elaine Floyd, Harold Grubbs, Roxanne Emmerich, Terri Kabachnick, Tim Celeski, Carol Peskoe Schaner, Judith E. Dacey, Annelie Chapman, David Zach, Richard Thieme, Greg Godek, Lisa Aldisert, Somers White, Nido Qubein, Aldonna Ambler, Dan Alcorn, Nancy Rosanoff, Arthur Cohen, Sharon Good, Marilyn Leiker, Claire Winslow, Sheila Delson, Barbara Hemphill, Julie Morgenstern, Lloyd Jassin, and Shana Ross. In addition, hats off to the numerous solo entrepreneurs and small business owners I've encountered in my seminars and travels over the last two decades; your stories have inspired this book and my work in countless ways.

Appreciation also goes to Leslie Newman, Colleen Kelly, and Flora Wong at Newman Design/Illustration in Seattle for the illustrations and design assistance. Thanks, too, to Barrie Selack for serving as the Working Solo Webmaster.

I am grateful to my agent, Joe Spieler, and publishing consultant, Tom Woll, for their ongoing support of the Working Solo vision. Thanks, too, to Mike Hamilton, Laurie Frank, and the entire publishing team at John Wiley & Sons for helping me reach solo entrepreneurs and small business owners through the Working Solo series.

And last, but certainly not least, I thank my husband, Robert Sedestrom, who has seen from the inside how a business is affected by smart strategies. I'm grateful to him for sharing his strategic ideas, and for his companionship on this entrepreneurial adventure.

Preface

Strategize. Politicians do it; athletes do it; armies do it. And it's the most touted activity in business today. But probably for no one are strategies more important than for you, the solo entrepreneur or small business owner. As the leader of a small enterprise, you can't rely on a big corporate marketing department to plan your promotional activities for the next quarter, a sales staff to pitch your product or service, a research department to tell you which customer base to target, or an accounting department to direct you when to spend and when to save. It's up to you, the individual who wears all the hats of marketing, sales, research, accounting—and CEO.

Based on my encounters with thousands of entrepreneurs over the past two decades, my guess is that you implement strategies on a daily basis as you struggle to grow your independent business. But I'd also venture another guess: that too often you create your strategies on the fly, on an as-needed basis. This is understandable. When you're trying to do it all yourself, or with a very small staff, you don't have time to strategize in advance. Unfortunately, while spur-of-the-moment plans can be inventive, they're often not very effective; nor do they always provide the best path for your company.

That's why I wrote this book: to give you smart ways to strategize, before you're in a crunch situation and running out of time, energy, and perhaps money. *Smart Strategies for Growing Your Business* is about being proactive, about taking preventive steps to care for your business and yourself during the always-challenging growth stages.

Smart Strategies for Growing Your Business is the successor to my first book, *Working Solo,* which I'm proud to say has come to be regarded as a classic small business startup guide. This volume, the fourth in the Working Solo collection (along with *The Small Business Money Guide* and *Working Solo Sourcebook*), fulfills my goal to provide you, the solo entrepreneur and small business owner, with a comprehensive yet easy-to-use source of expert advice, practical aids, and food for thought that will give you what you need to initiate, then institute, strategies vital to the ongoing and long-term success of your business.

I think you'll find this new addition to your Working Solo library a valuable tool in creating a strategically sound future for your company. It comes with my best wishes for your prosperity.

Terri Lonier
November 1998

Introduction

When you started your business, it was no doubt one of the most exciting—and overwhelming—things you'd ever done. After a short time, however, you also realized an even greater challenge was still ahead: keeping your business going. No one told you there would be endless days when you would feel as if you were slogging through quicksand.

It's true, growth *is* more difficult than startup. Once the adrenaline rush of launch wears off, you're on your own to build your company, day by day, brick by brick. Along the way you'll feel frustrated, annoyed, envious, angry, and pull-your-hair-out exasperated. Of course, at other times you'll feel elated, proud, confident, thrilled, and pleased as punch. Often you'll also feel dog-tired.

I've experienced every one of these emotions, and more, during my 20 years in business—the first 18 of them working solo—and for a lot of those years I was dog-tired, too. But somewhere along the way, I learned that it's not how *hard* you work that sustains growth, it's how *smart* and *strategically* you work. As a business owner, there's only so much of you to go around, and you have to make every day count.

More than a million people start businesses every year. But only a handful are able to turn their business dreams into reality. Most wear themselves out and either give up or go bankrupt before ever learning to work smart. By sharing with you the strategies you need to work smart and prosper, this book is designed to make you one of the handful whose professional dreams do come true. Its aim is to cut years off your learning curve, enabling you to grow the business you've always dreamed about more quickly and easily.

Think of *Smart Strategies for Growing Your Business* as a trusty guide, pointing you in the right direction when you're standing at the crossroads without a clue which way to turn. Filled with sound advice and real-life examples, these pages are brimming with valuable lessons that you can use as practical shortcuts to get you where you want to go. And, unlike many business books, this one was written with you, the solo entrepreneur and small business owner, in mind. As a small business owner myself, I understand the fact that you have limited time and energy, and that you need to-the-point information as you grow your business. This book's structure was designed to enable you to get help when you need it—quickly and easily.

Smart Strategies for Growing Your Business features a total of 50 "mini-chapters" in seven easy-to-follow sections: "The Power of Strategies," "Vision Strategies," "Marketing and Sales Strategies," "Operations Strategies," "Money Strategies," "Expansion Strategies," and "Momentum Strategies." Each chapter is a bite-size mental morsel, written so that even the busiest and most stressed-out entrepreneur will have time to read and digest the strategy—and then turn it into action.

This structure was designed so that you won't have to feel guilty about spending money on another business book that ends up in a pile somewhere in your office. *Smart Strategies for Growing Your Business* won't daunt you with too many words about the latest and greatest management scheme from someone who has forgotten what it's like to be exhilarated, scared, exhausted—and in need of help—all at the same time. This is a book you can use while you're traveling from here to there, when you're ready to take a short break during your day, or when you want a brief insight about a new business challenge. It's a book that lets *you* decide how much you can take in and implement in your busy schedule. And from my years of working on my own I know that it's better to tackle a few modest tasks than to set grandiose plans and never follow through on a single one.

This guide is set up so that you can read about these strategies in any order you choose, based on your current needs. Essentially, you can "shop," then "buy" only those that will help you in your particular situation. (However, if you're a new small business owner, or just thinking about going out on your own, I recommend you read the book cover to cover to give you the proper groundwork you need.)

But don't read the chapters and stop there. If you do, these strategies will have served only as an interesting mental exercise. To give you the power you need to succeed, they need to be put into the context of your daily business life. To get you started, I've included a series of "Take Action" steps at the end of each chapter—simple, doable activities that help you put the strategies to work right away in your business.

Smart Strategies for Growing Your Business is also a launchpad for your ongoing business learning. Throughout these pages you'll find details on books, audio programs, software, and other tools to boost your business knowledge. As a bonus, at the back I've created an extensive resource section—really a small book-within-a-book—that's chock-full of valuable business learning tools to help you build your company. It's all designed to connect you with the information you need and to lead you to experts who know you and your specific business best.

This book is a compilation (a collaboration of sorts) of my own experiences as well as those of countless individuals I've encountered over the years who have generously shared their stories. In that spirit, I hope you'll become part of the ever-expanding community of entrepreneurs who, though they don't see each other every day (and maybe *never* meet), nonetheless become colleagues in the true sense of the word.

So as you and your business grow, I invite you to stay in touch. Let me know which strategies work best for you, and if you've found new ways to tackle our entrepreneurial challenges. And if you're at the stage where you want or need more information, all you need to do is reach out your hand (well, technically, your mouse) for more Working Solo resources. You can check out our free e-mail newsletter and Web site at www.workingsolo.com.

Keep me posted on your business success.

Terri Lonier
terri@workingsolo.com

THE POWER OF
STRATEGIES

.

Chapter 1

Understand What Strategies Are

Meet Chris and Kim, two computer consultants. Both started in business seven years ago with the same background, the same skill level, and the same type of work. Today, Chris works 24-hour weeks, has the eternal glow of good health, and dines and relaxes in resorts around the world. Kim, on the other hand, eats half-cooked meals from the microwave, has a pasty, ashen complexion, works 75 to 80 hours a week, and is on a first-name basis with collectors for Visa and MasterCard.

The difference? Seven years ago, Chris sat down and wrote a list of growth strategies for the business, referred to them every day—and followed them *to the letter.* Kim said loudly to everyone who brought up the subject, "Strategies? They're for corporate stiffs. I'm an *entrepreneur.* I live by my creative instincts. My entrepreneurial spirit is what I use instead of strategies."

This not-so-far-fetched tale—representative of thousands of entrepreneurs I've encountered over the past 20 years—illustrates the power of strategies, from Chris's carefully planned success to Kim's crumbling venture. Chris saw strategies for what they are: the tools of the trade for successful business owners.

In fact, as entrepreneurs we're not very different from tradespeople or construction professionals such as architects and builders. No, we don't lay bricks or spread mortar. But we do draw up plans and lay foundations (granted, of a different sort) upon which we build our businesses. And instead of levels, hammers, and nails, one of the most important tools in our toolbox is the concept of strategies.

But just what is a strategy? Ask a dozen entrepreneurs about strategies, and chances are you'll get a dozen different answers.

Everyone has his or her own ideas about what strategies are and how to put them to use in a business. So before we begin, let me define the term as I use it in this book. Strategies are one of the four elements—along with tactics, goals, and vision—that make up a series of essential business plans and actions. (See Figure 1.1.) Each builds upon the others, creating power and momentum. By differentiating these elements, we can clarify our current business position and determine how to maximize the time we spend on each element.

Smart Strategy

Strategies are the tools of the trade for successful business owners.

Let's return to the construction analogy, because it's helpful to view these important elements as building blocks—that is, as part of the expansion process. Employing one without the others will result in a shaky foundation incapable of sustaining the structure you build on top of it. In short, you'll have a business that doesn't suit or support your needs and doesn't function as well as it could and should. Let's take a look at each of these elements in greater detail.

Figure 1.1 Strategies are an integral part of business success. They give focus to the often-scattered energy of tactics, and bring power to goals and your larger business vision.

Have a Vision

Let's start at the top: the *vision*. This word derives from the Latin verb meaning "to see," but a vision is much grander than just seeing: It's foresight, it's imagination, it's an awareness of possibility. In business terms, having a vision means you can see into the future of your company. Think of vision as what you can see on the farthest horizon—for your company and yourself. To enable this stretch in your thinking, ask yourself these questions:

✓   What are my grandest ideas?

✓   What am I ultimately striving for?

✓   What do I want to leave as a legacy?

Let's go still further with the construction analogy. Imagine the type of structure you want to build to live in during your professional life. Do you envisage a castle or a high-rise? Perhaps a sprawling ranch is more your style. The point is, your life is an open tract of land awaiting the construction—the realization—of your vision. But the building process cannot begin until you are clear about what you want and what suits you best.

Too many small business owners never take time to reflect on these questions. I cannot stress strongly enough that this exercise is essential, because the answers form the foundation of meaning in a business—and a life. Without cementing these building blocks, you can waste years not achieving maximum results because your energies are scattered in a dozen different directions.

There are no "right" answers to these questions, so let your imagination run free when you're defining your vision. No one's looking, so go ahead. Make your vision as big and colorful—or as small and black-and-white—as you want. Give this vision the deep reflection it deserves. Figure out what matters to you. Figure out how you matter to the world. Go beyond today; consider the impact you want to have. A word of warning: Don't back down. Don't say too much in life is beyond your control. Accept my challenge: Find out how much really *is* under your control.

Many of us entrepreneurs are so action oriented that we balk at sitting down and *thinking* about something; we want something to *do!* Well, we'll get to that, too. The coming pages include some exercises that will help you sort through these important questions and lead you to the fulfillment of your vision.

Define Goals

If our vision is the destination, the ideal structure we see on the horizon, then goals are the substance, the sustenance, that gives flight to our ideas. For example, assuming you've chosen the type of building you want, you can now decide how many rooms it will have and how they will be furnished—the style and ambience you want to achieve.

Business goals are as diverse as the people who establish them. Some are no-brainers, such as "win enough clients to pay the rent and my salary." A goal can be as specific as "install a new graphics program so I can target that client who demands this capability from its vendors." A goal might be as short-term as "get this job done by Friday" or as long-term as "in 10 years I want to be reporting $10 million in sales."

Goals are measuring sticks; but on these sticks, we get to draw the dividing marks. We determine what we'd like to achieve during a specific time frame; we design a particular outcome. You define your goals to meet *your* needs.

Goals are also your guideposts, established to keep you on the right path and to help you assess your progress.

Manage Tactics

We all wrestle with innumerable tasks that fill up our daily To-Do lists. Most new business owners (and many experienced ones, too) are all too familiar with activities that can take us in a dozen different directions at the same time, scattering our focus, until at the end of the day we're exhausted—but find ourselves wondering whether we've accomplished anything of importance.

No doubt about it, such tasks can derail the most capable business owner. That's why it's important to make the distinction between a tactic, an approach to accomplishing something, and an activity, which, while necessary, could be assigned a lower priority or delegated elsewhere, freeing you to keep your eye on the prize.

Formulate Strategies

Unlike establishing a vision, defining goals, and employing daily tactics, which are individual undertakings, strategies can be shared, adapted, and refined among other entrepreneurs in other fields.

Strategies are the blueprints you draw to help you achieve your goals; they are the systems you use to get yourself where you want to be. Employing strategies is putting brain before brawn, planning before you act. Strategies are so important that I had no difficulty filling an entire book with them! But to give you the power you need to succeed, strategies must be put in the context of your business "building"—integrated with your vision, your goals, and your tactics.

As you explore the strategies in this book, keep in mind the story of Chris and Kim, the two entrepreneurs we met at the beginning of this chapter. Chris and Kim were alike in so many ways when their business adventures began; the defining difference in their success was their individual approach to strategies. What Chris learned and Kim ignored is a key entrepreneurial lesson: More than money or title or intelligence, the important ingredient in business success is thinking—*strategically.* In the chapters ahead, you'll learn how to put this power to work for your business.

Take Action

1. Imagine your business as a building: What type of structure do you see? Take some time to brainstorm the possibilities.

2. Look back on the last six months of your business life. How have you spent most of your time? What percentage of your time was spent tackling low-level activities? How much time did you devote to seeing a bigger picture?

3. How has the structure of your business changed since the day you launched it? Has it haphazardly taken on a life of its own? Or has it expanded under your close direction, with your vision clearly in focus?

Chapter 2

Put Strategies to Work for You

Now that you have an understanding of what a strategy is and how it fits into the pyramid of business growth, let's take a look at how and when you can put strategies to best use in your business, starting with when to implement them.

Many business owners think that strategies come into play only during periods of intense planning. It's true that business planning periods generally feature the development and implementation of strategies. But strategic thinking should play an important role in the *daily activities* of any business that wants to survive and—more important—thrive in today's global and increasingly competitive marketplace.

Smart Strategy

Strategic thinking should play an important role in the daily activities of any business that wants to survive and thrive in today's global marketplace.

Study the following situations for hints on how you might more effectively use strategies in your business.

✓ *I'm just starting out.* At no time are strategies more important than when you're launching a business. They enable you to clearly think through what you want to achieve and streamline the process of getting there. If you're in this stage, it's essential that you take time to consider many different strategies, explore their power, and learn to use a few very well.

✓ *I've been in business for a while, and I need a boost.* The ongoing stress of keeping a business going can numb you to the world around you. Without your realizing it, your patterns may have become ruts, and exploring new strategies may seem equivalent to having a bucket of cold water dumped on your head: It's a shock, but it wakes you up and forces you to open your eyes to what's been happening while you were in a stress fog.

✓ *We just lost a major client.* You can often untie that knot in your stomach and quell the rising sense of panic this situation causes with some clear-headed strategic thinking. A business owner always has options, even if you have trouble believing it as you feel your way through the darkness of the down times.

✓ *We just gained a major client.* The thrill of expansion can quickly turn to terror if you don't carefully plan how you intend to take your business to the next level. There's risk in stretching too far too fast, so put on your strategic thinking cap and make sure you grow in a way that spells security to your business.

✓ *A new competitor has emerged.* In today's global marketplace, competitors can spring up overnight. Strategies can help you place them in perspective and point out ways to minimize their impact.

✓ *A terrific opportunity has presented itself.* When you're facing what seems to be a once-in-a-lifetime opportunity, be sure you can maximize its potential. Take a clear-headed look at what the potential benefits and pitfalls may be.

✓ *I can't choose among the many appealing options.* Sometimes we're like children in a candy store, distracted by all the possibilities. Our heads spin, and our business goes nowhere as we get caught up in the vacuum of not deciding. With strategies carefully in place, you'll always know the next step to take.

✓ *I'm drowning in the daily details.* No doubt about it, the mundane tasks of keeping a business running can obscure the grand plans you've set for yourself. To help you break through the mental and physical clutter so you can stay energized and focused on what's really important, you need to establish strategies.

✓ *A key staff member or associate is leaving.* No business ever remains in a state of equilibrium for long. When changes take place, strategies will help you remain on course and more smoothly make the transition to the next stage.

✓ *I'd like to retire or move on to something else.* When it's time to make the biggest change of all—to leave the business behind—you need to think strategically to maximize the results and minimize the impact.

Though I'm certain you can come up with other situations that leave you staring at the ceiling at 3 A.M. or distract you during your working hours, I'm just as sure you'll discover that designing and implementing strategies can guide you through any difficult or confusing period. By helping you clarify your thinking and take action, strategies can be both preventive medicine for your business and the cure for an already symptomatic situation.

Take Action

1. List the top three situations you are facing in your business today in which strategies can help.

2. Recall a challenge from your business past that you didn't meet as well as you'd have liked. Then ask: How well did I use strategies to address the situation?

3. Look outside your "own backyard": Is there someone you admire (in any endeavor, whether personal or professional) whose strategizing capabilities always help him or her to solve problems, ease difficult dilemmas, and in general make life easier? What can you learn from this person that would help you in your business?

VISION
STRATEGIES

Chapter 3

Know Yourself

There are a lot of different ways to create and/or choose the strategies you'll use to grow your business. Some you'll get from this book; others will come from the success of colleagues as they grow their companies. Perhaps you'll even tweak a few to make them uniquely yours. But no matter where your strategic inspiration comes from, it's important to remember this one guideline: For strategies to work, they must start from the inside out. You must know from the top of your head to the tips of your toes that the strategies you are about to implement will enable you to achieve even your loftiest goals.

Yes, this may seem obvious; but before you dismiss it as such, let me point out that knowing and believing something with such conviction is not so easy. In fact, it may be the most difficult part of growing your business—which is why most entrepreneurs never tackle it.

Why is it so challenging? Because it requires you to step back from your daily rush of activity and honestly assess what you value in your life and in your work. It forces you to answer questions about why you're devoting all this time, energy, and money to an entrepreneurial endeavor; it requires you to reclaim the clarity of your initial vision of your business.

Smart Strategy

For strategies to work, they must start from the inside out. You must know from the top of your head to the tips of your toes that the strategies you are about to implement will enable you to achieve even your loftiest goals.

Track Change

Chances are, when you launched your company, you had some fairly definite ideas about what you wanted to achieve. Maybe you had a certain income quota in mind; or perhaps you craved greater flexibility so you could spend more time with your family. Some of these ideas may just have been thoughts, unspoken guidelines that led you through the early stages of your business.

But as you no doubt have discovered, businesses become more complex as they grow. Opportunities emerge that can take you down paths you never imagined exploring. Suddenly you find yourself light-years away from your initial ideas, and you wonder how you got to the place you're at now.

This phenomenon is common to new homeowners. They buy a small, simple, but functional house that is beautiful in its simplicity. Then one day they decide to add a bedroom, then another bathroom. Suddenly the kitchen seems too small. Without really realizing it, they've built a whole new wing, doubling the floor space of the original structure.

How successful will the design of such a construction be? That depends on how well the owners planned the additions and how focused they were on their original vision for the house. We've all seen sprawling, unstyled homes that are the result of accumulated casual decisions made with no consideration for the relationship of each part to the whole.

Maintain Your Focus

Many businesses grow in the same uncontrolled, happenstance manner. Without a strong guidance system, an entrepreneur may suddenly realize that his or her organization has little in common with his or her original intentions.

Growth, of course, is natural, particularly in this era of global communication that enables us to respond so quickly—really, instantaneously—to marketplace changes. But "natural" often means haphazard for small business owners. We frequently wind up following this meandering trail, focusing only on the section that's immediately under our feet. It's only later, when we look up, that we are startled to find how far off our original course we've wandered.

To retain your focus, ask yourself this deceptively simple question on a regular basis: "What's most important to me?" I can't overstate how important it is that you clarify what you value in your business and your life. And if these values change over time—as they undoubtedly will—you must be honest about that, too. You are the only person who can answer this question. You can't delegate reflective thinking.

Identify Your Drivers

To jump-start your thinking about your values, consider these five driving factors, which I've labeled the "five Fs": fortune, fame, family, freedom, and fun. They are primary motivators for any entrepreneur. Let's take a look at each one.

- ✓ *Fortune.* Many entrepreneurs place fortune first on their list of goals. After deeper thought, however, they usually find that the accumulation of money, while certainly important, is not necessarily where they derive their greatest satisfaction. Probably more gratifying is acknowledging how closely their bottom line is tied to *their* efforts, talent, and capabilities. So though they may not strike it rich overnight, as they work to build their business, they will reap the rewards that come from being responsible for its growth.

- ✓ *Fame.* A healthy love of self is another key driver of entrepreneurs. They are very comfortable seeing their name in lights—or (more commonly) on company letterhead. Making their mark on the world is part of why they struck out on their own in the first place.

- ✓ *Family.* Many solo entrepreneurs seek a better way to balance the competing demands of their home and professional lives. They want to be able to spend more quality time with their families, and they want to provide a good livelihood for their loved ones.

✓ *Freedom.* Not surprisingly, more important than money to many entrepreneurs is the ability to call their own shots. Many turn down better-paying jobs because they place a high value on working for themselves; they want to set their own schedule, to ensure that it honors the needs of both their clients and their family. And they want the freedom to pursue new prospects when these come along.

✓ *Fun.* There often isn't a lot of tolerance (or respect) for self-expression in the corporate workaday world. Entrepreneurs in general are creative individuals who need an environment in which they can express their personalities in the context of a business. Incorporating a sense of self is also the way they ensure that those intangible inner, spiritual needs are met.

Rank Your Priorities

Once you've evaluated these important life drivers, it's time to prioritize them. Don't be fooled into thinking they carry equal weight—for example, assuming that fortune and family should have equal billing because you want a business that provides a good income for your family. In your daily life as a busy entrepreneur, chances are good that you'll have to choose between financial achievements and spending time with your family. You need to know for yourself, when it comes to that, where to place your emphasis.

The intent of this ranking exercise is to clarify your thinking, to free you to create a business that is aligned with who you are and what you want out of life both personally and professionally. Until you are clear about that, outside forces will continue to dictate your decisions.

So take the time to rank these five motivators—fortune, fame, family, freedom, and fun—and assess what they truly mean in your business and your life. Doing so will give you a rock-solid foundation for the all-important decision-making process that is part and parcel of running your own business. You'll also discover qualities about yourself that you may have overlooked or forgotten. Most important, you'll achieve a clarity of focus about your business that no book, coach, or outside resource can provide.

One final word: As you and your business develop and change, these priorities will as well. They'll also be affected when new opportunities arise and when your business grows in new directions. When you find yourself at a crossroad, unable to decide which way to turn, repeat the exercise. Ask yourself what means most to you. Let's face it: The answer is the core of who you are.

Take Action

1. Spend some quiet time thinking about what drives you in your entrepreneurial endeavors. Rank the five factors listed here according to the importance they have in your business today. Then rank them in the order in which you'd like them to appear.

2. List any traits or aspects of yourself that you would like to make better use of in your business.

3. Think about how you've changed since you launched your business. Have your driving factors altered? If so, what caused the shift? Do you like the changes? How might your drivers change in the future?

Chapter 4

Be Clear About the Business You're In

Now that you have clarified your values, it's time to refine your business focus. The strategy to help you achieve that is to define precisely what business you're in. This involves more than just being able to say or write down what you do and who your customers are.

This strategy, too, requires you to do some thinking. If you're the action-oriented type, you must persevere in this effort. I know you'd rather be out there *doing* something, but I assure you that the time you spend in thoughtful planning will pay off when it comes time to take action.

Consider Yourself a Piece of the Global Puzzle

If you ask most small business owners what business they're in, their responses generally will center on the activities they perform for their customers: "Oh, we do PR consulting," or "I'm a landscape designer," or "My company sells. . . ."

Smart Strategy

Be sure you can describe precisely what business you're in. This involves more than just being able to say or write down what you do and who your customers are.

There are two important elements missing from these answers: First, they completely overlook any marketing power that could come from a really powerful introduction. (We'll be discussing this in more detail in Chapter 11, "Craft a Powerful Introduction.") More important, they reveal that the business owners haven't taken time to step back and see how their companies fit into a much broader picture of worldwide business.

Some of you may be scoffing, wondering how, for example, a simple widget maker who may be operating a solo business could possibly fit into a global economy. Such a response is an indicator of an all-too-common narrow viewpoint. Consider:

✓ The widget company probably buys materials for its product from another (perhaps solo) business. These materials may come from nearby or from halfway around the world.

✓ The widget maker may use the services of an advertising firm (probably another small business) that may create the company's Web site to attract global customers.

✓ The widget company may distribute its product through a business dedicated to that service. It may ship its products to nearby locales or to distant lands.

✓ The widget maker probably purchases paper products (boxes, packing materials, and the like) from yet another business. Some of these materials also may come from another country.

Even if your company doesn't sell products or services directly to global markets, your business is still part of the world economy. Adopting this perspective will help you form a vision of the business you're in. Ask yourself: How do my activities as an individual, and my activities as a company, fit into the worldwide marketplace?

For most small business owners, the answer to these questions is both humbling and empowering. Yes, we may be pretty small potatoes in relation to the planetary picture, but on the other hand, the activities of our individual companies often become part of a remarkable chain reaction affecting other businesses, thus fueling a global economy.

Assess Your Capabilities

Another step you need to take to achieve clarity about your business focus is to determine which of your capabilities are unique and can be leveraged to serve your customers. Each business brings specific assets to the marketplace, ranging from something as tangible as a physical infrastructure to more intangible items such as proprietary methods or the intellectual firepower of a single individual. Which assets have you overlooked or underplayed in your company? Let the following examples jump-start your thinking.

Understand Your Market and Your Assets

The Williams Companies, a large corporation and a major player in the oil and gas industry primarily in the southern United States, was faced several years ago with the uncertain nature of the oil and gas market. Management took a long, hard look at the company's capabilities in conjunction with the future they envisioned for their business. They recognized that remaining solely in the oil and gas business was not the best option for future growth potential, so they looked at their corporate assets and where the market was going, and decided they could—and should—shift their focus.

One of the major assets of the Williams Companies was the 11,000 miles of pipeline they owned throughout the southern states. Management realized that the company's most important asset was not the oil and gas that traveled through that pipeline, but the network itself. In a brilliant moment of corporate clarity, they realized they were not in the oil and gas business, they were in the *distribution* business. Oil and gas were just commodities they were transporting.

After reviewing market needs, Williams took a bold move. They flushed out their vast network of pipelines and sent small robots into the system to clean it out. What replaced the oil and gas was the fuel of the future: fiber-optic cable. A new subsidiary, Williams Communications, was born, and is now one of the leading telecommunications companies in the world.

Gain a New Perspective

This shift in perspective can happen in the smallest of businesses as well. On a recent trip to Denver, Colorado, I hopped into a cab to get back to my hotel from the convention center where I had delivered the keynote speech. I always enjoy chatting with entrepreneurial types, and cab and limo drivers often are among the most creative in spotting and taking advantage of business opportunities. About 15 minutes into my ride, the driver handed me his business card while we were stopped at a traffic light, explaining that he and his partner would be pleased to be my "on-call" drivers during the rest of my stay in Denver. Intrigued, I asked him for details.

Jerry Gonzales and Andy Lohr have made the shift from taxi drivers to entrepreneurs in the prompt transportation business. They lease their cab from the taxi company, and, each driving 12-hour shifts, offer 24-hour on-call service, primarily to regular customers who schedule appointments for transport to doctors' offices, grocery stores, health clubs, even to the vet with their pets. The pair fill any open time slots with radio calls forwarded to them from the taxi company.

Jerry and Andy understand the unique capabilities they can offer their customers. Instead of waiting for radio calls to come in each day to make their fare quotas, they've created their own company-within-a-company. They're clear about the business they are in: the prompt transportation business. And to ensure that they're prompt—and that they maintain a loyal clientele—they keep a cell phone with them at all times so they can make appointments and alert clients when they will be more than a few minutes late to pick them up. They also keep the cab neat and clean so that customers are assured of a pleasant ride. And, as savvy business owners, they accept major credit cards.

Determining the business you're in often won't cost you a single cent from your budget, yet it can be invaluable to your business. The shift is one of attitude, outlook, and perspective. Think about your business as it exists now, and where you want it to be in the future. How does that image compare with the business it often *appears* that you're in? Now dig a little deeper and consider what business you're *really* in. What you find may surprise you—and lead you to an exciting new vision for your company.

Take Action

1. Examine your current business practices, then, based on what you've read in this chapter, consider what your business might become.

2. Identify the unique capabilities you provide to the marketplace through your business.

3. List three other uses to which you could adapt your current capabilities.

Chapter 5

Model a Mentor

No matter what size your company or how long you've been in business, no doubt you will often wonder, "What do I do next?" Standing in the midst of the forest that is your businesses, you won't be able to see the individual trees that line the path to your success. When you feel this way, it's time to seek out guides. Fortunately, in this digitally connected era, it's easier than ever to find them.

Face the Blank Page

Individual business owners approach the uncertainties that arise while their businesses are growing in different ways. Some are energized by the possibilities these uncertainties reveal, while others freeze in the track of indecisiveness; sometimes they engage in a back-and-forth approach, moving forward on the good days, staring into space on the bad ones.

Smart Strategy

In the absence of the perfect mentor, we have to take a patchwork approach to getting the help and advice we need. It's a process of piecing together the strengths, intelligence, and experience of many individuals along the way.

I call this the "blank-page syndrome," because it's similar to what writers deal with when first sitting down to write. Even professional writers can be terrorized by the vast, untouched expanse of paper or computer screen that seems to taunt them, daring them to say something—anything! Of course, there are those who dive right in, throwing ideas out as fast as they occur, knowing they'll sort them out later.

While growing your business, you can't afford to be paralyzed by indecision, nor can you waste your time trying out every single idea that crosses your mind. One way to balance the queasy sensation that comes from rocking between action and indecision is to enlist the help of mentors.

Seek Someone

In the early years of my business, I longed for a mentor, someone whom I respected and who was willing to take me under his or her experienced wing and guide me along the rocky decision-making and growth path. Needless to say, I envisioned this person to be kind, wise, and always there to sagely answer any question or solve any problem I had. Then, as my fantasy went, at the end of a decade or so, I would turn to this person and express how grateful I was for all he or she had taught me.

Snap! Just like that, my fantasy ended—as they all do—courtesy of reality. I looked high and low for this person for a long time, but I've yet to meet that individual who could devote the time and energy necessary to serve as my business guide.

Perhaps you've been one of the lucky ones. I have met entrepreneurs who have been greatly influenced and supported by a single person, whether it was the owner of a company at which they worked in their early years or a more experienced colleague with whom they bonded. My guess is, however, that your experience has been more like mine, and therefore that's the situation this chapter addresses.

In the absence of the perfect mentor, we have to take a patchwork approach to getting the help and advice we need. It's a process of piecing together the strengths, intelligence, and experience of many individuals along the way. In essence, you create your own mentor.

As you might guess, this mentor mélange has both benefits and drawbacks. Though you will have to spend more time reaching out to many individuals in a variety of venues, when you're finished you will have in hand the collective experience of a number of knowledgeable people, which far surpasses the wisdom any single person is likely to have.

But before you begin modeling your own mentor, you must identify those areas in your business in which you need guidance. This is necessary to avoid wasting your time as well as that of the professionals you choose to contact.

For example, if you're unclear about how to finance an expansion effort, spend some time determining what information you need. Then tap your network and set up interviews to collect ideas from business owners who have already been through this process. Ask them what worked for them, what they would have done differently, and—most important—what issues you may have overlooked in considering the matter. Also ask for referrals of others to interview. Compare notes from several such discussions, then craft the plan that suits you and your business best.

Make Virtual Contacts

A mentoring experience isn't always in the form of an in-person encounter. Long ago I realized that my chances of finding a single mentor were slim, particularly because I chose to remain in the relatively rural setting of New York's Hudson Valley. Therefore, my own mentors have derived from many sources, including books and other publications, audiotapes, and information gleaned from the Internet. I made it a practice to actively seek out the best and brightest business minds through the work they shared in print and other formats. In some cases, this has led to an exchange of ideas by letters and, more recently, by e-mail. As is the case with real-life mentors, many of these virtual mentors will probably never realize how they have influenced my work and that of others.

If you're struggling to gain some clarity and to find direction as your business grows, consider these actions that can help you to find the answers and information you need. One word of advice here: No matter how you choose to find mentors, always be sure to get *multiple sources* of feedback. This will enable you to compile the best course of action for your business.

   ✓ *Identify.* Write a list of those things that have been needling you—problem areas you realize you need help tackling, or decisions that you continually postpone because you lack the time to address them adequately or simply don't know where to begin.

✓ *Explore.* Look for articles in business or trade publications that relate to your questions. Keep your eyes and ears open to presentations in your community given by experts in the field that directly address your concerns. Go to the library and/or bookstore and cruise the shelves for relevant titles.

✓ *Seek counsel.* Choose the counseling approaches that work best for you. You may be more comfortable reading information, for example, than speaking with an individual after a presentation. Contact people through a letter or e-mail; this has the added benefit of allowing them to respond when it's convenient for them. And if the person you're interested in reaching is a fellow member of a professional trade organization, why not just pick up the phone and call?

✓ *Analyze.* Whether you need a one-time assist with a particular business decision or are looking for an active, ongoing coaching relationship, figure out how to set up the relationship to get the most from it. You may want to conduct a self-study course in your spare time, or attend a class or weekend workshop at a local community college. Make sure to choose sources and venues that fit your time frame and suit the way you like to get information.

✓ *Act.* Once you've identified several sources and made some decisions, start to implement them. Set up a schedule that includes reading, taking classes, or networking.

✓ *Evaluate.* Assign a time frame to your actions—say one new activity a quarter, or a once-a-week commitment to do research in the business section of your local library. This will enable you to more specifically evaluate the return on your investment of time, energy, and money.

✓ *Revise.* Step back once in a while and make adjustments as necessary. If you've been primarily reading articles and books, for example, it may be time to add some one-on-one contacts to your mentoring portfolio.

Consult the Mentor Within

As you sort through your business growth decisions, one often-overlooked strategy that can be very effective for many business owners is to consult the mentor within. People who are working solo or who are in charge often already have the answers in hand, but are too busy or too full of doubt to listen to themselves.

Sharon Good, a business coach in New York City, offers a simple but powerful method of tapping into this internal mentor. When her clients are faced with a challenge or decision, she encourages them to ask themselves a single question: "What would a winner do?"

This single query can jolt your thinking to a new level. It often forces you out of the muddle of confusion and mentally places you in a new position, from which you can gain a fresh perspective. Suddenly, you're no longer the harried business owner struggling to find the answers. You're the entrepreneur who has the courage to step out on your own, capable of moving forward to the next level of success.

Take Action

1. Look for an organization (preferably with a local chapter in your area) from whose membership you can identify someone that might be able to guide you through a problem area.

2. Take the most pressing business decision you're facing today and ask how a winner would approach it.

3. Check out SCORE (Service Corps of Retired Executives), a program partner of the Small Business Administration that provides free and low-cost business counseling at nearly 400 centers throughout the United States. SCORE volunteer advisors are also available for free online counseling via the SCORE Web site at http://www.score.org. To locate the SCORE office nearest you, call (800) 634-0245.

Chapter 6

Script Your Vision in Technicolor

W hen business owners talk about the vision they have for their companies, it's often described in financial terms: "We expect to generate *x* dollars in revenue this year." "We're targeting to increase our sales by *x* percent in the next six fiscal quarters." Without question, financial benchmarks are valuable ways to define your vision, but beware: By making them the primary indicators, you may render your vision one-dimensional.

In the same way a silent black-and-white film can't capture the full impact of emotion and action the way movies today can, numbers represent just one measure, one perspective of a business vision. If your vision is only the numbers written on a piece of paper or entered into the cells of a spreadsheet program, you will probably find it difficult to sustain the enthusiasm, focus, and commitment you had when you began your entrepreneurial career. Give your image—and thus your future—color and life. Make it real.

Direct a Mental Movie

One of the best ways to bring your future ideas to life is to create a mental movie of what it will be like when your future has arrived. This visualization technique has been used successfully by professional athletes for years.

Smart Strategy

Once you plant the image of a clearly defined goal in your subconscious, your mind goes to work making the goal come to fruition.

Recall the last time you watched Olympic skiers preparing for their descent down a near-vertical slope. Totally focused, many stand with eyes closed, gently swaying back and forth. They're tuning out the clamor and excitement all around them, concentrating on visualizing the achievement of their goal. They're playing a personal mental movie of each detail of their run: every turn down the hill, every bend of their bodies, every dip in the terrain.

Professional athletes know that to reap the power from this technique they must achieve mind over matter. This means understanding that the subconscious does not differentiate between the real and unreal. Once you plant the image of a clearly defined goal in your subconscious, your mind goes to work making the goal come to fruition.

Used in this way, visualization can be a powerful tool for taking your business to the next level. It's one way you can help transform the mental movie of your business vision into reality.

Embrace the Future

To help you create a vivid mental image of your future, I'm going to ask you to perform this simple exercise I often conduct with my audiences when I'm speaking around the country. In some ways, it's the equivalent of jumping into a time machine and transporting yourself a few years into the future.

1. To achieve the best results, find a spot that's quiet and comfortable. Have a blank sheet of paper and a pen or pencil handy. Relax; quiet your mind. Take as much time as you need to reach a state of peacefulness. Don't try to rush it, or the rest of the exercise will be a waste of time.

2. Now, imagine it's three years from now and you're walking into your favorite room (perhaps it's in that building you mentally constructed in Chapter 1). Figure out the precise date. "Feel" the season; imagine what the weather is like.

3. While you're three years into the future, and in your favorite room, go over and shake hands with *yourself.* Mentally record the ensuing conversation you're having with yourself. What

does this future you look like? What are you wearing? Where are you living? What are you doing? What is your life like?

4. When you're finished time-traveling, take 60 seconds to quickly write down your instinctive thoughts about this encounter. Don't analyze them; the point is to just capture your first impressions and as many details as you can recall.

5. Take a deep breath and then begin to review your experience with this exercise. Did you have difficulty imagining your life three years from now? Did you realize that you had never considered your future adequately before? How did your first impressions align with other ideas and plans you might have made about the future of your business previous to taking this exercise?

Often when I present this exercise I hear soft gasps as people meet their future selves. Sometimes it can be an uncomfortable feeling, but trust me, once you've taken this journey, your planning efforts will never be quite the same again. You will have opened a door to your future, one you won't be able to—and probably won't want to—close again.

Come Back from the Future

Now that you have a clear idea of where you'd like your business to be in three years, let's come back from the future to fill in those intervening years.

Two-Year Milepost

To start, I recommend you take one specific aspect of your three-year vision and consider what needs to happen *two years* from now for that single aspect to become a reality within the three-year time frame. For guidance, ask yourself some pointed questions, such as:

✓   What personal changes will I have to make to enable me to accomplish this goal?

✓   At what level of development will my business need to be? Will I have to hire help? Will I need more space?

✓ Will I need to learn new skills?

✓ Will new systems need to be in place in my business?

One-Year Milepost

Continue coming back from the future using the same question-and-answer process to get to the one-year mark. Develop a detailed list of what needs to be done every step of the way. Pull out a calendar and mark the milestones you've established for the next 12 months.

Be There Now

Your vision of your future will, of course, extend beyond just the next three years. But this exercise is a useful tool for getting you accustomed to thinking in a lengthier time frame. Often people have no trouble imagining where they'll be three years or five years from now, but have difficulty reaching, for example, to ten years from now. With practice, however, you'll be able to think as far into the future as you want, while working to ensure that your actions in the present are moving to take you there.

Take Action

1. Post your "future" where you will see it every day—perhaps on the refrigerator door or the bathroom mirror. And if you stop seeing it, really seeing it, move it to a new place.

2. If you don't meet one of your intermediary goals, take the time to regroup: Find out what happened; determine whether your failure was for legitimate reasons (for example, you got sick, your computer system crashed, and so forth). Be honest!

3. Increase your creative thinking skills by reading *99% Inspiration: Tips, Tales & Techniques for Liberating Your Business Creativity* by Bryan Mattimore (Amacom Books, 1994).

Chapter 7

Commit Your Vision to Paper

Keeping in mind the imaging exercise you just practiced to form a clear picture of both your long-term and intermediate three-year goals, let's explore additional strategies to help you move these ideas from a picture in your head to a tangible result.

Most successful business owners understand the power of putting ideas on paper, realizing that even the most simple plans remain fuzzy and frustratingly out of reach until they make the transition from image to paper. In fact, putting plans on paper may be the most important business strategy of all. Without it, your ideas may never become reality. Ironically, though they recognize the value of this strategy, most business owners resist writing down their plans, for two key reasons:

✓ It's hard work.

✓ They consider it boring.

The first objection is legitimate; writing business plans *is* hard work, and therefore requires a lot of energy. You have to think through all the details of your plan, and that can leave your head throbbing. But, I assure you, the results are always worth the effort.

As to the second objection, that writing business plans is boring, I disagree; it doesn't have to be. The key is to find your own style and give your natural expressive tendencies free rein. (And don't say you don't have expressive tendencies! We all do—it's just a matter of tapping into them.)

There are two distinct steps to the planning process:

1. Generate an idea.
2. Refine that idea.

Don't try to jump ahead to a finished concept; you must give yourself time to explore. And be sure to leave enough mental space to allow for unexpected possibilities to emerge.

Smart Strategy

Thought → word → deed: By committing your vision to paper, you clarify your ideas and give form to your future.

When my audiences take part in the exercise of imagining their future, each person creates a unique image. Some, for example, tell me they can't form specific pictures; instead they get inklings of ideas, or pieces of a diagram. There are even those who report seeing only fields of color.

These are all natural variations on a theme. Each of us, as a result of both our innate abilities and our training, will choose a different way to represent our ideas. No doubt, in this technological age, many would choose to sit at a computer keyboard and type out a paragraph or two of description. Others might grab a fine-line marking pen and itemize an outline on grid paper. Another group might translate ideas using colored pens or pencils on drawing paper. You get the picture (pun intended). The point is, none of these approaches is better or worse than another; however, there probably is one that is best for you, that enables you to express yourself most freely. That's the one you have to determine. To that end, let's take a look at some creative options.

Set Idea Nets

When you're trolling your subconscious for business ideas, it's important to set the right bait so that the "big-fish" concepts don't get away; often, it's important to set an idea "net," as well. The reason for this is that frequently you will go off on a fishing expedition to catch one type of fish, only to find that the waters you are in offer another option or opportunity you hadn't considered when you set out.

You've probably noticed that your flashes of insight usually don't occur in an organized, linear fashion. (There are those who believe that linear thinking operates independently of the creative process, and can even hinder it.) Consequently, insights may resist capture in a structure such as an outline. As you're trying to make sense of your ideas, your mind switches gears so quickly that logical development of the idea often is lost. Therefore, I suggest that the next time your ideas start to flow, you set one of these "nets" instead:

✓ *Mind map.* By mind mapping I mean that you should conduct a free-form brainstorming session on paper. To begin, jot down your main idea in a circle; let your mind wander to the next natural connection, then draw another circle for that thought and link it to the first. The goal is, at the end of your mind-mapping session, to have a map of the meanderings of your mind, which often reveals new ideas and relationships that you hadn't considered previously.

✓ *Diagram.* Diagramming your idea lets you show the relationships among parts of a whole. This can be a great way to get ideas down while simultaneously indicating the way the components relate to each other.

✓ *Flowchart.* Similar to diagrams, flowcharting is another way of jotting down your ideas and then watching the relationship patterns emerge from among those ideas. Flowcharts, however, establish a sequence to the movement of the ideas, for a more logical framework.

✓ *Color.* A lot of people do their best thinking in color, so if you're one of them, gather colored pens or pencils and paper and go to it. Let different colors suggest actions and emotional associations; use the entire spectrum; mine your subconscious for possibilities.

✓ *Clip and paste.* Inspiration can come when and where you least expect it. So be ready to be motivated by images all around you every day. And when you see something you want to use, be it in the newspaper, a magazine, or on the back of a cereal box, clip it out and file it. Then, when you have enough images, create a storyboard from them and see what evolves. Certain pictures will "talk" to you. Pull those out and arrange them on paper in ways that clarify your thinking and keep you motivated.

✓ *Index.* Working within a small, finite format such as a 3 × 5 index card is good for capturing those individual gems or fragments of a larger idea. A side benefit is that the cards readily lend themselves to organizing (indexing) later—into outlines or narratives. Change your plan? Just shuffle the cards into a new order.

✓ *Post.* Those how-did-we-live-without-'em Post-it Notes can function like 3 × 5 cards; you can jot and stick anywhere, anytime, then create a working outline that can easily be adapted, changed, or discarded. And now that these notes come in myriad colors and sizes, the possibilities are endless!

Each of these approaches is intended to tap into the nonlinear part of your brain—where those really good ideas are often lurking! Choose one or a combination to unleash the business artist within.

Fine-Tune the Picture

Once you've captured your ideas, it's time to translate them into an action plan. That pile of 3 × 5 cards may hold the next big breakthrough in your business, but how do you get there from here?

Now is the time to let that part of your brain that wants to structure and organize things do its work:

1. Review your ideas; analyze what steps you think you need to take to initiate the realization of each.
2. Try the reverse timeline approach described in the last chapter. For example, consider from the perspective of the completion date and go backward to the beginning.
3. Think in terms of timelines, milestones, calendars, or outlines.

Like focusing the lens on a camera, try to sharpen that mental picture you have of your business future using small movements.

Again, choose whatever form works for you: text, a well-thought-out diagram, or a flowchart.

Implement and Update

Having a plan, as crucial as it is, is only the first step. It's not an end unto itself; you have to *implement* the plan before it can add value to your business. So resist the temptation to file it away; instead, post it in your office where you can see it every day. Refer to it when you're planning next week, next month, next quarter, or next year.

I was impressed by an entrepreneurial colleague who faxed me his entire three-year business plan for a multimedia company on a single sheet of paper several years ago. It was a wonderfully detailed drawing of his vision for the company. And to stay focused on it, he pinned a copy on his wall and carried a reduced version in his wallet.

Finally, remember, the best plans are updated regularly. The goal is to craft a useful and powerful tool for your business.

Take Action

1. Develop a preliminary plan, using one of the methods (or your own hybrid) described in this chapter. Pinpoint the first three steps you'll need to take to set this plan in motion.

2. Refine your plan into a working document and/or diagram. Establish milestones and deadlines.

3. Check out business planning books such as *Business Plans that Work for Your Small Business,* edited by Susan M. Jacksack (CCH Incorporated, 1998) and Web sites such as Business Plan Pro at www.pasware.com and PlanMaker at www.planmaker.com.

Chapter 8

Track the Trends of Tomorrow

As you refine your business vision, be mindful of the environment in which your company currently operates, as well as where it might operate in the future. Take a page from H.G. Wells and do a little time traveling. Scope out new horizons, new ideas, and new strategies. No, you can't rent or buy a time machine, but you can use today's technology to tap into the future as envisioned by trend forecasters, and you can hone your own awareness of current events.

This chapter introduces a strategy that's not only fun, but that will also help you become comfortable initiating change rather than always responding to the actions of other people and businesses. The goal is to help you catch the wave instead of being swept up in the wake of others. You'll see quickly the competitive advantage you gain from being proactive, which will encourage you to be even more professionally adventurous.

Spot Trends

"To answer the question of where do we go from here, we need to know where 'here' is," observes futurist David Zach, a professional speaker and the author of *Zachronyms* (Innovative Futures Press, 1998). This process begins with getting a fresh perspective on our surroundings while discerning the underlying forces affecting our world. It also means spotting trends that may affect how, why, where, and when we do business, and then adapting them to the micro-scale of our small business.

To get you started, I've compiled 14 trend categories that you should take mental (and perhaps literal) note of, because some—or all—will undoubtedly have an effect on your business, whether directly or circumstantially. I've included some questions with each to fine-tune your time-travel antennae to the implications the category may have on your small business.

1. *Economic.* Today's economy is forcing people to take charge of their financial futures rather than leaving them in the hands of the Wall Street wizards. Does this trend offer opportunities for your business?

2. *Political.* No matter what the political climate to come, it's sure to affect your business. It's affecting your business now. Do you recognize how? Tune in to the direction it's heading. This is not a difficult trend to spot if you're paying attention.

3. *Technological.* You don't need a time machine to chart this trend. Digital communications and the Internet have changed—and will continue to change—the way people around the world communicate and conduct business. More important for small business owners is that these technologies enable them to compete with companies many times their size. As communication become even easier, faster, and cheaper, what impact will this have on your company? Are you making the best use of the new technologies?

Smart Strategy

Peering into the future helps you to initiate change rather than respond to the actions of others. Once you learn to do so, you'll see the competitive advantage you gain, which will encourage you to be even more professionally adventurous.

4. *Commercial.* Superstores. Boutiques. Electronic commerce. A lot's happening in this arena. What trends do you see specific to your industry, and what do they tell you about the direction your customers may be headed?

5. *Employment.* Two-career families are the norm. The average worker is predicted to change careers five or more times in his

or her working lifetime. The SOHO (small office/home office) market is the fastest-growing in this country. Will independent workers equipped with high-speed digital networks spell the demise of the corporate workplace? Will these trends continue? If so, how will they impact your business?

6. *Generational.* As Baby Boomers age and subsequent generations mature, changes will be reflected in the marketplace. What new products and services will be in demand?

7. *Educational.* Home schooling. Distance learning. Year-round schedules. Adult education and self-directed training. How might these educational trends affect you or your customers, and as a result, your business?

8. *Housing.* Ours is a society on the move. In making so many career changes, more people are moving more often. And the homes they build or choose to live in reflect their changing needs and lifestyles, as well as concerns for the environment. Small rooms are giving way to larger, freeform spaces; the kitchen is the entertainment center, home offices are the norm. What other housing trends do you see, and how might they affect your business?

9. *Medical.* As our society struggles to find the best way to provide health care for all, the trend is toward preventive health care. (After all, who wants to navigate the medical insurance maze? Better to stay healthy and not need to see a doctor.) Still, this country is addicted to junk food and sofa-centric television viewing. That dichotomous behavior affects several industries. How might your customers respond to these trends? And how might their decisions and choices affect the products or services you provide?

10. *Sports.* Michael Jordan single-handedly made basketball an international attraction. Interest in women's sports is growing. Soccer has a worldwide following. In short, athletes have become the modern version of ancient mythological heroes. All this has meant a spectacular rise in branding and global sales of sports apparel, sports drinks, and sports paraphernalia. Do these or any other sports-related trends offer business opportunities for you?

11. *Cultural.* Cultural trends are some of the shortest, and therefore the most difficult to exploit. What's hot today often is out tomorrow. Are you nimble enough to take advantage of notoriously fickle customers in the areas of art, dance, theatre, or music? If so, what can you learn from trends that are happening—or will be emerging—in the cultural arena?

12. *Leisure and entertainment.* Have you been paying attention to how the general public is spending its free time? Have you taken note of the impact of the new technologies in this area? Do you know what your target customers do for entertainment? What do leisure and entertainment trends tell you about the interests and values of your customers?

13. *Family.* The family continues to be redefined to include a broader interpretation of this core unit of society. Children are leaving the nest later, then returning home to live with parents; Baby Boomers are caring for aging parents; single-parent families are widespread; many children have multiple sets of stepparents, reflecting the still-high divorce rate. How do these multifamilial structures affect how you market your product or service?

14. *Spiritual.* As if in an attempt to keep up with the increasing pace of technology, people are looking inward for some peace and quiet. The spiritual climate today is one of personal exploration, featuring a stronger Eastern philosophical influence blended with traditional religious beliefs and the ideas of self-improvement gurus. Do these trends impact your business? What can you learn from observing and studying this shift in focus?

Go Back to Basics

"In times of great change, it's important to identify what should remain the same," cautions futurist Zach. "You must check with the outside world, but also examine your own principles to determine what makes sense for you." The clearer you are on what's important to you, the easier it will be to determine which future options are worth pursuing. So the next step is to look at these indicators and forecast how they might interact and affect one another in the future of your business.

To stay in touch with the choices your customers are making, it's important to track how your customers find you (upcoming in more detail in Chapter 18, "Track Your Customers"). With that data in hand, you can consider, for example, how technology and entertainment trends are beginning to intersect, bringing a wealth of new options—and business opportunities—in the form of movies, games, and other interactive leisure activities via the Internet and the World Wide Web. Or think about how the changing face of the family is being affected by the shift in medical care, how that might affect your customers, and what you might be able to do to capitalize on it. Look at the trends I've listed to determine other parallels and intersections that might affect your business. There are innumerable combinations that you might be able to turn into opportunities.

The goal of this strategy is to encourage you to lead, not follow, the pack as we head into an uncharted new business millennium. The most rewarding opportunities will open to those who map out the new paths.

Take Action

1. Investigate topics in books, trade journals, on the Web, and elsewhere that may seem totally disconnected from your specialty, such as anthropology if you're a PR consultant, medieval history if you're a Web site designer, or biology if you're a carpenter. You'll be surprised how creative your thinking will become.

2. Take a tip from futurist David Zach and look to what *doesn't* change as well as what does. Learn from philosophy, theology, and history. Read *The Lessons of History* by Will and Ariel Durant (Simon & Schuster, 1968); this classic work, based on more than 40 years of research and reflection, distills lessons drawn from the entire course of human history into less than 150 pages.

3. Check out these books on the future:

   Clicking: 16 Trends That Drive America, by Faith Popcorn and Lys Marigold (Harper Business, 1996).

   The Future Ain't What It Used to Be: The 40 Cultural Trends Transforming Your Job, Your Life, Your World, by Mary Meehan, Larry Sanuel, and Vickie Abrahamson (Penguin Putnam, 1998).

   The Future and Its Enemies: The Growing Conflict Over Creativity, Enterprise, and Progress, by Virginia Postrel (The Free Press, 1998).

Chapter 9

Form a Success Team

I meet with thousands of entrepreneurs each year, and it never ceases to amaze me how few of them take the time to pick a team of advisors to help them achieve success. This one simple strategy, when pursued actively and sensibly, can make a significant difference in the level and rate of your business growth.

Choose Your Advisors Carefully

Frequently new business owners use what I call the default method of selection for choosing their advisors—people who could mean the difference between success and failure for their companies. For example, one day they realize they need a banker, so they go to their local branch and choose whoever is available to handle their banking needs. Or a legal question pops up and a neighbor says, "Oh, I have a friend who's an attorney," and that's who they hire to answer legal questions. They gather marketing advisors, computer consultants, and other support service providers in a similar, lackadaisical fashion. All I can say is, if you're looking for trouble, this is one sure way to find it.

Smart Strategy

Never underestimate the impact advisors can have on your business. Always be on the lookout for new talent for your team.

Another mistake many entrepreneurs make is to think that choosing advisors is a one-time strategy—that once you pick 'em, they're yours forever. Wrong. When you're just starting out, you need the best advice you can find to help you make the right decisions for getting started in your business and for adjusting to the impact the business will have on your life and on those in your life. Then, as your business grows, your needs will demand greater levels of experience and specialized advice. If you're lucky, some of the advisors who guided you when your business dream was a mere glimmer of an idea will have grown along with you in their expertise, and will be able to continue to offer you valuable insights. But that's a big if. More often, business owners have to seek out new advisors with broader skills, or other professionals who specialize in business operations that have expanded since startup.

Let's take a look at some of the types of advisors who should make up the team you and your company need to succeed on the playing field of business growth. As you review this list, note where your team is strong and/or weak. To help you with this, I've included a pointed question you should be able to answer in each area.

✓ *Legal advisors.* This includes attorneys who deal with general business matters, as well as others who specialize in areas such as intellectual property, real estate, or other matters that could affect your business. It's not unusual these days for entrepreneurs to retain several attorneys to ensure that they have the best legal representation they need.

   How strong is your legal team? Do you feel confident in its abilities to support your efforts as your company grows?

✓ *Financial advisors.* These include your banker, accountant or CPA, bookkeeper, and others who guide you in managing the money matters in your company. Your choices here can dramatically affect every aspect of your business. (I talk about financial advisors in greater detail in Chapter 34, "Assemble Your Money Team.")

   Do you have a strong money team in place? Does it share your big vision as well as keep you grounded in *daily* financial management?

✓ *Marketing advisors.* This category can range from large marketing firms that prepare in-depth PR campaigns to individual pros in fields such as direct marketing or newsletter design. Your business needs and budget will dictate the number and kind of marketing advisors you'll hire. In this area in particular, you'll see the need to change advisors as time goes on and your business grows. Savvy business owners get past the "I can do it myself" syndrome and learn that their companies need more professional promotional materials as they mature.

> How much of your marketing are you still doing yourself? Would you have greater success if you outsourced some of these programs?

✓ *Technology advisors.* Technology plays a central role in most small businesses these days, yet few entrepreneurs have the knowledge—or patience—to keep up with this rapidly and constantly changing field. In larger companies, full-time tech support pros are on hand to ensure that mission-critical technology is always operating at maximum productivity. For small companies, nearly *all* technology is mission critical: Most small businesses would come to a grinding halt if their phone systems, computers, printers, photocopiers, fax machines, or other equipment failed. Your technology advisors may include the 16-year-old who lives down the hall from you, or the computer enthusiast who's on your speed dial and ready to answer late-night phone calls. The key is to have this part of your team in place before an emergency disrupts your business.

> What havoc would result from technology failures in your business? Do you have plans in place to address such situations?

✓ *Insurance advisors.* When it comes to disasters such as fire and theft, too many small business owners go into denial rather than face the consequences. But with systems and strong advisors in place to guide you in selecting insurance, any risk can be offset. Be sure to review your insurance coverage and insurance team once a year.

> Are you working with insurance professionals who understand your business needs and risks? Is it time to review your team and your coverage?

✓ *Support services.* By support service professionals, I mean such people as day care providers, personal trainers, hairstylists, clothing consultants, and any others who help to ensure that you are at your best at all times. These individuals play an important role in your business development, too, but because they interact with us on a more personal level, we often leave them out of the advisor picture. Don't. Especially in small companies, personal and business lives often intersect. The level of professionalism your support advisors exhibit will impact your business, so choose them with care.

What support services do you have? Is it time for you to upgrade?

Seek and You Shall Find

Where do you find individuals to make up your advisory team and companies to serve your business? Candidates are everywhere, but you must have a discerning eye to choose the best match for you.

The most effective screening process starts with asking for referrals from colleagues who operate businesses similar to yours. Fellow entrepreneurs will be remarkably candid about the positive and negative aspects of working with someone. (A side benefit to this process is the insight you gain about how referrals happen; it's often what *your* potential customers are doing to select you!) Candidates may also be members of a professional association or networking group to which you belong. Or, a current advisor may suggest a professional colleague he or she has worked with before (for example, your legal advisor may recommend a CPA who serves the attorney's other small business clients).

Whichever way you find your advisor candidates, be sure to conduct due diligence before bringing them on board. Ask for an introductory meeting (which should be at no charge) and prepare both general and specific questions about the candidates' qualifications, experience, fees, methods of working, and other capabilities your business requires. Ask for names of current clients to contact for recommendations (which will likely be given to you after the advisor has contacted them for permission first) and any other relevant background material.

Take time to make your decision, and don't be afraid to reject someone if the chemistry between you is not right. Be patient with yourself if your initial choices don't work out, but be proactive in quickly moving to another individual or firm that can serve you better. Also be prepared if your advisor leaves you. For example, I've been through three CPAs in three years, due to a marriage, a dissolution of a partnership, and a job transfer. While frustrating, this has taught me a lot about the right questions to ask (!) and has enabled me to become clear about the specific needs I have for my business.

Synergize

If it's at all possible, it's a good idea and a truly valuable undertaking to periodically gather all the members of your advisory team together—particularly your legal and financial advisors. This will help them gain a more well-rounded view of your business. Your firm may also become involved in projects in which your advisors will have to work together (not just *through* you), and having the members of your team know each other will facilitate such activities.

Though such a gathering is not always easy to orchestrate, it is possible. Consider hosting a meeting or luncheon once a year. Or, if your advisors are geographically dispersed, put technology to work: Schedule a conference call; find out about videoconferencing. Be imaginative. There are more options for achieving this than you might think.

Take Action

1. Make a list of your advisors in each category. Which categories are weakly represented? Are there any areas where you have too many advisors? (This can be a drain on your time and financial resources, as well as creating confusion if you're getting conflicting advice.)

2. For which areas do you still need to get support? What tasks are you still doing that you could be outsourcing? Examine your business operations for areas that you should turn over to others to handle.

3. If you need to change advisors—either by choice or circumstance—could you make a transition smoothly? Create a list of potential advisors who could serve as backups.

Chapter 10

Make Master Mind Connections

To close this section on vision strategies, I want to share with you a strategy that has played an important role in my own business over the last year and a half. Deceptively simple, it can unleash creativity and insight and allow your business to expand in ways that will surprise you. If there's one vision strategy that can boost your business growth more than any other, this is the one.

What makes this strategy so powerful? To explain, let me begin by defining the concept of a master mind. Napoleon Hill, in his classic book *The Master-Key to Riches* (Fawcett Crest, 1965), defined a master mind as "an alliance of two or more minds blended in a spirit of perfect harmony and cooperating for the attainment of a definite purpose." Hill, an advisor to two presidents and a friend of Andrew Carnegie, spent 20 years compiling case histories of some of the wealthiest men of the twentieth century for his book *Think and Grow Rich.* Hill professed that the master mind was "the basis of all great achievements, the foundation stone of major importance in all human progress." In short, creating a master mind is about tapping into group wisdom.

In the same way that choosing essential advisors (as we discussed in Chapter 9) frees you from worrying about legal and financial issues, having a collective of trusted colleagues frees you, too—but in a more creative way. It's like the feeling of being in a hot-air balloon just after the tethering cords are cut. Remarkable things happen as you mentally ascend: Self-limiting habits are revealed, current problems come into perspective, doubts fade into the distance, new horizons open up.

Teach an Old Concept New Tricks

The idea of a master mind has been used by successful entrepreneurs for decades. Putting a group of entrepreneurs together can really make the sparks fly! It is, as Hill wrote, an environment in which "every human brain is both a broadcasting station and a receiving station."

Smart Strategy

The object of a master mind is to form "an alliance of two or more minds blended in a spirit of perfect harmony and cooperating for the attainment of a definite purpose."

Unfortunately, most solo entrepreneurs and small business owners often find themselves too busy to actively seek out other individuals to create a formal master mind group. Sure, they may run into Harry at the copy shop and shoot the breeze about a current business challenge, or swap resources with Jeannette while standing in line at the grocery store, but that's not what I'm talking about here. I'm talking about *committing to a regular meeting* with other business owners. Believe me, I know how difficult it is; I've chosen to live in a rural area, and though I'm digitally connected to the world, initially the notion of tracking down three or four kindred spirits in my neck of the woods to whom I can bare my business soul seemed to me very time-consuming and emotionally risky.

In response to any hesitation you may have, I offer you a modern-day alternative to the in-person master mind gathering: the master mind teleconference.

Build a Master Mind Phone Bridge

Through the wonders of modern telecommunications systems, a master mind group can meet via teleconference. No longer do you need to be geographically close to achieve the benefits of such an alliance. Members can be located anywhere in the world, as long as they have phone access. This is a liberating realization, because your universe of candidates for creating a master mind group has now become limitless. The members of my group, for example, hail from Arkansas, California, Minnesota, Missouri, and New York.

The ideal master mind size is four or five individuals; any more and it becomes too difficult to keep the voices distinct during the phone meetings, and the calls become too lengthy. Members should be passionate about their businesses and ideally be diverse enough to contribute unique capabilities and know-how. Here's how it works:

1. Members commit to regular meetings, which are scheduled by consensus. The meeting comes to order when, at the specified date and time, all members dial into a telephone bridge number that links all parties into a teleconference.

2. Groups generally speak twice a month, for an hour, although some prefer to talk weekly. When members are in different time zones, meeting times are planned to accommodate members' schedules as best as possible.

3. Each individual is allotted approximately 10 to 12 minutes to share news of accomplishments, ask for advice and feedback, and establish one goal that he or she wants to complete before the next session.

4. One person acts as timer, one as scribe, one as leader. Roles rotate for each meeting, either informally or on a schedule. At the close of the session, the scribe recaps each member's self-assigned goal, and the group chooses the next meeting date and time. Within a few days, the scribe e-mails a brief summary of the session to the members.

A number of telephone service providers now offer teleconference capabilities. While there is a range of pricing and call options, most offer two increasingly standard formats:

✓ A toll-free number that everyone calls to be connected. The per-minute rate is generally 20 to 30 cents higher than standard long-distance rates. Each participants pays his or her own charges.

✓ A standard long-distance number that members call plus a single per-minute surcharge for establishing the link. Members pay their typical long-distance charges and a leader pays the additional per-minute conference call charges (currently averaging 20 cents per minute).

Most services offer both operated-assisted and direct-dial conferencing options. Once your account is set up, many services allow you to reserve your calls via an automated system by punching in codes from your telephone keypad.

Because telephone technology is continually evolving and a master mind group can be such an important business tool, I've set up a special section of the Working Solo Web site for the most up-to-date information on telephone conferencing services (see the Take Action section of this chapter).

Maximize the Magic

I can attest that the power of a master mind is remarkable. In the 18 months since my group has been active, each member has achieved significant breakthroughs in his or her business, advances that we know would not have happened as quickly—or at all—without our collective brainpower at work. For example, with group guidance one member salvaged an unhappy client relationship and turned it into a win/win experience that boosted her annual income significantly. The master mind helped another member sort through priorities and refocus his business, enabling him to cut his workload by 30 percent without sacrificing revenue. And in writing this book I've relied on the master mind as my brain trust to help me develop my ideas and make sure the information is on target for entrepreneurs.

If you'd like to create such a group—or if you'd like to take a group you're currently with to the next level—here are some tips:

✓ *Choose members carefully.* Approach people you know are willing to meet the commitment of participation. Cancellations and absences should be strictly limited, primarily through self-imposed guidelines. Choose individuals to balance one another—you don't want four financial consultants and one attorney, for example.

✓ *Give the meeting structure, but keep it flexible.* I recommend that you divide each person's allotted 10 to 12 minutes of time into thirds, averaging 3 to 4 minutes during each third. During the first third, members recap what they've been doing, including their "wins" since the last meeting, so the others can help to celebrate achievements. During the second third, members present a goal or a challenge they're currently working on for which they'd like feedback. Reserve the last third for brainstorming for solutions, at the end of which each member assigns him- or herself a simple, achievable goal to be completed by the next meeting.

✓ *Know that trust will build over time.* The "personality" of any community takes time to form. As the months pass, members of the group will become more comfortable with one another and will grow to trust each other and themselves more as well.

✓ *If possible, schedule an in-person get-together at least once a year.* This should be a fun event, geared to help bond the group in ways that meeting over the telephone cannot. It's also a prime time to conduct annual planning.

✓ *Learn how to be a consultant, colleague, and friend.* The goal is to let the other members come to their own right conclusions. As a participant it's your job to coach, not provide answers or dictate actions.

✓ *Appreciate the value.* In dollar terms, you cannot calculate the collective value of spending an hour this way. But you will be able to count the value in the results you see in your business.

If you choose to create your own master mind group, I promise you'll find it worthwhile. You'll feel exhilaration as you make breakthroughs alongside your colleagues. You'll enjoy the camaraderie of support and encouragement—and you'll come to realize, as I have, that a collective creative mind can take your business to levels you might never reach on your own.

Take Action

1. Make a list of colleagues you'd like to invite to a master mind group. Photocopy this chapter and give it to them along with the invitation.

2. Talk with your long-distance provider about setting up a bridge call. If your provider doesn't offer this service, check out the master mind resources list on the Working Solo Web site, http://www.workingsolo.com.

3. Canvas your group to determine the date and time for the first call.

MARKETING AND SALES STRATEGIES

Chapter 11

Craft a Powerful Introduction

Ask a number of small business owners what their primary concern is, and a high percentage will tell you it's getting more customers. After all, sales of your products or services are the most tangible way of determining your success, and are among the most potent ways of achieving personal and professional satisfaction.

To lead off the marketing and sales strategies, I'm going to start by explaining a strategy for introducing *yourself.* This is unquestionably one of the most valuable strategies, yet it costs nothing to implement.

Smart Strategy

Introductions are your verbal business cards, and they need to be designed just as carefully as those professionally printed gems you carry in your wallet, briefcase, or suit jacket.

In a professional interaction, the first words out of your mouth can be a powerful marketing tool. Unfortunately, most entrepreneurs don't realize this fact and therefore squander this moment. The degree to which you master the skill of introducing yourself can determine whether you'll walk in through open doors to remarkable opportunities or be shut outside, wondering what the magic word is to open the doors.

To begin, I ask you to consider your answer to the deceptively simple question, "What do you do?" Chances are, a standard phrase or two automatically popped out of your mouth. Now I ask you to reevaluate your comments: Is this really the best way to represent yourself and your business?

Introductions are your verbal business cards, and they need to be designed just as carefully as those professionally printed gems you carry in your wallet, briefcase, or suit jacket. Verbal business cards should be thoughtfully crafted, too, packed neatly and concisely with pertinent information about yourself and presented in an appealing manner that is easy for the recipient to understand. When handled with care, your introduction sets the stage for a successful presentation of your business message. Let's examine how to produce an artful verbal introduction.

Brag Effectively

Obviously, we all want colleagues and potential clients to recognize the value our companies offer. But if we can't or don't effectively communicate that value, is it valuable at all? Too few business owners take the time to actively analyze and choose the specific words they use to introduce themselves. If you're among them, or if you have tried and failed in this attempt, I have a suggestion that has been proven to work.

In *Working Solo,* my first book in this series, I detailed the process of introducing yourself that I call the "five-minute brag." This technique has become one of the most popular among readers of that book; it continually generates positive feedback and some very interesting stories from the many entrepreneurs I encounter in my travels. I think the reason it's so successful is that it's such a simple method, yet it can generate powerful results. I'll review it here.

The "five-minute brag" is a time-delimited exercise designed to help you carefully construct phrases that represent you and your business in the best possible light. It is intended to prepare you to be able to speak interestingly and convincingly for *up to* five minutes, which is usually a lot more than you may ever get in an actual business situation. Its premise is this: If you aren't prepared to speak comfortably, unself-consciously, and effectively about your business for up to five minutes, chances are you'll fall back onto safe subjects such as sports, the weather, current events, your children, or your pets. Later, walking away from the encounter, you'll be frustrated and angry that you squandered another opportunity to make a good connection.

Your goal in crafting your self-introduction is to be able to express briefly the central value that you and your business can bring to others. The five-minute brag is the time to focus on company benefits, not to highlight personal accomplishments.

Customers will not care, for example, how many degrees you've received from prestigious universities; they want to know if you can get them out of a jam and help them meet that deadline tomorrow or that you can help to generate more profits for their company. The response you want to motivate in the listener is: "Wow, that's really interesting. Tell me more!" not, "Yeah, so what's that got to do with me?" To achieve this, you must keep your message simple, and you must tap into the listener's emotions.

Speak Simply and Carry a Big Message

Sometimes in trying to impress people, we resort to using language we wouldn't ordinarily incorporate into our daily speech. Usually this only serves to put people off. Remember, your listener must immediately be able to understand what you mean. So, instead of saying, "My company assists in building customer retention," say, "We make sure your customers come back to buy again and again." Don't say, "My company is tasked with making your systems fully compliant with market standards," when you can say more simply, "It's my job to guarantee that your communications equipment will work anywhere, anytime." Or, a financial planner might say, "I want to help you to have enough money so you can relax and spend time with your grandchildren," rather than, "I'd like to establish adequate financial planning guidelines for your retirement." Don't make your listener have to translate business-speak or guess at what you mean.

One of the best ways I've found to analyze whether a message I'm trying to convey is simple enough is to think about it as a show-and-tell for a third-grade class. If you were invited to speak to a group of rambunctious nine-year-olds, which words and phrases would you use to explain what you do? Remember, these are people with short attention spans, who are easily distracted and probably aren't particularly interested in what you have to say. Sounds a lot like a group of potential business prospects, right? If your words could hold this group of imaginary third-graders, you're on your way to creating a powerful self-introduction.

Ideally, your message should strike an emotional chord in your listener, too. In the perfect situation, your words create a bond with the potential customer so that his or her inner voice says, "Hey, this person speaks my language. I want to work with him (or her)." To do this, it helps to have some understanding of the individual's needs. Because even as you are creating a clear image of your service or product in his or her mind's eye, you want to be touching on a potential need or want as well.

Put Yourself in Their Place

One of the best self-introductions I've heard recently came from Marilyn Leiker, a solo entrepreneur who owns a word processing and desktop publishing service in Syracuse, New York. I've met hundreds of people who offer this type of business, and most will try to impress a potential client with descriptions of the types of computers and printers they use. In contrast, when someone asks Marilyn what she does, she answers:

> I'm the person people come to when they can't meet their dead-lines with word processing, desktop publishing, proofreading, or editing. I'm fast, I'm accurate, and I have lots of experience.

Then Marilyn hands the person her business card and says, "I'd like to help you get your work out on time." Powerful, isn't it? She's saying, "I know what it's like to need help to get a project out. I understand how difficult it is to get good, reliable help. I am that help."

How can you translate Marilyn's approach to your own business? When crafting your introduction, try to put yourself in the position of the potential customer, who may be under pressure to meet some deadline or solve some problem. For example, Marilyn makes it clear she knows firsthand about the dread of deadlines, the fear of the consequences if they're missed, and the desire to get them met. Without preying on the fear of her potential customers, she paints a picture of how working with her can bring them some big benefits. She builds rapport and establishes camaraderie, and it works like a charm.

Take the Time It Takes

No matter what business you're in, your self-introduction can be as successful as Marilyn's. And the cost of developing this powerful marketing tool? Time: the time to carefully analyze the result you want, the time to carefully craft the phrases, and the time to practice and refine your message. And you don't even have to steal the time from your work schedule. Try out your introduction when you're driving to the store for that container of milk you forgot earlier. Or, if you're a city dweller, tune out the crowds on the bus or train and mentally practice your words. At first, some phrases might not work or will generate a lukewarm response. But keep at it until you see that a single sentence makes a lightbulb go off for someone. That someone is your new customer.

Take Action

1. Draft a five-minute brag and practice it in front of a mirror or on tape until it becomes easy. Then practice it on one or two colleagues and refine it further.

2. Create an "express elevator" version of your self-introduction to use when you only have time for a very brief exchange.

3. If you have (or want to have) a diverse clientele, script several versions of your introduction to keep in your "brag bag," so that you can pull out the one that best suits whatever situation you're in.

Chapter 12

Create an Identity

Business *identity:* For a lot of people, that term conjures up images of business cards, stationery, and maybe a logo. But identity is much more than the image of your business on paper. A business identity is formed from the myriad details that make up your customers' perception of you and your business, and can include the way you or your employees answer your phone or the marketing and packaging of your products; it can even include the clothes you wear, especially if they're distinctive or idiosyncratic in some way (I know one creative entrepreneur who has 37 different pairs of stylish eyeglasses).

A business identity has the power to invest in or detract from the presence you create in the marketplace. Each and every day people make instantaneous judgments about your company based on this identity, whether you've created it purposefully or by happenstance. This is particularly true for solo business owners, for whom the line between business and business owner often disappears. Consequently, how you create, maintain, and build your company identity can have a substantial impact on the growth and success of your business. And if you're one of those whose business identity evolved without any conscious thought, it's especially important to consider tactics you can employ to bring this strategy out into the open, where it can work for you as you stock your marketing toolkit.

Smart Strategy

Your identity is formed from the myriad details that make up your customers' perception of you and your business.

Make a Good First Impression

You know the saying about first impressions: Everybody leaves one, either good or bad, whether they like it or not. Obviously, as someone trying to build a business, you'd rather leave a positive impression of your company in the minds of your potential customers. How do you achieve this? You must form an identity. Every business, no matter what size or in what market, needs an identity made by choice and with great care.

And thanks to digital technologies, even the smallest of companies can create a big presence through fax, phone, and the Internet. Using these relatively inexpensive methods, a bare-bones operation, through a well-executed identity program, can become much more—quickly.

A strong identity can reinforce the perception that your company is as big or successful or as qualified as others larger and more well established. Identity "flags"—logos, business cards, stationery, signage, a Web site, and much more—are all items that you can, and should, plan and control.

Cause a Psychological Impact

A company's identity has one primary purpose: to present a distinct message that elicits a response in the viewer. For most companies, that viewer is ideally a potential customer. The task for the designer (and you, as the business owner) is to create an identity capable of walking the fine line between good looks and performance—although the latter should always rule. Never forget the importance of communication.

"It's all about perception," says Seattle-based identity specialist Tim Celeski. "Identity is 90 percent psychology and 10 percent design. A good designer crafts not only the visual elements but also the viewer's response."

No business can survive by relying only on the marketing reach of person-to-person interaction. As entrepreneurs, we all leave something behind, whether it's a simple business card, a glossy color brochure, or a Web site address.

Make Your Mark

At the core of any identity program is a logo, or mark, generally made up of a simple image or symbol, perhaps stylized lettering, or even an abstract configuration, designed to capture the essence of your business. Over the last 25 years, Tim Celeski has created dozens of graphic identities for companies of all sizes, in industries as diverse as housing, health care, food, high tech, and consulting. He stresses how important it is that business owners recognize the value of a strong identity, and, conversely, that they recognize the harm a poorly rendered identity can cause.

A finely crafted identity is an invaluable asset that can give your business credibility and establish a quality of professionalism. So invest the time and money to work with a professional who can help you determine the unique attributes of your business and then translate them into an easily identifiable image. "You can look home-grown in the blink of an eye if you don't do it right," Celeski warns, recalling the dozens of successful companies he's seen whose weak identity marks undermined their other marketing efforts.

Celeski offers three guidelines for small business owners who need to create or upgrade their identities.

1. *Hire a professional.* Don't ask your cousin Jim or a colleague's son or daughter whose design degree still has wet ink. "It's absolutely the worst thing you can do," observes Celeski. "Make sure your designer has a good understanding of your business, and is experienced in logo design as well as digital media." A good sign of a professional designer is that he or she will spend a lot of time *listening* to you, getting a feel for your company's individual style. Good designers not only have artistic ability, but also understand how the public interprets imagery and thus how your customers are likely to respond to your identity markers.

2. *Make sure the designer you hire is knowledgeable about current media options.* In today's competitive business world, identity may extend from that business card in your wallet to a presence on the World Wide Web. "Transferring a logo to digital format for Web presentation is not as easy as it

sounds," Celeski says. "You'll get a superior integration of your print and online message, as well as a more powerful image, if the designer approaches the task knowing that you want your mark to work in many media."

3. *Don't try to put too much into an identity mark.* If your company does four or five different things, don't feel that an identity has to carry the entire burden of describing all of them. It's more important to convey the character and unique qualities of your business than to try to literally symbolize it all. Simpler is definitely better.

Celeski also cautions business owners who are looking for professional help to be suspicious if the designer resists your request to keep it simple. Keep in mind that you want to make it easy for the viewer to understand quickly what your image is aiming to express. The best marks are straightforward in design and message.

Logo creation is a unique segment of the design field, and not all designers are qualified for this specialty. Make sure you hire someone who is experienced. Carefully review his or her work and ask for references so you can check the person's work ethic as well—you want assurance that what you paid for will be ready when you ask for it.

Know the Necessary Ingredients

A good identity tells the world, "I'm a success and I'm going places." In addition to hiring a professional designer, you must take responsibility for knowing what makes a good mark. Here are some common characteristics:

✓ *Distinctiveness.* The best marks stand out from others. This is becoming increasingly difficult to achieve: For example, there are more than 10,000 registered marks using the diamond shape.

✓ *Uniqueness.* Your mark must be a "one and only," particularly if you want to trademark it. Though it may call to mind elements found in other marks in terms of color or style, it should clearly establish the meaning and value you intend.

✓ *Legibility.* To be effective, your mark must be easily understandable to viewers. Consumers are bombarded daily in all
media by thousands of marketing messages; if yours is too
difficult to read or understand, it will be passed over—or
worse, derided and then dismissed. The best marks can be
carried out effectively in both color and black and white.

✓ *Consistency.* To retain its power, a mark must be deployed
in a consistent manner. The color, layout, design, and other
elements must transition smoothly into every application,
from the tiniest business card to the largest billboard on the
highway.

✓ *Simplicity.* I've said it before and I'll say it again, less is
more when choosing an identity design. Think of the Nike
swoosh or the Apple Computer logo. The simplicity and
directness of these marks have turned them into icons.

✓ *Memorability.* Most of all, you want your mark to be memorable. Not every viewer may like it, but if they all remember
it, the identity has done its communication job successfully.

Needless to say, few marks or logos are successful in incorporating all of these elements at a high level. Those that do (and we all
know which ones they are) become classics, valued highly and used
wisely, for they carry a significant part of a firm's marketing weight
and translate directly to the bottom line.

Mark Your Future

Does every small business need to invest in a logo or a professional
identity program? Not necessarily, but make no mistake: All companies have an identity, whether it's a well-designed set of print
materials or a box of economy business cards from the local quick-
copy shop.

Ultimately, it comes down to controlling the message you want
to leave with your customers. Realize it's human nature to make
decisions based on appearance. You may work in sweats and tennis
shoes, but would you make an initial sales call to a valuable prospect
in that wardrobe? Your identity carries your message before you
arrive and after you leave. Make sure it works as hard as you do.

Take Action

1. Think about the different ways your company's identity is communicated to potential customers: business cards, letterhead, signage, your wardrobe, your car, voice mail, and so forth. Take an identity inventory of your business.

2. Single out two areas of your identity you'd like to improve.

3. Check out these two resources, representing very different approaches to graphic identity:

   The Business Card Book: What Your Business Card Reveals About You . . . And How to Fix It by Dr. Lynella Grant (Off The Page Press, 1998)

   From Lascaux to Brooklyn by Paul Rand (Yale University Press, 1996). The late Paul Rand, the master of graphic design who created such famous logos as those for Westinghouse, IBM, and CBS, was also a respected author and university professor.

Chapter 13

Be a Brand

The strategy of branding is closely related to identity. A brand, however, often can take on a life of its own, with its own personality and emotional appeal. When developed well, a brand becomes a powerful marketing force that is a magnet for attention—and profits.

Let's take a look at three powerful contemporary brands: Starbucks, Nike, and Harley-Davidson. Each is linked to a company of the same name, yet the brand name generates more of an emotional, instinctive response, rather than calling to mind a company per se. These brands spark a feeling, or the recollection of an experience that relates to, say, a Starbucks' iced latte on a hot summer day, the expression on your son's face when he got his first pair of Nike shoes, or that thrilling ride you took on the back of a friend's Harley-Davidson "hog."

Smart Strategy

Small businesses and solo entrepreneurs can glean insight from the branding efforts of large companies and then "downsize" them for incorporation into their own marketing efforts.

Over time, a brand becomes imbued with a spirit that creates a strong link with customers. It's an unspoken promise that says to customers, "I know the type of special person you are and what you like, and I can deliver it to you."

Open the Umbrella Effect

A brand's ability to generate positive responses and instill customer loyalty is particularly valuable in today's economy, where product cycles have shortened. The ever-changing demands of customers today have companies big and small scrambling to meet those demands. In the fallout, new products and services are often scrapped before they have a chance to prove themselves in the marketplace.

Enter a brand, which acts as an endorsement for a range of products and/or services, in essence serving as a marketing umbrella. Instead of increasing the visibility of individual products or services, companies put their efforts into building a brand, which has wider reach and longer life. Therefore, Starbucks can market not just coffee, but other products related to coffee beans, including bottled iced coffee beverages and coffee-flavored ice cream, that are sold in more traditional outlets such as grocery stores. Nike can spend millions promoting its brand, but spread that cost over promotions for shoes, clothing, and other related sports items it sells. And Harley-Davidson can garner visibility for its renegades-with-a-penchant-for-quality personality, and retain customers so loyal that they tattoo the brand onto their bodies. Talk about making a marketing impression!

Too many small business owners make the mistake of thinking that branding is only for the big guys, the major corporations who can invest megabucks into brand creation, development, and maintenance. Certainly, major brand campaigns *are* limited to companies that can underwrite the investment required to build a national or international presence for their products and services. But small businesses and solo entrepreneurs can glean insight from the branding efforts of large companies and then "downsize" them for incorporation into their own marketing efforts.

Let's take a look at a few branding concepts, and, prompted by the question that follows each, consider how to adapt them to your smaller, nimbler company.

✓ *Brands are more than logos.* Many elements combine in a brand to generate an emotional bond with a customer. Consider Tiffany's trademark aqua-blue box that is always tied with a white ribbon and a bow. Tiffany employees are trained to wrap and tie those ribbons just so. This seemingly small service has become such a symbol of the store that many customers rewrap an empty box and keep it as a remembrance of the gift they received. Is that blue box part of the Tiffany logo? No, but it communicates the brand awareness better than words or a graphic image ever could. And what about Cinnabon, the company that sells those tempting cinnamon rolls in shops appearing in a growing number of airports? If that aroma wafting hundreds of yards down the concourse doesn't count as branding, I don't know what does.

What elements of your business could become symbols for your company? Remember, think beyond words and pictures.

✓ *At its core, branding is about trust.* In today's fast-paced market environment, we are all bombarded daily with buying decisions. A brand name offers customers stability; they know what they are getting in exchange for their investment. A brand that is marketed well and with integrity instills confidence and reduces the sense of risk on the part of the customer. Branding also simplifies buying decisions: a Wal-Mart brand and a Nordstrom brand have clearly distinguished levels of quality. Customers can therefore choose wisely based on their budgets and needs.

How can you communicate trust, which is an intangible, to motivate the buying decision for your customers, which is a tangible?

✓ *Brands are about personality.* Let's say you're craving a fast-food burger. On the same stretch of road, you can choose among McDonald's, Burger King, or Wendy's. How do you make your choice? Face it, the food is very similar, in spite of promises of a special sauce, a cooking method, a garnish, or a sesame-seed bun. If you're like most people, you've developed a preference over time even if you've never thought about it before, and probably couldn't put it into words. You're buying the brand, the personality, the experience.

What is your company's personality? How can you capture and communicate it to potential customers?

✓ *Brands need tending.* Brands, an inherent part of a company's reputation, must be managed with care and protected from misuse that may degrade the customer's trust. Tylenol learned this during the package tampering scare several years ago. Likewise, Burger King had to overcome the stigma caused by the discovery of tainted meat in some of its products a few years ago. Savvy companies know that their brands must be updated and safeguarded to meet consumer needs and concerns.

What can you learn from companies that have reinvented themselves in the face of trouble or in order to stay in tune with a changing marketplace? Are there elements of your marketing scheme that have grown stale?

Do Some Virtual Branding

Cyberspace opens unparalleled opportunities for small businesses to establish a brand presence. Because entrepreneurs don't have to invest in the traditional business infrastructure that encompasses office space, inventory, or staff, even one-person firms can generate as much visibility as considerably larger companies.

The disadvantage to virtual branding, however, is that it is more difficult to assure a customer connection with a brand. As Jeff Bezos, founder of the popular and successful online bookstore Amazon.com explains, "Online, people have few visual clues. [Whereas] if I'm walking down the street and spot a large bookstore, I don't even need to notice the name to have a pretty good idea of what the experience will be like."

To offset this shortcoming to virtual branding, Bezos and his staff have steadfastly built the Amazon.com brand among online customers one at a time. "A brand is a relationship between you and your customer, and ultimately what's important is not what you send out to them in advertising, but what they reflect back and how you respond to that. The entire experience of Amazon.com is shaped and created by our customers," he says.

Since its debut, Amazon.com has focused on creating an online experience that offers a well-rounded and thoughtful selection of books, which generates the emotional responses of inspiration and discovery. As Bezos states, "Word of mouth has been incredibly important to us, and ultimately that's what a brand is: the things people say about you when you're not there."

What are people saying about your business when you're not there?

Take Action

1. Determine what you want your brand to say about your company.

2. Ask some colleagues for feedback on your business identity and brand. How do their impressions differ from the ones you were hoping to hear?

3. Identify one step you can take to further your brand identity. Take it.

Chapter 14

Become an Expert

As their companies grow, most small business owners become discerning about their marketing strategies. No longer willing to chase any and all far-flung prospects, they narrow the focus of their efforts. Experience teaches them that no business has to—or should—reach every person, just those interested or potentially interested in buying.

One of the best ways to narrow your market efforts is to set yourself apart in your field, to become an expert, with the goal of attracting a specific group of customers—in other words, to create a niche. By promoting yourself as an expert to a target audience, you can establish what will become the backbone of your entire marketing program.

Smart Strategy

Becoming an expert is a proactive strategy. You must go after the leadership role; it won't be handed to you.

As an expert, you add value to your business in three key ways:

1. You tend to attract higher-level prospects, with the probability of turning them into long-term, loyal clients. The result? A better return on your investment of time, effort, and money from your marketing endeavors.

2. You attract the media, who are always looking for solid information and insights from knowledgeable spokespeople from all areas of the business world. This is a definite "you scratch

my back, I'll scratch yours" undertaking: By providing the media with valuable up-to-date material or commentary, you position yourself as a respected source, which builds your visibility—and, more important, your credibility.

3. You gain personally. When you're always on the alert, looking for new ideas, trends, information, and material in your industry, you will come to greet each day as a fresh challenge.

Identify, Then Refine, Your Niche

The adage "There's riches in niches" says it all. By focusing on a niche market, you can narrowcast your marketing message and pinpoint your ideal prospects, maximizing your impact and minimizing your expense.

Once you know your niche, the next step is to analyze it and who its current experts are. Then decide either how you could join their ranks, or create a new category in which you are regarded as one of—or even the only—preeminent authority.

Both these tasks probably will take some time to complete, so don't be hasty. First and foremost, your niche choice should spring from your passion; this is not something for which you can fake a commitment. Your enthusiasm will keep you interested and intent on finding the next new morsel of information that will strengthen your position as an expert.

Your choice should also spring from your unique combination of knowledge and experience. For example, a businesswoman who launched a desktop publishing business several years ago rode the wave that arose from the novelty of the technology in its early years. Initially, her business soared. Then, as she began to face increasing competition from a broadening field—including college students who, subsidized by university equipment and facilities, undercut her pricing to levels she couldn't match—she reconfigured her business. By integrating her background as a paralegal into her desktop publishing services, she showcased her expertise in both areas. Now she serves the legal profession, whose professionals appreciate her understanding of legal terminology, procedures, and deadline pressures. As a result, she can command higher fees—and watch with pride as her revamped business continues to grow.

Leave Your Reluctance at the Door

Becoming an expert is a proactive strategy. You must go after the leadership role; it won't be handed to you. As communication coach Granville Toogood explains in his book *The Articulate Executive* (McGraw-Hill, 1996), bold thinkers are charismatic. "They add value to what they are saying by taking a position," Toogood points out. "They have a point of view, and they press their case with conviction. They believe."

And because they believe, so do others, thereby cementing the experts' place as experts. But experts never take their status for granted. They know it must be safeguarded and continually reestablished in the hearts and minds of their target audience. One of the most effective ways to do this is to "share the wealth."

Share Your Knowledge

When you extend your expert status, you also become a resource. Wise experts share their information widely, and often without expectation of direct compensation. They understand the fundamental cyclical rule: By giving, you get.

This process begins with ramping up your research and learning efforts to encompass absolutely everything available on your chosen area of expertise. At first, this may seem a bit overwhelming, but if you set aside a small amount of time each day or week to study, you'll find the cumulative effect to be remarkable. As you immerse yourself in your specialty, suddenly new ideas and opportunities will appear. Your aim is to provide valuable information for customers and your industry. Ask yourself:

1. What do people in this field want and need to know most?
2. How can sharing my expertise help them and my business?
3. What's the best way of reaching this audience?

Let's say you've come up with a novel marketing technique that's effective and economical for your industry. Or you've surveyed the marketplace and discovered some unusual and potentially valuable data. Maybe you've created a handy checklist to help customers make a buying decision. The possibilities are endless.

Once you have the information in hand, it's time to choose the appropriate vehicle through which to disseminate the information. A few common options include:

✓ *Publish.* If you have writing skills, consider putting what you know on paper and submitting your articles to publications ranging from your local freebie weekly to an industry or association monthly or even a nationally distributed magazine. Choose your target publications strategically by first carefully analyzing their readership. Make sure your audience is reading the publications you target. For example, if your business is a lawn-care service, you might submit a series of articles to the local paper that answer common questions about lawn-care problems. You'll gain free publicity—and probably new customers.

✓ *Make speeches and give presentations.* The thought of public speaking makes most people quake in their shoes, but if you want to attain expert status, it's a must-master skill. Again, establish what you want to attain and whom you want to reach. Choose your venues by the audience makeup; verify that the audience can contribute to your business growth. Your venues may range from local service clubs such as Rotary to regional or national industry conferences. Later, if appropriate for your market, consider teaching a continuing education class at the local community college. To polish your skills, join Toastmasters; if you choose to develop into a professional speaker, check out the National Speakers Association (details in the Take Action section of this chapter). Be sure to circulate copies of your published articles as handouts at your presentations. Often the questions from participants at these events will inspire future ideas.

✓ *Answer FAQs.* Frequently Asked Questions pages are a staple of most Web sites, and thus a great avenue to showcase your expertise and offer value on your own or another company's site. The Web is also a great place to solicit ideas for research and writings. By posting a request for questions, you can find out what your customers are thinking and need to know. (We'll explore this in greater detail in the next chapter.) Furthermore, the Web offers an immediacy that print publications can't match, a quality you can use to leverage your position as an expert with up-to-the-minute information.

In our information-hungry era, truly knowledgeable people with fresh insights and perspectives will always be in demand. If you choose to use the expert strategy to grow your business, know that there will always be a need for that level of commitment, no matter what market you work in.

Take Action

1. Define your niche. How crowded is it? How can you refine it to make it uniquely yours?

2. Investigate joining Toastmasters [(714) 858-8255; http://www.toastmasters.org] to improve your public speaking skills; if you want to become a paid professional speaker, check out the National Speakers Association [(602) 968-2552; http://www.nsaspeaker.org].

3. Read Miriam Otte's helpful guide, *Marketing with Speeches and Seminars: Your Key to More Clients and Referrals* (Zest Press, 1998).

Chapter 15

Listen Between the Lines

We entrepreneurs love to talk. We're brimming with new ideas, unique experiences, and great suggestions that we love to share with anyone we come in contact with. Talk, talk, talk. Wind us up, push the button, and we'll talk for days. But it's just as important to flip that coin: to listen. Otherwise, we cut ourselves off from valuable feedback that can help us grow our companies. If all the information is flowing out, it stands to reason that nothing is coming back in.

My strategy for changing that dynamic is based on a technique I've dubbed "listening between the lines." Just as developing the ability to read between the lines enables us to discover things that may not be apparent at first, listening in this manner opens us up to insights we can use to move our businesses to the next level.

There are seven key areas where listening in this manner will assist in your business growth. Consider the impact of each as it directly relates to your company.

1. Listen to Your Customers

Particularly during a sales situation, silence and attentiveness can pay off big time. When you talk to prospects, listen as much to what they don't say as to what they do. Human beings transmit a lot of important information through body language and innuendo. When a customer is confident that your interest is genuine, he or she is much more likely to reveal what's *really* on his or her mind about the product or service you're trying to sell. This information can literally change your entire business.

By listening to customers, you may also learn to identify incremental changes you need to make in your business, points that get overlooked when we talk too much. Most people today are comparison shoppers—and they can bring you remarkable feedback about your competitors. This info is yours for the listening.

Smart Strategy

When talking to prospects, listen as much to what they don't say as to what they do. Human beings transmit a lot of important information through body language and innuendo.

Another way of listening to your customers is by eliciting their feedback on surveys and other response forms. Such methods can serve as guides when you are revamping certain business operations or want to improve customer service. And note: Your survey process should include acknowledgment of and appreciation for the customer's participation.

Last, but certainly not least, listening to customers can lead to the creation of exciting new products or services. Countless solo entrepreneurs have had their entire businesses change as a result of a casual comment such as, "Hey Marie, I know you usually only do food catering, but can your company do the floral arrangements, too? I want to make sure my theme is carried out consistently." After taking a deep breath, Marie realizes it's a bit of a stretch, but decides to go for it and replies, "Sure, we can do that for you." Bingo! She connects with a floral specialist and she's off and running with an expanded capability to promote.

2. Listen to Your Competitors

When you're among a group of your competitors, you often will reap greater benefits if you can keep your mouth closed. Granted, for most entrepreneurs this is a challenge, since the competitive spirit runs deep within us, compelling us to tell one and all how we think things should be done.

Resist the urge to compete in this arena, because listening between the lines can bring you valuable information about another company's plans, strategies, and financial status. No, I'm not suggesting that you make your business decisions solely in response to what other firms in your field are doing; what I am saying is that the best offense is a good defense, and the more you know about what your competitors are doing, the better able you'll be to not only defend your turf, but expand it.

3. Listen to Your Colleagues

Feedback and advice from fellow entrepreneurs can be the most valuable guidance you receive. They understand what it's like to be a solo flyer, and therefore can give you hints and share "learned-it-the-hard-way" information that can save you hours of time, thousands of dollars, or headache-producing frustration—but only if your ears are open to their advice.

In my own case, a single comment from a colleague—"Terri, why don't you bundle your products together and offer customers a package price?"—unleashed a flood of new ideas and increased my revenues an additional 20 percent the next year. In terms of a marketing return on investment, those few seconds of attentive listening were of greater value than six months of pondering potential marketing plans.

4. Listen to Your Staff

If you have staff, whether part-time, full-time, volunteer, or "virtual," stay tuned in to their comments, for those comments can translate into a big boost for your company. These people understand your business from the inside out, and often have a perspective you lack because you're running the whole show. I recommend you have a forum in place for encouraging input from your staff on a regular basis. Their suggestions could translate into a savings of time or money. They may give you insight for handling a difficult client, or may suggest new product ideas. Listen up! And be sure to acknowledge any and all staff contributions.

5. Listen to Your Family and Friends

It's true that we often tune out those we care about most, dismissing their suggestions for solutions to our business problems with the thought, "What do they know about business?" In fact, they just might know plenty. Don't forget: They know you better than anyone—maybe better than you know yourself—and therefore can give you a perspective that you can't get from anyone else.

Furthermore, because they're not wrapped up in the inner workings of your business, they often can ask really pertinent, insightful questions that lead you to the solution you've been searching for in vain. Like the combination to a stubborn lock, their query can cause all the tumblers to fall into place, releasing the treasure behind the door of the safe.

6. Listen to Yourself

A good deal of the time, we know the answers to our questions, the solutions to our problems, the step we should be taking next. But that information will reveal itself only if we can quiet the inner yammering and stop running, running, running to get the next task accomplished.

To achieve this inner silence, some entrepreneurs turn to meditation; others find a quiet time each day to be alone with their thoughts. I like to walk or swim, because while focusing on the movement I clear my mind so that I can reconnect with myself. Once your mind is quiet, prompt yourself with a simple question, such as "What do I think about this?" and note the first response that comes to mind. Keep probing. Ask again: "Yes, but what do I *really* think?" After asking three or four times, you'll find yourself digging deeper into the issue, uncovering layer after layer of meaning, emotion, insight, and other substance that you didn't even know existed. It's all inside if only we take time to actively listen.

To gain fresh perspectives, I "time-travel." For example, I'll ask, "If I were looking back 10 years from now, how would I find that I had resolved this situation?" Or I'll become the "future me," and ask that older, wiser person to offer some insights. It doesn't matter how you manage to engage yourself in this inner dialog, it only matters that you do it. It can bring some remarkable results.

7. Listen to the World

Today's business world encompasses the farthest and deepest corners of the Earth. All business owners, no matter how big or small their firms, operate within a complex system of global activity. By listening between the lines to what's taking place in this worldwide arena, we can align our companies with the trends that are shaping the global marketplace.

You may not think that what's happening on the other side of the world will impact your small business, but, as in nature, everything and everyone is interconnected; you never can tell which ripple started by a stone thrown halfway around the world may affect your business or your customers a week or a year later.

Unless we open ourselves to the broader perspective and absorb what's happening on a global scale, we limit ourselves to thinking small. Listen big to think big.

Take Action

1. Ask your customers, colleagues, or staff for feedback about you and/or your business. Listen attentively, then compare and contrast what you've heard.

2. Ask your friends, family, or significant other for input about your business and about you as a business owner. Make sure you let them know how much their feedback means to you.

3. Establish a time and a method for regularly getting in touch with yourself.

Chapter 16

Drive Appropriate Marketing Vehicles

How you spend your marketing dollars is one of the most important—and most difficult—decisions a solo entrepreneur or small business owner must make. Faced with myriad options, too many newcomers navigate using hunches or whims, or fall prey to the persuasive pitch of ad sales reps. In the early years of running my pottery business, I recall thinking that I'd probably have just as much success standing on the corner and handing out dollar bills than with the so-called marketing methods I was using.

Fortunately, as your business acumen develops, you learn to make better choices. Yet even after many years' experience, many entrepreneurs still feel they're playing the lottery when it comes to promoting their services and products. Though there will always be unknown factors that can derail any marketing approach—no matter how well planned and researched—the strategy presented in this chapter will show you how to teach yourself the discipline it takes to reduce the risks you take while increasing the success you gain from your marketing investments decisions.

Chart Your Choices

To help you understand your marketing dollars at work, take a look at Figure 16.1. The grid I've designed is based on two axes: cost (left vertical axis) and reach (bottom horizontal axis). They determine how much "bang for the buck" your marketing dollars might generate. *Reach* indicates how many individuals will receive your message; *cost* reflects the amount of money you'll have to spend to contact them.

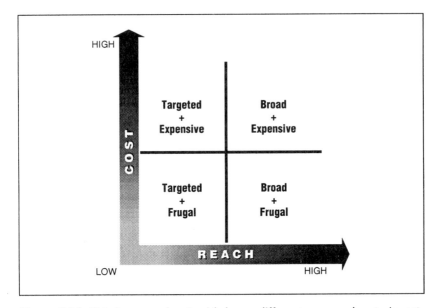

Figure 16.1 This four-quadrant grid shows different approaches to investing your marketing dollars. The bottom horizontal axis represents *reach,* or how many individuals will receive your message; the left vertical axis represents *cost,* or the amount of money you'll have to spend to contact them. Most solo entrepreneurs and small business owners have greatest success with marketing methods from the lower left quadrant category, targeted plus frugal. For examples of specific marketing approaches that fall within each quadrant, refer to the chapter discussion.

By working your way around the four quadrants, you'll be able to get a clearer understanding of where your business fits into the grid and where it makes the most sense to invest your marketing budget. Let's begin in the upper right quadrant.

Broad Reach, Plus Expensive

Marketing options in this category work best for companies with a goal of maximum impact on a large, diversified audience. They may utilize vehicles such as billboards, television and radio spot advertising, full-page ads in general daily newspapers, and so forth.

This mass-media approach is designed to build widespread awareness for a product or service, particularly when a company isn't quite sure exactly who its customers are going to be. It's rarely effective for small businesses, since it's so broad—and expensive. Expensive, of course, is a relative term. In general, it's best to steer clear of a single marketing option that consumes your entire budget. It's too risky to tie up your total marketing investment in an approach that has such a broad focus.

When might a small business use marketing vehicles in this area, such as billboards, television and radio ads, or full-page ads in general newspapers? Rarely. Keeping up to date with these marketing options is an important part of your business education, however.

Broad Reach, Plus Frugal

Moving down one quadrant in a clockwise direction, we come to an approach that mixes broad reach with frugality. If you're convinced that you need to reach a mass-market audience, but haven't identified your specific buyers yet and have to find a way to do so on a limited budget, you may find that you get a greater return on investment (ROI) with marketing vehicles such as broad-based direct mail, flyers and inserts, custom stickers, ad specialty products, and so on.

Smart Strategy

The value of tracking many types of marketing—even if it's outside the realm of possibility for a business of your scale—lies in the lessons you learn about how, and why, customers buy.

In this category also fall PR efforts such as submitting articles, news releases, or story ideas for local media, mentioned in Chapter 14. This extends your message more broadly, and your time is your primary expense. (Keep in mind that by frugal here I do not mean cheap. If your marketing materials are poorly rendered, it won't matter who you send them to—they won't work.)

Can small business owners effectively reach customers by focusing on this quadrant? Again, not often. But sometimes the idea behind a product or service is unusual enough—such as the entrepreneur who launched a pet taxi service in California's Bay Area—that the media will offer extensive coverage at little cost to the small business. As the "buzz" spreads to the general population, legitimate prospects contact the business directly and it reaps the benefits.

Targeted Reach, Plus Frugal

Moving one quadrant to the left, we come to the effective combination of targeted reach on a tight budget. This is where most small companies should focus their marketing efforts.

Many of the methods in this category fall into the realm of guerrilla marketing, an approach that relies more on wits and imagination than the brute force of big budgets. According to guerrilla guru Jay Conrad Levinson, creator of the best-selling book series on this topic, "Your size is an ally when it comes to guerrilla marketing. If you're a small company, a new venture, or a single individual, you can utilize the tactics of guerrilla marketing to their fullest."

Examples of successful marketing approaches in this category include personalized mailings to a current customer base or to highly qualified prospects; piggybacking inserts into mailings going to a specific organization or association; classified ads in trade magazines; articles written for publications delivered to a target audience; and any other low-cost, high-return method that connects to a focused market.

Courtesy of today's technology, anyone can create professional-looking marketing materials on a limited investment. All you have to do is put on your creative thinking cap. Collect examples of marketing pieces you like, and refer to and "borrow" from them. And be sure to ask for feedback on your designs from colleagues or graphics professionals you may know.

Other benefits accrue from the targeted plus frugal approach:

✓ Because you're not spending a lot of money, it's easier to track your expenses.

✓ Fewer materials go to waste—that is, reach the wrong audience.

✓ By targeting a focused group of recipients, you can more easily respond to prospects.

Guerrilla marketing is about a mindset as much as a choice of marketing vehicles. The ultimate in guerrilla marketing tactics is exemplified by the pizza parlor that offered a discount to customers who brought in the Yellow Pages ad from the restaurant's competitor. The campaign was wildly popular, and essentially destroyed the future effectiveness of the competition's advertising.

Low cost, high creativity, big results. That's guerrilla marketing at its best, and that's why it's such a favorite of clever, resourceful small business owners.

Targeted Reach, Plus Expensive

The last quadrant also describes a targeted reach, but on a bigger budget. When your product is designed to serve the needs of a tightly defined group of customers, your best strategy may be to choose your marketing options selectively, so you can reach specific customers making specific buying decisions. You don't scatter your efforts like so much buckshot, hoping that the numbers will work in your favor; rather, you take careful aim at the needs of your potential customers.

Marketing vehicles that fall into this category include advertisements in glossy trade publications whose readership parallels your market (timed to coincide with an industry event or a product launch, perhaps), a tasteful, well-designed direct-mail piece, or a promotion specifically designed with the prospect's interests in mind.

For example, consider the Las Vegas casinos that woo high-spending clientele with limousines and lavish hotel suites brimming with fruit baskets, caviar, and champagne—all provided at no charge. The casinos underwrite this expense for only a select group of individuals: high rollers who will gamble away much more than these perks cost. As smart business owners, the casino executives know the marketing must match the level of the intended audience; in this case, that means it must be filled with glamour, obvious wealth, and the adrenaline of risk. It's a marketing approach that works, reeling in satisfied customers and mega-profits for the casinos.

Would such an approach work for smaller companies? Only if you have high-ticket products or services with big *margins* (essentially, the difference between your sticker price and your total costs to produce the product or deliver the service). Without this profit potential—and a highly targeted client base—it's too risky to invest in marketing this expensive. It's not out of the question, but it requires a special match between prospective customers and your product or service.

Whether you adopt any particular marketing vehicle depends on many factors, including your financial goals, your intended customers, the specific product or service, and more. The value of tracking many types of marketing—even if it's outside the realm of possibility for a business of your scale—lies in the lessons you learn about how, and why, customers buy.

Take Action

1. Pick the marketing quadrant that's the best fit for your business today. Then pick the most unlikely choice. Analyze what the two have in common, and what makes them different.

2. List the places your customers are most likely to be when making a buying decision.

3. Check out the *Guerrilla Marketing* book series by Jay Conrad Levinson and the Guerrilla Marketing Web site at http://www.gmarketing.com.

Chapter 17

Spread the Word

Of the numerous marketing options available to you—and new ones are emerging every day—it's an old standby that still works best for small businesses: word of mouth. A positive review of your product or service, passed from one client or customer to another, carries more weight than any self-promotion you can do, because it offers the credibility that comes only from experience. The trust this instills in a potential buyer is golden, something even the most expensive marketing campaign can't promise to deliver.

Smart Strategy

Actively solicit and empower others to support you and your business. Enlist others to endorse and recommend your company.

Business owners know this instinctively. We realize that referrals streamline the decision-making process for clients and reduce the time it takes to build trust between you and them. The sale is made almost automatically. What most entrepreneurs don't realize, however, is that we can actively control these referrals; in essence, we can proactively assemble a "cheerleading squad" for our companies. That's what this strategy is all about.

Identify Your Cheerleaders

The foundation of this strategy lies in soliciting and empowering others to support you and your business. Your aim is to enlist others to endorse and recommend your company. Why would people be willing to do this? For many reasons:

✓ The most obvious is that they used your company's products or services, it was a positive experience, and they're willing to say so.

✓ They may know you on a personal level and believe you to be hard-working and conscientious.

✓ You may have shared a common professional experience with them in the past, such as being co-workers, and they are willing to support your efforts.

✓ Perhaps you embody the entrepreneurial dream, and they admire your courage for going out on your own.

Whatever the reason, you want to strengthen any preexisting bonds with such people and add them to your ranks of supporters.

To begin, make a list of all the people you know who have been enthusiastic champions of your past endeavors and of your current undertaking. Rank them as best you can according to the weight their endorsements would have with potential customers. For example, though your parents or spouse may be spirited supporters, they may not carry any actual weight with the market you're hoping to attract, whereas there may be individuals on your list who have expressed appreciation or admiration for your business efforts in the past who may be willing to serve as a source for referrals. Don't forget to add your mentors; they may head the list!

Your original list may contain 5 or 50 names. The number is irrelevant; it's quality you're after, not quantity. Two enthusiastic cheerleaders can make as big a noise as 10 lukewarm supporters. In time, however, you'll want to expand your squad to a core of about 10 to 40 individuals, depending on the type and size of business you're growing.

Establish Regular Contact

Once you've ranked your potential cheerleaders, it's time to enlist their support. Set up a schedule and method to contact them on a regular basis. "Regular" can vary; again, it depends on your business. For some, it may mean a weekly phone call or e-mail. For others, it may mean a postcard once a month, or a quarterly newsletter.

Maintaining regular contact is important for two reasons:

- ✓ You want these individuals to know how highly you value your relationship with them.

- ✓ You want to maintain your position in the front of their minds, and on the tip of their tongues, so that when a referral opportunity arises, they automatically recommend you.

How aggressive you are in soliciting an individual's support depends on your style as well as theirs. Some entrepreneurs take the direct approach and candidly ask, "Will you call Jim and tell him how my company is the best one for the job?" Others prefer a more indirect method of keeping cheerleaders informed of their activities and letting referrals occur more casually. Often, it comes down to a mix: You'll have individuals you can always comfortably ask for outright endorsements as well as champions who emerge for a specific project and then fade until another project lights them up.

Be Vigilant

Your relationships with your cheerleaders will need tending if the bonds are to be long-lasting and happy. And like all relationships, each will have its own character; don't expect them all to progress in the same way. Some may lend themselves to regular in-person contact, while others may be better served through phone calls, e-mails, or mailings.

Choose the best method of interaction by evaluating all members of your cheerleading squad on three factors: the role they can play in your business, the amount of time they have, and how they prefer to communicate. For example, if an individual is a primary source of referrals to your target market, but is out of the office frequently, you may find it best to connect by voice mail or e-mail. Others you may be able to take to lunch every four to six weeks. It can be a fine line to walk, balancing your business needs while respecting people's time and work as well, but finding a way to do this is central to making this strategy work.

Provide Referral Tools

Once you have your cheerleaders ready, willing, and able, you need to provide them with their "megaphones"; that is, any tools they may need to help them recommend you professionally and easily. You'd be surprised how many entrepreneurs overlook this seemingly obvious step in the referral process.

Let's assume you provide tax preparation services, and Mary, a self-employed travel agent you have done some work for, has agreed to be one of your cheerleaders. What you don't want, for example, is to have Mary say to a potential referral, "I can recommend Greg Harris, but, darn, I don't think I have his number." Your job is to make sure Mary has not only your number, but perhaps a brochure or other promotional material as well. And don't forget to send Mary regular updates about your company. Then Mary can say, "You're interested in having someone do your tax return? You should call Greg Harris. I just heard from him the other day, and he's really up to date on all those new tax law changes." Arm your cheerleaders with the information they need to promote you and your business. This might include:

✓ Newsletters
✓ Brochures
✓ Postcards
✓ Annual report or updates
✓ New product announcements
✓ Copies of articles that mention you or your company
✓ Clippings with information related to your field
✓ Books or articles that you've written
✓ Flyers from conferences you've attended or at which you've spoken
✓ Audio- or videotapes featuring you or other related information

Be creative with these tools. For example, when the first edition of my original book, *Working Solo,* was published, I had a few thousand color postcards printed. I then went through my Rolodex and sent five cards along with a letter to about a hundred colleagues and friends with the message, "You've all been telling me for years to write this book. Now I have, and I'd like your help in spreading the word." These cheerleaders shared the postcards with people they knew who wanted to start their own business. In this way, I succeeded in launching the book via a powerful grassroots effort. It was an effective method of involving my extended team of cheerleaders, and what better way to launch a book for entrepreneurs?

Show Appreciation

Word-of-mouth promotion is a strategy whose power increases with time. Managed well, it can supply an ongoing stream of referrals and other benefits to your business. But it must be tended carefully.

Take time to make the extra effort to show your appreciation for any and all endorsements or referrals you gain from your cheerleaders. This doesn't have to be expensive or time-consuming—a simple note sent via fax or e-mail can do the job nicely. And in this impersonal digital era, a short handwritten note of thanks carries more weight than ever.

Take Action

1. Make a list of your potential cheerleaders. Plan how to engage their services on your behalf; once you have them on board, determine how often you will be in touch with them.

2. Brainstorm methods to educate your cheerleaders about your business.

3. Explore other creative ways to promote your business by reading Raleigh Pinskey's *101 Ways To Promote Yourself: Tricks of the Trade for Taking Charge of Your Own Success* (Avon Books, 1997).

Chapter 18

Track Your Customers

A fter you've determined how to get your message out, you need to find out how effective your marketing methods are. If I asked you to give me a breakdown of where your customers come from, could you tell me? If not, you're putting your business in jeopardy—and probably wasting a lot of time, energy, and money as well.

As dependent as they are on a stable client base, it's surprising that the majority of entrepreneurs have only a vague notion about their source(s) of customers. Don't fall into the trap of getting swept up in creating marketing materials and then ignoring the results they generate.

Start with Six Magic Words

Compiling this valuable information is easy to do. You don't need special or complex equipment (although a basic database or spreadsheet program will help to more efficiently and accurately calculate the results); nor does it take a lot of time or effort.

To start requires only an awareness that you want to gather this information. You and anyone on your staff must be trained to ask these six magic words when they come in contact with a customer:

How did you hear about us?

The answers to this question can tell you volumes about the effectiveness of your marketing efforts. They will reveal whether the $600 you spent for that ad in the Yellow Pages was a better investment than the $16 you spent hanging up flyers all over town—or the

$6,000 you invested in a Web site. But if you never ask, you'll never find out.

Go to the Source

Your source data can benefit you in three important ways. First, it can pinpoint where your referral network is strong and/or weak. As we discussed in Chapter 17, having a team of cheerleaders for your company is a powerful way to grow your business. But to ensure that those referrals keep coming, you need to acknowledge the source of new business. If you don't ask the "magic" question, you won't know who deserves the thanks, either. And without acknowledgment, trust me, even the most ardent of cheerleaders will soon lose his or her enthusiasm.

Smart Strategy

Don't fall into the trap of getting swept up in creating marketing materials and then ignoring the results they generate.

Second, the data may be able to give you a jump start on a strong relationship with a client. For instance, if you learn that a new client was recommended by Janice, you can contact Janice for more background information. Perhaps she can give you details that can help you serve the new client better or make your sales presentation hit the right mark. If you don't ask the source, this valuable cycle cannot begin.

Third, source data can give you control over the mix of new customers coming into your business. Let's assume that Brian, a graphic designer who is a good source of business for you, has been sending you—an events planner—only corporate customers, when in fact you'd like to expand your individual client base to weddings, parties, and the like. With this as your goal, you can tactfully ask Brian to include more of this type of client in his referrals in the future.

Monitor the Market Pulse

As you accumulate source data, patterns will emerge that can offer valuable guidance as you continue to grow your business. And if you enter that data into a computer, you'll have a wealth of valuable information at your fingertips. For example, in addition to determining where you're getting the best payback on your marketing dollars, you'll be able to monitor factors such as:

- ✓ *Seasonal demand.* Do customer orders peak at a certain time of year? If so, how can you maximize this period? How can you compensate during other times?

- ✓ *Geographic preferences.* Are orders for specific products or services coming from a single geographic region? Is that what you intended? If not, what tactics can you use to maximize your marketing impact geographically?

- ✓ *Price sensitivity.* Do certain items sell better at a specific price? Is it worth raising or lowering the price to sell more?

- ✓ *Age or gender preferences.* Are your products or services selling better to customers of a certain age? Do they sell better to men or women? Knowing this can help you design marketing materials tailored to their buying patterns.

- ✓ *Overall sales trends.* Are some of your products or services fading in popularity? Are others turning into classics and continuing to sell well? Your data can help you monitor which may require more marketing and which you should probably eliminate from your business.

Evaluate Data Regularly

All this data won't do you a bit of good if you don't set time aside to review it on a regular basis. It's like driving around lost with the road maps tucked in the glove compartment. Pull 'em out and reach your destination directly!

If you're puzzled about how to set up a database to capture this information, or how to generate reports and analyze the data, call in some professional help. A few hours of consulting time can result in systems that can help you monitor your marketing expenses and results simply and clearly.

Today's software database programs are easy to use and simple to set up. Many packages come with predefined templates for business activities, so you can be up and running in no time. (See resources in the Take Action section of this chapter.)

You've heard the quip "use it or lose it"; well, it applies to this strategy. Sure, it may be more exciting to plan and generate snazzy materials trumpeting your products or services. Less attractive is the analysis required to make sure those marketing dollars were well spent. But if you don't do the numbers crunching, you'll end up having to do budget crunching, which is an even less appealing task.

Take Action

1. How do your customers usually find you? What's the best investment you made in marketing your products or services during the past 12 months? How can you improve on that success?

2. Make a list of the information you need to capture on each of your customers.

3. Set up (or refine) a customer tracking database. Check out software programs such as FileMaker Inc.'s FileMaker Pro, Microsoft's Access, Symantec's Act!, and Qualcomm's Eudora Planner and Now Up-to-Date. (For additional contact information, see the resources section in the back of the book.)

Chapter 19

Go Beyond Satisfaction

One of the thrills of being an entrepreneur is becoming your own boss: no more catering to the whims and idiosyncrasies of someone who could secure or deny your professional advancement. It's startling then to realize that you've traded one boss for many. Those bosses are our customers. And your job is to keep them all happy.

Needless to say, that's a tall order. That's why this chapter's strategy is designed to help you discover ways to create a loyal customer base eager to buy from you again and again.

Debunk the Satisfaction Myth

Can you remember the last time you were totally satisfied as a customer? If you can't, you're not alone. Why? Some would say that customer service has gone the way of the dinosaur, unable to survive at the business pace of today. Few companies have the time to ensure that each and every customer is satisfied. Consider, too, that the satisfaction bar has been raised. For example, only a few years ago, if you had ordered something by mail, you probably thought it acceptable to expect it in a week or so. No longer. If we order something today, we want it tomorrow, via FedEx or UPS. And if some company found a way to get it to us the same day, that would soon become the baseline standard.

Let's face it, today's communications technologies have also upped the ante in the satisfaction game. For over three decades now, Moore's Law (actually an observation made in 1965 by Gordon Moore, formerly of Intel)—that microprocessor technology doubles in power and drops in price every 18 months—has proven true. As a result, businesses large and small are faced with trying to satisfy a world of consumers who believe the natural progression of goods and services is faster, cheaper, and better over time.

Smart Strategy

Personalization is something at which small companies can excel. We can relate to a customer as an individual, because that's our own frame of reference.

How can a solo entrepreneur or small business maintain such a pace? We can't. Instead, we have to change the rules of the game.

Make It All Personal

A paradoxical development to the digital networking of our world is that at the same time we're becoming more interconnected, we're also becoming more isolated, because many of us interact more with machines than other people. The fallout is that customers yearn for a one-on-one personal interaction, even if it's just with the telemarketer on the other end of the phone at Lands' End.

Fortunately, personalization is something at which small companies can excel. We can relate to a customer as an individual, because that's our own frame of reference. All you have to do to get in this mindset is to ask yourself, "How would I feel about my company if I were the customer?"

Learn to Love Your Data

Once you've metaphorically put yourself in your customer's shoes, there are also practical systems you can put in place to cement this bond with your customers. Recall our discussion in Chapter 18 of the importance of creating and using a database. Your database will serve as the central repository of the many elements of information that, when crunched, will give you a competitive edge.

Savvy entrepreneurs use this technology to strengthen their links with customers. Harold Grubbs, a financial planner based in Little

Rock, Arkansas, sends a personalized gift basket to his clients on the anniversary of the date they first started working with his firm. "It's a small investment, but it consistently gets great response," he explains. "It's a celebration of when we first started our relationship, and it shows my appreciation for their ongoing business." Grubbs uses another small business in town to provide the baskets; when new clients come on board, they're added to the database with notes about their favorite coffees, teas, chocolates, and other food preferences. The system has been running for several years now; it is easy to implement and generates a great payback in customer loyalty. "I often get calls from gruff, seasoned businessmen who pick up the phone to say thanks," Grubbs says. "That's when I know my message of appreciation has hit the right note."

As a bonus, Grubbs's personalized approach generates referrals (remember our discussion in Chapter 17?), but not just for his firm— the basket creators have also picked up several new customers along the way.

Calculate Your Entertainment Value

Today's customers treat the shopping and buying experience as a form of entertainment. This is reflected in the emergence of the megastore-as-tourist-attraction syndrome, exemplified by such monoliths as NikeTowns and Sony superstores. The alliance of Barnes & Noble with Starbucks is another example of this retail-as-entertainment phenomenon.

Central to this trend is the customer attitude that says, "If I'm going to give you some of my hard-earned money, I want to have some fun in the process." If you can tap into this attitude, you can build a loyal group of customers who'll keep coming back to your business, and for whom price won't be the only issue.

Robert Stephens, founder and president of the Geek Squad, a 24-hour, on-site rapid response computer task force, understands the power and appeal of fun. He's made it the central quality of his Minneapolis-based company. Specializing in computer support and repair, Stephens and his crew have made high tech high camp. Adopting a style straight out of the *Dragnet* television series of the fifties, Stephens and his crew sport gray fedoras, flash Geek Squad patrol badges, and have titles such as "special agent" and "cadet." The fun extends to the company cars, which include a black-and-white 1960 Ford Falcon and two ice-cream trucks painted SWAT-team black and sporting the orange-and-black Geek Squad logo.

Stephens, the chief inspector (natch), says the company humor eases the intimidation and fear many people feel when faced with computer glitches. "People like to have us around," he says. "They get a kick out of our style." Underlying the light-hearted approach is a serious business staffed by knowledgeable professionals who deliver quick response and quality repair work to hundreds of clients in the Twin Cities area. Voted Best Computer Repair Service two years in a row, Stephens's Geek Squad has mastered the mix of delivering service with fun.

Sell a Piece of Yourself

Entrepreneurs such as Harold Grubbs and Robert Stephens understand that when customers patronize a solo or small business, they're buying more than a product or service; they're buying a piece of the entrepreneur as well. This personal connection is what can set you apart from larger, more impersonal firms. In these days of ATM machines, voice mail, and e-mail, think how much you appreciate making a one-on-one link with someone. Do the same for your clients. You'll both feel better for it—and your business will enjoy the results, too.

Take Action

1. Think about the last time you were a satisfied customer. Jot down the name of the company that provided you with that experience, and that perhaps earned your loyalty in the process. Try to identify exactly what it was about that experience or that company that made it a pleasure to do business.

2. Make a list of three ways you can personalize your relationship with your current customers. Come up with at least one innovative or fun solution. For more ideas, read *The One-to-One Future* by Don Peppers and Martha Rogers (Bantam Doubleday Dell, 1997).

3. Implement a reward or thank-you program for your customers. It can be simple and inexpensive, but it should also be unique and thoughtful.

Chapter 20

Think Long-Term

I think of entrepreneurs as a sort of Polaroid camera crowd. We get a flash of insight or an idea and want to be able to just push a button and see the finished results in seconds. Yes, we want instant gratification.

Wishful thinking aside, we're aware of the long-term effort required to develop and then maintain the various elements that make up our individual efforts. Nowhere is this more true than in building a strong customer base.

Oh sure, our marketing ideas may come fast and furious, but the results take time to achieve, and even more time to assure over the long haul. Like grains of sand falling on one side of a scale, your efforts may not at first seem to be effective. But as you persevere, the tiny bits of sand pile up, until the cumulative weight of the sand slowly tips the scale in your favor.

Keep this imaginary scale in mind when it comes to crafting and later evaluating your marketing and sales efforts. It's all about a long-term perspective. Without this vantage point, you'll scatter your energies, take on boatloads of frustration, and squander time and money.

Go for a Cumulative Impact

Generally, no thriving business can point to a single event, campaign, or program and say with confidence that it is responsible for the total success of the firm. For the most part, three factors make up a successful marketing campaign: mix, consistency, and persistence. Let's take a look at each one.

Mix It Up

If you've been relying on some "no-fail" promotional methods and, as a result of the data evaluation you did in Chapter 18, you realize they're not as successful as they once were, try to inject a little variety in your marketing mix. Savvy entrepreneurs attack marketing from more than one angle. To grow your business, you'll need to take some risks and try new things.

You don't have to go overboard and overhaul your entire marketing strategy. Just stretch a little and try one new thing, then monitor it closely. Let's say you're a printer specializing in party invitations and the like, and you've been relying on Yellow Pages pickups—customers who found you while cruising the phone book. But you recognize that these pickups have been dwindling the last six months. Why not consider printing an invitation for *your business* and distributing it in your target area at link businesses, such as the bakeries around town who bake all those cakes for all those parties for which you print invitations?

This doesn't mean you should abandon what's been working. In fact, that leads us to the second important factor.

Be Consistent

I recall speaking after one of my presentations a few years ago to a woman who created unique, one-of-a-kind hats for the entire family. Over lunch, she explained how she was frustrated because her sales had been slumping. Intrigued, I asked her about her company's sales history and her marketing efforts. She said her sales were fairly stable all year long, and that her primary marketing was word of mouth and the distribution of a brochure she had created ages ago. I asked her if anything had changed recently, and she explained that she had run out of brochures and that she hadn't bothered to print more.

I reminded her that customers have a short attention span and of the importance of being a consistent presence in the marketplace—any marketplace. I urged her to get her brochures reprinted and in circulation again. Several months later, she sent me a note reporting that sales again were on the upswing, and she attributed the improvement to the redistribution of her brochures.

One reason entrepreneurs often fall into this trap of letting ongoing marketing efforts decay is boredom. We irrationally think that because we've seen our marketing materials for years, our prospects will find them boring as well. Nothing could be further from the truth. Commit to consistency.

Be Persistent

The average person is exposed to more than 3,000 marketing messages each day. It makes sense, then, that it will take repeat exposure to *your* message to make it register with your prospects. It takes persistence to build momentum, that powerful marketing force that all businesses need to propel them into success. It may cost a little more initially to keep your message out and about, but you know the old saying, "You have to spend money to make money." Don't be discouraged by early slow returns on your investment; time is on your side if you're persistent.

And don't forget: As you roll out your marketing program to your potential customers over an extended period, make sure it's developing the intended image you want in their minds. Each item should not only attract their attention but also reinforce your company identity.

Make Customers for Life

In traditional marketing, costs are often calculated on a metric of cost per thousand, or CPM, which refers to the dollars it takes to reach a thousand people with your message. This approach is faulty, however, because as a business owner you're seeking qualified prospects, not just random individuals. A newer, more far-reaching notion takes into account the lifetime value of the customer, or how much revenue a business will receive from a single buyer *over the course of his or her buying lifetime.* When you take this longer view, it brings into sharp focus how important even the briefest encounters can be in determining the success of your business.

I remember when my first book was nearing completion several years ago and I had to find a photographer to take a publicity shot. I got the names of three professionals with the intention of checking out their portfolios. I called each one and experienced dramatically different responses. The first just wasn't interested. The other two agreed to meet with me in their New York City studios to show me their portfolios and to discuss the shoot.

Smart Strategy

The question you need to answer is "Am I treating my customers as lifetime investments or as one-time hits?"

I made the appointments back to back (which I realize in retrospect highlighted the difference between these two photographers even more). At the first photographer's office, I was left standing alone for several minutes before his receptionist told me it would be a few minutes and to have a seat on the couch. While waiting, I perused the photographer's portfolio and was impressed with the quality of his work, specifically the way he captured his subjects. Twenty-five minutes later, I finally met the photographer, and he very briefly explained how the shoot would proceed and what his fees were. He didn't apologize for keeping me waiting, nor, more important, ask why I wanted the photograph taken. As I walked outside, I thought perhaps my expectations were too high, although common courtesy hardly seemed like a high expectation.

With less enthusiasm, I went to my second appointment. As I rode the tiny elevator up to Arthur Cohen's photography studio, I was filled with uncertainty. What a difference. Within two minutes of my crossing the threshold, Arthur came out and immediately asked about me, my work, and what I wanted the photo for. He seemed genuinely interested in every detail. For the first 15 minutes, we spoke only about my book, not about the photo shoot, the schedule, or his fees.

As I came to know Arthur better, I learned that his "interview" is not just his natural enthusiasm. It's a way he can test the waters to determine how easy or difficult a potential client will be to work with and how he or she may react with a camera zooming in, capturing every imperfection on film.

Arthur's interview method also reveals an understanding he has gained from years in business: that a prospect—any prospect—can become a customer for a lifetime. The other two photographers probably regarded me as worth $500 to $1,000 for them from a single shoot, whereas Arthur recognized that my value to his business could be 10 times that amount. And he was right. I've returned for several other sessions and recommended him to fellow authors and other business colleagues (and now to you, the readers of this book!).

The question you need to answer is: Am I treating my customers as lifetime investments or as one-time hits? If your answer is the latter, my advice to you is to rethink your marketing approach.

Take Action

1. Plan to implement one new marketing tool in your business next quarter. Track it to measure the results it generates.

2. Check your marketing methods for consistency.

3. Who are three long-time customers? Do you know why they're still with you? If not, ask them and find out.

Chapter 21

Develop Your Sales Skills

New business owners want to be the boss; experienced business owners want to be master salespeople. Why does this change in focus occur? Simple: Seasoned entrepreneurs understand that sales is at the heart of any business. This is an important strategy to learn. If you can't make positive and profitable connections with customers, your business will ultimately fail.

Nevertheless, a high number of business owners I come in contact with still try to build their companies without having a true understanding of the selling process. Many are convinced they aren't "any good at selling," and thus they avoid it whenever they can. It reminds me of the perception of a four-year-old who covers his face with his hands and says, "You can't see me now." Adapted to an entrepreneurial setting this translates: "If I don't want to do sales, or I'm not good at it, then my business doesn't need it."

Smart Strategy

There's one clear indicator of a company's chance for success: the attitude of its owner toward sales.

What is it about selling that generates such negative responses? For one, sales is a profession that has been ridiculed and denigrated in this society—and continues to be so. I know a retailer in New York City where Tuesday is "sales day"; that is, all the sales reps for the retailer's suppliers visit the retailer to make their pitches or to maintain contact. The retailer's staff, a rather casual and ordinarily friendly crowd, routinely roll their eyes as the "suits" start to file by;

many go out of their way to avoid the salespeople, claiming important meetings or luncheon appointments they must attend. I know this attitude is not unusual, and that sales professionals in every industry face this rudeness on a daily basis. With this kind of reception, it's no wonder many small business owners would rather not deal with sales!

Another factor that complicates the attitude regarding sales is that many of us believe that salespeople "are born, not made." In reality, this is just an excuse we use to let ourselves off the hook for not doing our sales work. The truth is, anyone can develop sales skills much as we develop computer skills or administrative skills. If you want to be a successful independent businessperson, you must face that fact.

There are three important concepts that business owners must master if they want to grow their companies: Strike an emotional chord; think solutions and value; and learn when no is the best answer. Let's take a look at each.

Strike an Emotional Chord

Experienced sales professionals know that to sell a product or service they must highlight its benefits, not just its features. This concept may seem confusing to new business owners. Here's an example: A washing machine's *features* may include size of the tub, its automatic controls, how it loads, and how quietly it runs. But its *benefits* to the consumer are how well it cleans clothes, how easy it is to use, and how reliable it is.

In general, features are distinguished by just-the-facts-ma'am descriptions—color, size, model, cost—whereas benefits are *emotionally charged* factors that make your product or service irresistible to buyers. Remember: All buying decisions are made on an emotional level, so it's the benefits of a product or service that make the sale.

Here are a couple of service examples: An accountant's "features" are that he or she can organize your business records, generate detailed reports, and help you satisfy Uncle Sam. But what you're really buying is the benefits the accounting service offers: peace of mind and the knowledge that your finances are being handled by a competent professional. A printer you hire features the capability to produce a die-cut brochure for you in six colors. However, the benefit you're buying is the capability to win new customers, make more money, and—as an extension of this emotional progression—have the life you desire.

With the distinction between features and benefits in mind, the first step to developing your sales skills is to ask yourself two questions: "What do my customers really want?" and "What are the emotions behind those wants?" Most buying motivations usually include one or more of these elements:

✓ Convenience
✓ Easy solution to a difficult problem
✓ Time-saving alternative
✓ Prestige
✓ Fear
✓ Fun
✓ Comfort

To learn these answers, don't forget to incorporate what we discussed in Chapter 15, "Listen Between the Lines"—and never *assume* you know all the reasons your customers buy!

Think Solutions and Value

Once you've clearly identified the benefits of your product or service, it's time to ratchet your sales preparation to the next level: assigning a value to what your business offers.

Adopting this strategy means you must take a close look—from your customers' perspective—at what you're currently delivering. Ask what problems keep your prospects awake at night. Once you have that answer in hand, set about determining how your business can offer a solution for their sleepless nights.

The power of this method is that it ties your sales message to emotion, the first concept we discussed. More important is that, by positioning your company as a solutions provider, you set yourself apart from other firms that only tout features. With this approach, the customer views you less like a commodity and more like a colleague. As a result, you can charge more for the value you bring and competitors fade from view.

Let's take a look at Sharon and Elaine, two independent wedding caterers. New to the business, Sharon presents clearly detailed bids to her clients, outlining menu and service prices at a competitive rate—and wonders why she never gets much work.

Elaine, on the other hand, understands that good food at a good price is the baseline. Her years of experience have taught her that a wedding caterer is part chef, part party host, and part therapist at these stressful events. In her presentations Elaine points out the value she offers in coordinating her efforts with the florist, musicians, and other service providers.

Elaine understands that her client's ultimate need is not food, it's a desire for a once-in-a-lifetime flawless event. She paints a picture of how her firm can easily and effortlessly deliver that dream. And while Elaine's fees are higher, the customer accepts them willingly as worth the added value.

A note of warning: Don't assume your customer understands or appreciates your value. It's your sales task to clearly identify the compelling reasons why *your* company's products or services are the best solution to the customer's vexing problem. You must not only point out the benefits of why customers should buy, but also convincingly demonstrate why they should buy *from you*.

Take No for an Answer

We all hate rejection, taking no for an answer. But experienced sales professionals know that *no* is not the word to fear; it's *maybe*. *Maybe* leaves you hanging. Does it mean the customer is really considering your offer, or just wants to get rid of you? Should you invest more time (equals money) on this person? In short, *maybe* precludes closure, whereas a simple, honest *no* frees you to move on to the next prospect.

One of the most important skills you'll learn is to discern between a *maybe* that is being said to graciously end a conversation and save you from rejection and one that signals genuine interest worth a revisit. Unfortunately, this skill is born only of experience—but you will learn when to push forward and when to take no for an answer.

Invest in Sales Training

To close the discussion of this strategy, I want to strongly encourage you to supplement the three concepts just discussed by investing in your development as a sales professional. Today, more than ever before, valuable resources are available to small business owners, ranging from books, audiotapes, and videos to CD-ROMs and Web sites as well as seminars and classes. Implementing one or more of these aids will give you an almost immediate return on your investment as you put the material you learn to practical use.

One word of caution: Sales skills can never be totally mastered, and therefore can be an ongoing source of both excitement and frustration. But if you focus on the excitement, your attitude will be one of optimism, seeing the opportunity in every interaction with a customer who can benefit from your products or services.

Take Action

1. Practice asking your customers why they buy from you, and write down their answers. Whether or not you use this feedback in subsequent presentations to other customers is up to you, but you'll have the benefit of this knowledge to drive your sales.

2. At least once a year, focus on one aspect of your sales development that needs work, and sign up for a seminar or workshop to address it.

3. Start your sales training simply. Buy a book or audio program that addresses your particular concerns and capabilities, then really use it! Here are a few suggestions to get you started (look for others in the Resources section in the back of the book):

   The Sales Bible, by Jeffrey H. Gitomer (William Morrow & Company, 1994)

   Selling for Dummies, by Tom Hopkins (IDG Books Worldwide, 1995)

   Outrageous! Unforgettable Service, Guilt-Free Selling, by T. Scott Gross (Amacom, 1998)

   Guerrilla Selling, by Jay Conrad Levinson, Bill Gallagher, and Orvel Ray Wilson (Houghton Mifflin, 1992)

   The Psychology of Selling audio program by Brian Tracy (Brian Tracy International, 1995)

   Selling the Dream, by Guy Kawasaki (Harper Business, 1992)

Chapter 22

Leverage Technology

Twenty years ago, when I started my first solo venture, the business world was running at a much slower pace. Desktops, if they held any machinery, sported typewriters, not computers. Human beings still took your messages when you were out to lunch, not some electronically disembodied voice from the phone system. Memos were circulated by hand or interoffice mail, not via e-mail. Schedules were longer, too, because even the simplest marketing materials took days or weeks to typeset and print. And if you wanted something delivered in a hurry, you used first-class mail.

Today it's hard to imagine how anything got done. What, no fax machine? No laptop? No cell phone, pager, or e-mail? And how would we start our day without the espresso maker or juice machine? Yes, technology has changed our lives in countless ways.

For small businesses, the impact is particularly evident in marketing and sales capabilities now available to them—capabilities formerly reserved for those companies with big budgets and bigger staffs. Today an individual can operate a business out of a tiny home office tucked into the corner of a room and compete with companies many times larger—anywhere in the world. The playing field, while not completely leveled, has been redesigned.

That said, having access to state-of-the-art technology doesn't necessarily translate into being able to use it effectively. To get the most from today's technologies—by which I mean generating a positive impact in your business—you must *leverage* these high-tech tools and use digital capabilities as a fulcrum for those business challenges you're facing.

There are three levels on which to utilize technology in your marketing and sales efforts: adding a digital flair to traditional marketing practices, marketing with new media, and transforming the essence of your business. As you move up through the levels, you begin to leverage technology in a more effective way, thereby gaining additional competitive advantage.

Add a Digital Flair to Traditional Marketing

The first level is where you adapt traditional marketing materials to new technology. This usually involves printed materials such as business cards, brochures, catalogs, and so forth.

For example:

- ✓ Digitize your logos to incorporate your graphic image consistently across all your business materials.
- ✓ Store images of your products on your computer for quick and accurate reproduction in any format.
- ✓ Generate marketing materials with high professional quality.
- ✓ Design and publish a newsletter for your customers.
- ✓ Produce limited-edition or one-of-a-kind marketing materials for special customers.

All these efforts take advantage of technology by saving you time and money, and at the same time improve the professionalism of your output. In no time, you can present a big-company image on a small-company budget. And be aware that today this higher level is a *baseline standard,* meaning that customers *expect* this professionalism from a business—any business, large or small.

At this level, you've paid the entrance fee to the theme park, but you don't have any ride tickets yet.

Market with New Media

At the next level you begin to explore ways to expand your marketing reach through new uses of the technology. For example:

✓ Research your prospective clients by conducting data searches on the Web.

✓ Stay up to date on industry news and trends by subscribing to—and checking in with—online information services.

✓ Clip articles you find in your news scan and send them to select customers using e-mail.

✓ Create an e-mail newsletter to send valuable, up-to-date information to your key customers.

✓ Set up an autoresponder on your computer or with your Internet Service Provider (ISP) to give your customers instant e-mail access to commonly requested information, 24 hours a day, 7 days a week.

✓ Create a Web page that highlights pertinent information about your company. Later expand that page to a full Web site, and feature a detailed catalog of your products and/or services, plus lots of helpful information to draw your customers back.

✓ Institute electronic commerce capabilities on your site so you can conduct sales on a global, 24/7 (24 hours a day, 7 days a week) basis.

A growing number of businesses are using technology at this level today—and, because of the swift pace of new developments, all of these methods will become easier to implement and subsequently commonly used even by very small companies in the near future. The point is, you'll have to keep up to stay competitive. Again, once it becomes commonplace, you lose your marketing advantage.

At this level, you're in the park and have been on a few good rides, but the renowned roller coaster awaits.

Transform Your Business Essence

At the third level, it's time to approach technology in an entirely different way. From this point on, you won't be considering how it can support your traditional marketing efforts or boost your sales to the next level; instead, you'll analyze technology trends with an eye to how they can completely transform the essence of your business.

In Chapter 4 I spoke about the need to clarify what business you are in, illustrated by examples of companies that had taken a close look at their capabilities and shifted gears to embrace new business opportunities. To leverage technology to its fullest, you must do the same. You must take a look at your current business, analyze where technology is heading, and see where the two may intersect.

Smart Strategy

Access to state-of-the-art technology doesn't necessarily translate into being able to use it effectively. You must leverage these high-tech tools and use digital capabilities as a fulcrum for those business challenges you're facing.

The new business opportunities that await you are being generated, in part, by *digital convergence*—the coming together of many different types of information and media through the 1s and 0s of computer programming code. Everything begins to overlap, and thus the lines start to blur: Music becomes computer-based audio, video is integrated into multimedia, words become interactive programs, and on and on. Companies that can create innovative content—and communities of enthusiasts for that content—become the leaders of brand-new markets.

For solo entrepreneurs operating idea- and information-based companies, this convergence opens many doors. For product-based firms that are nimble and creative enough to make a unique new blend of product, media, and distribution, the opportunities are almost unlimited.

Futurize

What will these new businesses be like? Ah, that's the crux of the matter. Because they'll be either brand-new inventions or new combinations of traditional formats, there's no way to predict what will emerge and, of those companies that do emerge, which will go the distance. Some indicators do exist, however, such as the firms creating one-of-a-kind music CDs to customer specifications by licensing the individual songs from larger music firms. It's an old product (music), packaged in a new way (to order, on CDs), capitalizing on a current trend (personalization), by leveraging technology. The songs are all digitized, so the cuts can be previewed and the order of the tracks can be shifted with ease.

Or consider Wally Bock. With a background in military intelligence and experience in police work, Bock became a technology enthusiast back when mainframes were state of the art. Bock has come full circle. By leveraging technology and his background in intelligence, he has launched a successful firm that conducts online business intelligence (www.bockinfo.com). He understands that companies need information—about themselves, about their industry, about their competitors—but don't usually have the time to track it down. His business has taken a long-standing need, transformed it with the power of technology, and created a novel service with open-ended growth potential.

This type of convergent thinking is how entrepreneurs of all stripes can take advantage of opportunities in the near future. To achieve maximum results with technology, however, you must be willing to leapfrog your thinking to several years down the road. Then add your unique abilities to the mix. The combination can be formidable—and can signal the beginning of an exciting new business.

Needless to say, this is the roller-coaster ride, marked by the stomach-dropping twists and turns of the digital business landscape. But for individuals who want to grow their businesses in exciting new ways, this is virgin territory, the technology version of manifest destiny.

Take Action

1. If you haven't done so already, have your logo and promotional and product photos digitized. Unless you are skilled with this process, hire a designer to do this for you.

2. Build a long-term technology marketing plan for your company. Think of the ways you'd like to see your business grow over the next several years, then consider how technology can be integrated into the plan.

3. Increase your understanding of the role and impact of technology by reading books such as:

   Blur: The Speed of Change in the Connected Economy, by Stan Davis and Christopher Meyer (Addison-Wesley, 1998)

   Release 2.1: A Design for Living in the Digital Age, by Esther Dyson (Broadway Books, 1998)

   Technotrends: How to Use Technology to Go Beyond Your Competition, by Daniel Burrus (Harper Business, 1993)

   What Will Be: How the New World of Information Will Change Our Lives, by Michael Dertouzos (HarperCollins, 1997)

Chapter 23

Network Your Way
to Business Growth

R emember as a teenager hearing your parents warn you: "Choose your friends carefully. They can make a big difference in your future"? Of course, these comments likely fell on deaf ears as you struggled to establish your independence and identity. Later, however, you no doubt looked back and realized the wisdom of those words.

This same advice, with slight alterations, can be applied to you now, while you're in the process of growing your business. "Choose your colleagues carefully; they will have a greater impact on your business success than you may realize today."

The strategy of networking is so important that I'll take it a step further and state: The quality of your professional network has a direct correlation to the rate of your business growth and the level of success you attain.

Smart Strategy

The networking strategy is about choosing our colleagues as deliberately as we make our business decisions.

No, this is not just another way of saying "It's not what you know, it's who you know"; it's much more than that. The "who you know" implies that personal connections (often, those you have not earned, but "inherited" from family and friends) will open doors for you. And while that's an aspect of the benefits that come from a strong network, your close associates affect you on many other levels as well, from the way you view your business to the reaction you have to defeat or failure and the practical ways you handle daily tasks and challenges.

We small business owners are sponges for information and input—we soak up ideas, methods, viewpoints, biases, techniques, and so much more. The networking strategy asks you to choose more carefully and consciously what you soak up. It requires that you be truly aware of your environment and those who populate it.

Read the Roster

Take a look at your roster of close colleagues. I daresay you'll find individuals who stumbled into your life by happenstance—through a mutual friend, shared interests, repeated run-ins at industry or business shows or events, or simply because you clicked.

This serendipitous accumulating of colleagues is not unusual, but it is in direct contradiction to how we try to arrange most other aspects of our business lives—which is usually by careful thought, sometimes lengthy decision-making, and careful implementation of a plan or procedure.

The networking strategy is about choosing our colleagues as deliberately as we make our business decisions. If you want to grow your business, you must seek out and choose colleagues who can support and guide you in your efforts. Become more aware of the types of colleagues you need in your business life, and consciously seek out ways to make connections with them.

Weave Some Networks

To expand your professional connections, I recommend three main avenues to explore, each of which will bring you in contact with different types of individuals:

✓ *Industry associations.* Fellow members of industry associations can help you navigate the ins and outs of your particular field. They understand the marketplace in which you're working, and can be valuable allies in keeping you apprised of news, gossip, opportunities, or insights. You can share referrals, team up on projects, and create mutual visibility.

✓ *Other business associations.* Connections with peers from different industries can bring you a fresh viewpoint on your own field. The solutions to problems you may be facing may be more obvious to outsiders. Both your business and personal life will be enriched as you discover the similarities in the challenges that all business owners confront, no matter in what particular niche they may be working.

✓ *Personal associations.* Non-work-related relationships can sometimes offer the most well-rounded support of the three network structures, because these are the people who know your entire self and can therefore offer comprehensive suggestions. They can serve as a reality check, to force you to make sure your work goals are part of a larger vision; they can also help you sort out the meaning behind your long hours and hectic life. Besides, what better way to get a new perspective than to spend a few hours with a close friend—hiking, seeing a movie, or sharing dinner—and *not* talk about business?

The cross-pollination of ideas and inspiration from these three types of networks is vital to your business growth—and to your personal life as well. So take time to review your current network, then invest time in expanding it to include individuals from all three categories.

Work Your Network

Once you've identified areas in your network that you need to strengthen, it's time to put your network to work. Your connections are only as valuable as the amount of attention you pay to them. You must define what role you want them to play, and then direct the show. Here are some things to keep in mind:

✓ *Think reciprocity.* Approach your network colleagues with a goal of mutual success. You don't always want to be tapping into your network for support without giving back; nor do you want to be the one always giving.

✓ *Stay in touch just to stay in touch.* We've all had the experience of hearing from people only when they want something from us. It sours a relationship—quickly. Stay in contact with the individuals in your network even if it's just to say hello.

✓ *Connect on different levels.* Staying in contact has many different manifestations in this digital era, and each conveys a slightly different message. Use these methods strategically. For example, use e-mail to send a short response to a question or to share an idea. But, as I've mentioned before, to show appreciation, a handwritten thank-you note will go a lot further.

Be aware as you develop your networking skills and preferred methods that the true value of a connection may not be revealed immediately or even for some time. Don't be shortsighted when new acquaintances come into your business life. Someone with skills, interests, and colleagues in an entirely different field could turn into a priceless link for your company in ways that you can't imagine right now. Similarly, that junior staffer with seemingly no influence on a current project may advance to another company and to a higher-level position, with the power to hire your firm. Don't count anyone out.

Tend the Network Garden

A network is an organic entity, and as such is in a process of continual transformation. Consequently, you'll be seeing growth spurts as well as decay. As your business develops, you'll need to become a gardener for your network. You must plant new seeds to grow new contacts; you must water diligently, so your current connections stay strong and healthy to be there when you need them; and of course, you must weed out the growth that is inhibiting *your* growth.

Like a bed of hearty perennial flowers, a well-tended network grows fuller and more attractive as time goes by. If you make a conscious effort to develop your business network, you'll see that it expands exponentially within a very short time. Then the personal and professional riches of this strategy will come back to you manyfold.

Take Action

1. Draw up a wish list of networking contacts. How many do you already know but need to strengthen the connection with? How can you meet the others?

2. Write down ways that you can bring value to each of these individuals. List how you'd like them to aid you in your business.

3. Read Susan RoAne's *The Secrets of Savvy Networking: How to Make the Best Connections for Business and Personal Success* (Warner Books, 1993), then commit to improving your networking skills.

Chapter 24

Move Up the Value Chain

W hile many of us solo entrepreneurs or small business owners planned and plotted and saved for years to "do our own thing," a surprising number of individuals have entrepreneurship thrust upon them. They may have been downsized or laid off by a long-time employer, decided they'd had enough of the so-called security of corporate life, and opted to strike out on their own rather than follow the traditional job-hunting route. Others, while working full-time jobs, begin by making extra money from a free-time avocation or passion and realize they could make a living doing something they really love.

But however they get to small business ownership, too many entrepreneurs, even those who were well directed at launch, later let the marketplace dictate their subsequent development, which in a sense is again giving up control. The strategy in this chapter helps you determine where your business is located in the value chain, so that you can *consciously* move up the chain how and when you want. It enables you to reposition your company in the marketplace, and, as a result, increase your revenues and profits.

Follow the Brigade

To understand the notion of a value chain, let's take a behind-the-scenes look at the kitchen of a typical five-star restaurant. At first glance the activity may seem chaotic. But on closer inspection, you'll find that a finely tuned system keeps everything in order and ensures that the food and service are of the highest quality.

Internationally renowned chef Auguste Escoffier was the innovator in the late 1800s behind this hierarchy of food preparation, called the brigade system, still in use today. Escoffier devised processes and procedures to streamline the kitchen operations of London's elegant Savoy Hotel. In addition, he also defined each staff member's position, with specific responsibilities so that there was no question who was supposed to be doing what, and when.

Smart Strategy

Moving up the value chain enables you to reposition your company in the marketplace, and, as a result, increase your revenues and profits.

In today's grande cuisine restaurants, this system also serves as a way for younger chefs to move up in the kitchen hierarchy all the way to chef. For example, a recent cooking school graduate might begin as a pantry chef, in charge of preparation of cold food such as salads or cold appetizers. He or she might advance to station chef (in larger kitchens, these line cooks focus on one particular preparation, such as fish, grilled foods, fried foods, or vegetables). Next in the hierarchy is the sous chef, the second-in-command or "underchef." He or she is typically responsible for scheduling, assists the line chefs, and fills in for the chef as necessary. Finally, at the top of the hierarchy is the chef de cuisine, also known as the executive chef or simply "the chef." He or she runs the show, from supervising every detail of food preparation to creating the menus. In today's environment, many chefs have become celebrities for the creative flair they bring to fine dining, as well as for the high-profile clientele they attract.

Like a member of a grande cuisine kitchen staff, your company is one of the links in the business world hierarchy. For many solo entrepreneurs and small business owners, this position—your status—is one of default: You saw a marketplace opportunity and turned it into a business. But that's for beginners.

Lead the Brigade

Now it's time to move up in the business value chain, and this is something you want to control. (Don't forget, one of the main reasons you became a business owner was because you wanted to be your own boss, in charge.) Taking this step will clarify the context in which your current business operates. It also will enable you to take your business to the next level—to take charge rather than react to the idiosyncrasies of the marketplace.

To begin, you need to analyze how your business relates to other businesses in the value chain. For example, let me introduce Dan, a direct mail copywriter. For one of his projects, he has been assigned to write sales letters for his client to generate customer response, and ultimately, profit. When he's done with his part of the project, Dan turns over the letters to the client's in-house marketing team whose various members put the other pieces of the project together: One contacts a list broker to obtain the best names, another works with a designer to create the mailer, a third negotiates with a printer and secures a mailing house to prep the finished piece for delivery.

In Escoffier's brigade system, Dan's making salads. Though salads are an important element in a well-rounded meal, and Dan makes very good salads, let's face it, he's not going to be the one called out of the kitchen to accept customer kudos at the end of the meal.

So Dan decides he has made enough salads to last a lifetime and commits himself to growing his business by moving up the value chain. First he reviews his copywriting work and his options. After several years in business, Dan knows which list brokers have the most reliable databases of names to rent; he also knows the printers who give competitive prices and the mailing houses that guarantee their work. With this information in hand, Dan's ready to pull himself up.

He decides to reposition his company by offering additional services, knowing this will also mean he can charge higher fees for his expertise. Instead of just writing the copy, Dan contracts to obtain the mailing lists and brokers the printing and mailing house services. He points out the additional benefits and savings of having it all handled by one outsourced firm. Wisely, he implements these changes slowly, so he can monitor the responses he gets (recall what I said in Chapter 18 about the importance of tracking customers). He also decides to work in conjunction with other independent professionals from time to time on those projects he knows will overwhelm his capabilities or where his experience is limited. (I discuss this further in Chapter 42, "Expand Virtually.")

As a result of this ranking analysis, followed by his conscious decision to move up the chain, Dan is able to increase his revenues over a few years. And as a bonus, he has expanded his skills and networked with some interesting and valuable professionals, which will make the next move up even easier.

Break the Consulting Chain

In the discussion of this strategy, I want to single out those solo businesspeople who call themselves consultants. Because this is a vague title, meaning different things depending on the type of business, consultants often operate for too long at the bottom of the hierarchy, taking any and all jobs a client may offer that fall remotely within their field of expertise.

If you market yourself as a consultant, I can assure you that by adopting the approach outlined in this chapter, you can migrate your practice—and your income—up the chain. This process is particularly effective for consultants who have identified their unique set of skills and abilities—and have mastered a way to sell the value of their expertise to clients. (This is covered in more detail in Chapter 47, "Refine and Reinvent.")

Coupled with experience and time, this strategy can enable you to move away from executing your clients' plans to *creating* their plans. Think of it as moving from chopping vegetables to choosing the menu.

Know When to Stay Put

Not every strategy in this book is for everyone or for every business, and this is one that works better for some than others. You may find, for example, that your comfort level—indeed, your happiness—is in one particular area, or that you don't want to transition your company to, say, take responsibility for other tasks or staff. Frankly, some businesses don't lend themselves to this type of upward strategy. For example, if you're a Web site designer, you may not want to incorporate other services, such as Web site hosting, where technical support calls would be demanding. Or if you have a mail-order product-based firm, expanding into distribution or opening retail outlets may not suit you.

But whether you adopt this strategy or not, there is great worth in stepping back and evaluating your business in the context of a value chain. You'll become clearer about the options you have to market your business, as well as the role your skills and contributions play in the broader business environment. You'll also come to realize that no matter how small a cog you are in the commerce machine, you're still vital to ensuring that it operates smoothly and efficiently.

Take Action

1. Ask and answer: Where am I in the value chain that operates in the marketplace I serve?

2. Identify what it would take to transition your business in the marketplace. Are there areas that seem like logical choices for moving up?

3. Explore a more detailed discussion of the value chain hierarchy in modern business by reading *The Profit Zone*, by Adrian J. Slywotzky and David J. Morrison (Times Books, 1997).

Chapter 25

Upgrade Your Customer Base

This strategy is similar in spirit to the last, "Move Up the Value Chain," in that it asks you to *choose* to upgrade your position in the marketplace rather than stand pat. It explains how to grow your business by focusing on acquiring and retaining specific types of customers. This strategy is also a prime example of the concept that the simplest ideas are often the most powerful—and the most frequently overlooked.

It's a basic tenet of Business 101 that your customers are the source of your revenues and profits. But let's go beyond the obvious: Though it's patently clear that customers buy your goods or services, and therefore complete the cycle of commerce, what often remains unsaid is that it's the *type* of customers your company serves that is the actual determining factor in the level of profits you generate.

What's discussed even less frequently is that your profits are directly tied to your customers' financial capabilities. Put more bluntly, if you target a market that is financially restricted, you're limiting the growth of your firm. This is particularly problematic for solo or very small businesses, where the additional limitations of time and staff create a wall so high it effectively can't be scaled.

Shift Focus for a Better Return

Let's look at an example of a solo businesswoman who realized the value in upgrading her customer base. Susan is a financial planner in southern New Mexico. In the first years of her practice, just anxious to build a clientele, any clientele, she accepted every job that came her way. After many long hours and a lot of hard work, her business slowly began to grow, primarily by word of mouth and referrals.

Smart Strategy

The financial capabilities of your customers will determine the heights of your success.

Then one day, a longtime client referred her to a wealthy colleague. Susan was a bit unnerved at first, since this prospect's financial portfolio was larger than anything she had handled to that point in her career. So even though she would be in charge of only a small portion of this client's holdings, Susan approached the project with particular diligence, determined not to squander the opening to another level of achievement. She even pursued additional studies of financial matters, and in many other small ways put extra effort into managing the details of the new account.

As time passed, Susan observed three important things. First, the paperwork and other tasks associated with managing the wealthy client's portfolio were not substantially different from that for her other clients. Second, in some ways, the wealthy client proved to be an easier case, because he was too busy with running his business affairs to be calling all the time. After all, that's what he had hired Susan, a fellow professional, to do—relieve him of the concerns of managing his money. Third, the fees Susan earned were higher because they were based on a percentage of money under management.

It took a while for Susan to realize the impact that this client had on her business. But once she did, she decided to focus all her marketing efforts on attracting more upscale clients. That too became easier, because the best leads in this upscale market came from referrals, so the only marketing she had to do was to satisfy her clients to ensure they would pass on her name.

Susan's business is now primarily made up of high-income clients, although she retains a number from her earlier business incarnation with whom she enjoys working. Her other lower-income clients she has passed along to a younger associate she trusts and stays in contact with to make sure none of her former clients' accounts are mismanaged. Today, Susan is working just as hard, but she finds it much more fulfilling—and profitable.

Upgrade Any Business

Though not all businesses are such clear-cut cases for customer upgrading, I assure you it can be done in any business. It all comes down to being selective about your customers. It's a simple equation, really. To grow your business, you can either take on more customers worth your current level of income or take on the same number of customers at a higher level. Far too many entrepreneurs struggle year after year in business, trying to capture just one more account—any account.

The more effective—and saner—approach is to leverage your time and effort to generate more revenue from each client, not from more clients at the same level. This means either increasing the amount that current customers will pay for your product or service or migrating to new customers who will pay more.

Analyze the Best

This process begins with a financial analysis of the sources of your current revenue. Financial software can easily generate reports that will clearly indicate which customers are most valuable to your company. As experienced entrepreneurs will tell you, don't be surprised if you discover the customers who take up the greatest amount of your time end up being those who bring in the least amount of revenue.

This is the celebrated 80/20 rule, or Pareto principle, named after the Italian economist Vilfredo Pareto, who applied mathematical theories to income distribution. Pareto observed that 80 percent of the wealth came from 20 percent of a town's inhabitants. This law of distribution is applicable to remarkably diverse situations, and it's invoked frequently in contemporary business analysis. In small business terms, Pareto's law translates to the common situation in which 80 percent of a firm's revenues come from 20 percent of its customers.

Your task is to always know which customers occupy the top-level ranking. Armed with this information, you can strategically assess where to direct your marketing efforts. You can weed out non-productive segments of your business and build in areas where you have greater return on your investment. In just a short time, patterns will emerge, and you'll be able to see which types of customers will enable you to reach your growth targets.

Some solo entrepreneurs chafe at the thought of targeting upscale clients. And as the director of your own business, it's up to you to decide. But before you do, I remind you: There's only so much of your time and energy to go around. There are many ways to grow a business. If you want to become the best, why not work for those who can appreciate and pay for the best?

Take Action

1. Analyze the return on investment for your clients. Track the time you spend on each of them and compare it against the income they're generating for you. Does the 80/20 rule apply? Does the time spent on any single customer exceed the "budget" you've set for him or her?

2. Plan for the upgrade. Increase your capabilities and skill level. Get the word out, and ask friends and colleagues for referrals. Be ready to serve your new clients well.

3. If you find yourself resisting upgrading your customer base, ask yourself why. Perhaps you still doubt yourself and your capabilities. Give one of your mentors a call (remember Chapter 5?) for a confidence boost.

OPERATIONS
STRATEGIES

Chapter 26

Design Your Workspace for Functionality

As small business owners, we spend a lot of time making sure we offer and then provide excellent products and services. It's a bit ironic, therefore, that we don't give equal time to the space that facilitates the delivery of those products and services, to the design and function of where we spend most of our waking hours—and where our livelihood is generated.

When you improve the efficiency of your office, you'll reap several benefits:

✓ Your stress level will go down.

✓ Your response time will speed up.

✓ Your productivity will improve—as will your bottom line.

I know you understand that what I'm saying here is true, but I'm equally sure you find it difficult to carve out the time to create an office environment that can support you in this way. That's what this strategy is about.

Put Your Invisible Assistant to Work

When your office is designed well—by which I mean to meet your needs, not some *House Beautiful* fantasy of functional—it serves as your invisible assistant, supporting you in everything you do. (One of my former solo businesses was as a photographer's agent, and in that role I witnessed the preparation and styling of many interior office locations before a shoot. Believe me, the workspaces you see featured in magazines resemble the photos for only about six hours—until the photographers leave, that is. Then they revert to reality, with papers strewn on the floor and Post-it Notes stuck all over computer monitors.) When the layout of your workspace is poor, you'll expend needless energy to make things work, and thus be more tired at the end of the day, with probably a lot less to show for it as well.

Smart Strategy

There's a subtle but important distinction between layout and organization. Layout affects workflow and productivity, but it cannot compensate for the strength or weakness of the underlying systems. The two must work in concert.

After 20 years of working on my own, in eight different office spaces, I've learned some important pointers about office design that have improved my productivity—and profits:

✓ *Design your office desk as a cockpit.* All essentials should be within easy reach. For most people, an L- or U-shaped configuration is the most efficient. Matched with a chair that swivels, this setup lets you maximize your productivity. You'll also have the confidence to do your best work, knowing your tools are at hand.

✓ *Limit the items on your desk to the essentials.* Store that extra box of paper clips somewhere else, move the unopened mail (see the next point). And that's not yesterday's cup of cold coffee lingering on your desk, is it? The less clutter on your desk, the more focused your mind.

✓ *Set up a mail center, where you open and sort mail.* Mine is next to a trash can and a recycling bin—because 75 percent of the incoming mail ends up there within minutes of being opened (sometimes even before). I strip mail of its envelope, packing material, and advertising, which goes a long way to reducing paper clutter. Ditto for cartons and large boxes. I break these down for reuse or recycling and make a weekly run to the recycling center.

✓ *Plug in your printer within reach and your fax machine out of earshot.* After years of juggling the placement of these two devices, I've concluded that it's most efficient to have the printer nearby, so I can easily grab output. The fax machine I prefer farther away so that the noise it makes doesn't interfere with my thinking or while I'm making phone calls. Furthermore, it forces me out of my chair several times a day, which keeps me from forgetting to get up and move, which in turn keeps me energized.

✓ *As difficult as this may be, try to keep at least one horizontal space completely clear to use as a work zone or project staging area.* I have one table that is off-limits for anything but temporary special use, such as collating project materials or preparing items for a road trip. Nothing stays on this table for longer than two days.

✓ *Invest in a good chair.* Your office chair is your most important piece of furniture. In fact, you'll likely spend more time in your chair than you will in your bed—or anywhere else, for that matter. You may have to do some research to find the one that's just right for you. There are hundreds of well designed and ergonomically sound work chairs out there. Take time to find one that will support you, literally and figuratively, while you work—and remember, it's tax deductible.

✓ *Pay attention to lighting and ambience.* Environmental conditions can greatly affect your attention span, endurance, and energy level, not to mention your mood. These add up to how productive you will be, as well as how much you enjoy your work. If you're unsure where to start, many good books are available at your neighborhood bookseller. Also, talk to a lighting specialist at your local home supply center for some practical tips and suggestions.

✓ *Analyze your daily workflow and activities, to make sure the office layout works in harmony with your actions.* Sometimes the smallest changes can bring unexpected benefits. For example, I found that placing my printer on a table with wheels enables me to more easily change the toner cartridge, fix paper jams, clean it (which otherwise I would do rarely, if at all), or move it to another location should that become necessary.

Above all, make your workspace a reflection of you and how you prefer to work.

Model for Mobility

If you're one of the growing number of solo entrepreneurs and small business owners who have to travel frequently, you may also have to design an alternative office space, which may be the trunk of your car or your briefcase at 30,000 feet in the air. Though these spaces are substantially smaller, you must organize them with as much care as your regular workspace. Here are some tips for setting up an office on the move:

- ✓ *Invest in special equipment.* This may include luggage designed for easy access to interior spaces, your laptop, and accessories. Shop around for compartmentalized storage units for your car to keep materials organized and safe from spillage caused by the motion of driving. If you find yourself saying, "There's got to be a better way to do this," you're probably right. By using your ingenuity and keeping your eyes open to potential solutions, you'll discover ways to streamline your work processes and boost your productivity when your office is on wheels or wings.

- ✓ *Share ideas and experiences with fellow travelers.* A single tip or source for equipment can simplify a task and result in increased savings of time, energy, and money.

- ✓ *Adopt a mobile mindset.* If you're a traveling professional, review your office-on-the-road needs on a regular basis. This is where you spend valuable time, and if don't you invest in the proper equipment to support you, it can directly impact your business growth.

Call In the Pros

When it comes to office design, nothing beats having a professional guide. Even a brief consultation can introduce changes in layout, equipment, lighting, and other elements that can improve your work environment and productivity. Don't overlook the value of a fresh pair of eyes. We often are so intimately bound to our offices that we become blind to the surroundings and can't imagine any other way to shape the space for better efficiency.

A related group of advisors—many of them soloists themselves—are called professional organizers. These individuals are masters at making calm out of office chaos. But note: They are not designers or space planners, nor are they there to clean up your office. Rather, they objectively analyze your office activities and establish systems to help you function more productively. Many are members of the National Association of Professional Organizers (NAPO). Over the past few years, I've worked with several NAPO members with great results; their systems have helped to streamline my office dramatically (see resources in the Take Action section of this chapter).

The popularity of office design and organizational pros points out the need for—and value of—properly developed office systems. It also points out the subtle but important distinction between layout and organization. Layout affects workflow and productivity, but it cannot compensate for the strength or weakness of the underlying systems (which we'll cover in the next chapter). The two must work in concert.

Take Action

1. Sit down at the end of a particularly long and tiring day and ask yourself how much of your weariness is attributable to bad office design and/or equipment. Do you need a larger desk? A staging area that doubles as conference center for meeting with clients? New files? Better task lighting? Should you invest in off-site storage?

2. This month, look through some of those office supply catalogs before you toss them on the recycling heap. Get some ideas of design options and pricing. Cruise some home office supply and office furniture stores. Sit behind some desks, switch on some lights, and ask questions of the staff. Check out Neal Zimmerman's book, *Home Office Design* (John Wiley & Sons, 1996), to help clarify your thinking.

3. Contact the National Association of Professional Organizers (NAPO) at (512) 206-0151 (or on the Web at http://www.napo.org) to find the names of professional organizers near you. Call them and discuss their services and your needs.

Chapter 27

Establish Systems

If the public view of a company is the glitzy exterior, its business systems are the interior wiring. They may not be much to look at, but they keep the power running to light the entire structure. Unfortunately, too many small business owners pay attention only to the outside views of their companies, not realizing until too late that their neglect of the support systems is costing their companies untold amounts of wasted time, energy, and money.

Once set up, systems form the safety net under all you do. They are the oil that keeps your business engine humming smoothly. Well-designed and carefully implemented systems free up your time and liberate your mind from unproductive worry.

To assess how your company's systems are functioning, I've compiled brief descriptions and checklist items that correspond with the five primary operations areas of a business: marketing, sales, administration, personnel, and finance. See how your company stacks up in these areas.

Devise Marketing Systems

As discussed in earlier chapters, everything your company does to reach out and attract customers can be thought of in marketing terms. With that in mind, consider how well your marketing systems function by reviewing this checklist.

❏ Does your letterhead and all other printed material contain full contact information, including your e-mail address and/or Web site, in easy-to-read type?

❏ Have you created an overall look and feel for your company that carries through on all your marketing materials?

❏ Are your printed materials fax-friendly? Can they be read clearly by the recipient?

❏ Do you have a process in place to respond to information requests quickly and easily? Phone, fax on demand, e-mail, Web?

Smart Strategy

Once set up, systems form the safety net under all you do. Well-designed and carefully implemented systems free up your time and liberate your mind from unproductive worry.

❏ Have you made it easy for customers to order? Do you offer multiple ordering options (mail, phone, fax, online, and so forth)?

❏ Do you have a telephone system that can route or handle customer requests efficiently?

❏ Do you track inventory of your most popular marketing materials so you know when you're running low?

❏ Is there a core group of marketing and media contacts you are in contact with on an ongoing basis? Is this database updated regularly?

Organize Sales Systems

The sales process makes handshakes happen and gets contracts signed. How well are your systems in place to support your growing company?

❏ Do you have a lead-tracking system that moves the sales process forward?

❏ Have you developed software templates to streamline your paperwork processing for proposals, letters, contracts, and other forms?

❏ Are your customer contracts easy to read, execute, and file?

❏ Is there a follow-up system that enables you to check on new customers and that presents additional buying opportunities?

❏ If you sell by telephone, do you have a script that all (even new or temporary) staff members can follow?

❏ Are your salespeople trained to cross-sell other products or services, to maximize each and every sale?

Fine-Tune Administrative Systems

Once the sale is made, do you follow procedures that guarantee the product or service is delivered properly and on time to the customer? What about your daily office operations?

❏ Have you set up a mail center in your office? (See Chapter 26.)

❏ Are your shipping fees and instructions clearly indicated on your order forms?

❏ Is your street address printed on all materials, particularly if you operate a post office box?

❏ Have you established accounts with more than one parcel delivery service and overnight carrier, in case of a labor strike?

❏ If your product has to be assembled, are instructions clearly written and included with the packaging?

❏ If you use packing slips, are they generated at the same time as invoices to reduce duplication of efforts? What about mailing labels?

❏ Do you have a database in place to capture and track customer information?

Manage Personnel Systems

No matter what size your business, you will no doubt interact with some type of staff or with independent contractors. How strong are your systems for dealing with staff and independent workers?

❏ When you hire an independent contractor, do you use a template for your written agreement that clarifies your relationship and outlines each party's legal and tax responsibilities?

❏ When you hire an employee, is there a system in place to welcome the new person to the company and to ensure that all the proper paperwork is completed?

❏ Do you conduct regular performance reviews for each staff member? Does your staff get regular feedback from you on their work? How do you encourage feedback from your employees about the business, their jobs, your clients?

❏ Are your work hours clearly spelled out? Do your staff members know your policies for sick days, personal days, overtime?

❏ Are you on top of what your employees really want? Do you know what benefits they value most and what additional training they may wish to receive?

❏ Do you have a backup system in place in case one of your independent contractors is unavailable to work for you? Do you maintain an active list of potential talent?

Build Financial Systems

Financial details are the foundation for any successful business, but they are often ignored or handled haphazardly as a new business struggles through early development stages. To navigate growth, you need a strong understanding of finances; we'll be covering that in more detail in the next section. In the meantime, review this check-list to prompt the establishment of strong financial systems.

❏ Do you have an efficient method for submitting and tracking invoices?

❏ Have you written policies regarding discount schedules and prepayment options?

❏ Do you have financial software installed on your computer? Does it generate reports—including an income statement, a balance sheet, and a statement of cash flow—that you review on a regular basis?

❏ If you deliver a service such as consulting, have you established quantitative milestones for interim billing?

❏ How long would it take you to determine the current financial state of your company?

❏ If you carry inventory, do you have systems in place to monitor its quantity and value?

Streamline to Maximize

The answers to these questions are indicators of the strength or weakness of your business systems. If any one of these items is not implemented well in a business, the impact would be far from critical. But mismanaging or overlooking several could have a devastating effect on your company's operations—and future.

There are no standardized systems for small businesses. Each company must create its own, based on the experience of its owner and wisdom gleaned from others. Let the questions I've put forth here guide you in developing your own systems set, recognizing that the ideal collection of business systems will remain elusive. You'll have to continually tweak them to reflect the changes in your business practices. As this strategy shows, it pays to be always on the lookout for methods to streamline your daily operations and maximize your efforts.

Take Action

1. Use these checklists to conduct a systems inventory for your business. Pinpoint the weak spots and the areas that lack a system altogether.

2. Determine which tools you'll need to get your infrastructure in place. New forms or letterhead? A customized contract? Database software? A voice mail system?

3. Implement your system, then give it a test drive. Set aside time—your own or a staff member's—to institute the new systems.

Chapter 28

Manage Your Time

E ven if you've been in business for only a few months, you've become aware (perhaps even painfully) of the importance of managing your time. Stating that "time is your most valuable resource" is preaching to the converted. You don't need platitudes, you need effective and easy-to-implement time management strategies. That's the purpose of this chapter.

Know the Value of an Hour

The best way to appreciate the value of your time is to calculate the financial worth of a single hour. Let's assume you've established a revenue target of $200,000 a year. That translates to $100 an hour for a 40-hour workweek for 50 weeks a year.

Now think about a recent typical workday: Probably you took a couple of coffee breaks, extended a few phone conversations with idle chatter, were left on hold with a tech support call or reservation clerk, rummaged around for misplaced papers, were interrupted with telemarketing pitches, got caught up in distracting activities, and so forth. Over the course of the day, these nonproductive minutes could easily add up to two hours or more.

I think you see my point: In small chunks, time slips away unnoticed. Using our example, the lost hours would calculate to $200 a day, $1,000 a week, or $50,000 a year! Even more compelling is to realize that it adds up to more than an entire day a week, or a quarter of your entire work time. Gone. Vanished. Irretrievable.

Doing these calculations is the first step in this strategy. It hammers home the importance of time management and how it directly relates to your bottom line. The next step is just as important: You must heighten your awareness of how you spend your time.

Smart Strategy

The best way to appreciate the value of your time is to calculate the financial worth of a single hour.

To do this, for a week, chart how your spend your time in 15-minute blocks. I know this may seem tedious, but I encourage you to persevere for five days, because at the end of the week you'll have taken a very revealing snapshot of how well or poorly you invest this resource.

If you've done a similar exercise before, do it again—and on a regular basis. Whenever I find my business going off track, I pull out the chart and find out where my time is being spent. The results help me to strategically assess where I'm getting the best return on my most valuable asset.

These two exercises—calculating the value of an hour and charting your time usage—should provide you with compelling motivation to take command of your time. Think of them as tactics to *push* you toward mastery. Their complement, establishing goals, will *pull* you toward achievement.

Single Out Seven

Earlier, we discussed the power and value of establishing a vision for your business and translating that vision into specific goals. How you integrate the individual goals into your daily work schedule is the puzzle piece that completes the picture.

One technique that I've found particularly effective in this endeavor is to create a To-Do list of seven activities that are directly tied to my goals and vision. I call them the Solo Seven. I write them down at the end of each day to give myself a head start on the following day. It's an approach I've adapted from that of sales expert Tom Hopkins, who has used a similar technique for years with great success.

Don't, however, get caught up in the number seven. Sometimes you'll come up with only six things; other days you'll have eight or nine. Seven is just a good target number; it's enough to stretch your thinking, yet is usually manageable in a day.

Creating such a list achieves several things:

✓ *It's a good way to bring closure to a day.* You can assess what you've achieved and what you have left to do. It clears your mind so you can have a good night's sleep, because you have tomorrow's plan on paper.

✓ *It jump-starts the next day.* This is invaluable if, like me, you're not a morning person and you have a tendency to let a whole morning slip by before you've started the first task of the day. This list serves as a focusing tool to push you to dive right in and make the mornings productive.

✓ *It's very satisfying to go through the list and see what you've accomplished.* What's more liberating at the end of a long workday than to check things off of a list?

✓ *It's a way to chart your progress.* Keeping your lists in a datebook or bound notebook lets you monitor challenges and accomplishments.

✓ *Most of all, the Solo Seven focuses your attention on what's really important.* This list holds you accountable.

Think Achievement Rather Than Activity

Your list should include items that are directly linked to your business vision as well as to specific goals. Unless you make this link, you will fill your days with activities, not achievements.

Your list items should also be reasonable. By that I mean don't add something you know you can't accomplish during a single day. Learn to reduce your goals into bite-size pieces.

Too many entrepreneurs sabotage themselves by putting items such as "Write a book" on their To-Do list, right between "Pick up suit at dry cleaners" and "Fax proposal to Stevens Corporation." You're much more likely to get that book written if your Solo Seven list contains items such as "Draft one-page outline of book concept" or "Create profile of target reader of book."

Extend Your Time Horizon

The last part of this strategy requires you to take a fresh look at how you view the future. Do you remember how long the summer seemed to be when you were in grade school? Now the years pass so quickly we sometimes can't recall what month it is. That shifting sense of time passage also happens in your business. In the early stages, each day is filled with so much new activity that time seems to move more slowly. Your focus is on the coming month or quarter. As you and your business mature, however, your time horizon lengthens, and you begin to plan a year or two in advance.

To successfully grow your business, it's important to adopt this longer view, and to plan two to three years—or more—into the future. At the same time, you must remain nimble enough to react to a changing marketplace. This will serve you well as you chart your growing company's next steps. It will force you to think not only about the immediate results of an action, but how that action may impact your business down the road. Like a chess master, you need to begin to plan strategically—not just the initial and intermediate moves, but future moves, too. Checkmate!

Take Action

1. Find a calendar or datebook you like—and use it! It can be one you buy or one you create on your computer or by hand. Realistically plan your work hours so you don't overcommit and can stay on schedule.

2. Keep track of your time in 15-minute increments for one workweek. Be sure you go back over the data you collect at the end of the week to see where you need to make adjustments.

3. Create your own Solo Seven list. Try this technique for one week and see the difference it can make in your sense of accomplishment and your productivity.

Chapter 29

Choose and Use Technology Wisely

Take a moment right now to conduct a mental survey of the various technologies at work in your office. Even among you die-hard Luddites, I'll bet there are several tools you can't imagine not having as you go about your daily operations. Today's entrepreneurial efforts thrive—indeed, often depend—on state-of-the-art technologies to communicate, produce, and most important, compete. Savvy small business owners understand this power, and with the aid of everything from computers, fax machines, and voice mail to video conferencing and Internet technologies, they're reshaping the way their businesses operate.

Weave a Web, Not a Trap

Because office operations today rely on a number of these new technologies, they've become the source of both remarkable power and endless frustration for most small business owners. Yes, they give us a competitive edge, but not without a price—and I'm not talking just about dollars.

The challenge for small business owners is to know *which* technologies to use and *how* to use them to enhance their work while not letting them become an overwhelming distraction or pool of digital quicksand that sinks operating dollars. Getting comfortable with the digital domain (for most of these technologies are digitally oriented) and learning how to deal with it on your terms is an important part of growing your business.

To help you navigate the high-tech world as you grow your business, here are some guidelines to keep in mind:

✓ *Determine the appropriate technology to use.* When you're approaching a task, realize that the appropriate technology to help you complete that task may not always be the "highest" (that is, newest) form of technology. If scissors and scotch tape will do, pull them out and put them to work. On the other hand, if what you need is a "bells and whistles" presentation, don't try to wing it; put that state-of-the-art graphics software to work and give it the high-quality professionalism you need.

✓ *Invest wisely in technology.* If you think of the money you spend on technological improvements as investments, rather than purchases, it will help you to make better decisions. Do your homework before you buy: Solicit input from technology-savvy colleagues, read computer magazine product reviews, peruse the bookstores for a title that explains the ins and outs of the product, talk with sales staff at several stores. If possible, try out the item before you buy it.

✓ *Be aware of the total cost of ownership.* You might have seen the acronym TCO in the technology media a lot lately. Short for total cost of ownership, it refers to how much it *really* costs to own a piece of technology after you pay the purchase price—including the learning curve, maintenance, how soon it will become obsolete, and its true capabilities. It happens more often than we care to admit: We buy a product that features a new, highly touted technology, and realize too late it wasn't worth it. Don't let your business be sunk by what I call the Titanic effect—your purchase price is only the 10 percent that's visible above water. Make sure you calculate the total cost of your technology investment, including installation, supplies, maintenance, possible repairs, and so forth. A little research time up front can save you a bundle (of dollars and frustration) later on.

✓ *Follow my six-month rule.* If you know precisely the purpose a piece of technology will serve for your business, and are confident you can put it to good use during the next six months, buy it. If not, wait; it probably will become faster, better, and cheaper in those months. This became very clear to me in 1991 when I purchased my first laptop. I looked at the price—ouch!—but knew it would enable me to get work done on the road I couldn't do otherwise. Within six months the computer was paid for, just from the work I was able to do while crossing the country at 30,000 feet.

Smart Strategy

The challenge for small business owners is to know which technologies to use and how to use them to enhance their work, and not to let them become an overwhelming distraction or pool of digital quicksand that sinks operating dollars.

✓ *Talk the talk.* A good way to increase your knowledge and comfort level with the constantly evolving technologies (and their accompanying jargon) is to read on a regular basis one or two of the technology trade publications. Adding *Home Office Computing* and either *PC Magazine* or *Macworld* to your reading list is a smart decision. They review new products from a problem-solving perspective, bring you operational tips, and can keep you informed about upgrades and new developments that can impact your business.

✓ *Surf the Internet.* All major computer software and hardware manufacturers operate Web sites. A visit can give you a feel for their customer service style and reliability. You can also compare the features of specific models and track current pricing. Some sites, such as the one operated by Dell Computer, establish personalized tech support areas based on the specific model of computer you've purchased. It's a way to save valuable time when tracking down a technology solution. And read the Frequently Asked Questions (FAQ) document relating to any new product you're considering. Often, any questions you have, others have, too, and the answers probably are already out there.

✓ *Be safe rather than sorry.* If you don't have a backup system in place, you're asking for trouble. You don't have to be a techno-wizard to know that the issue is not *if* your system will go haywire, it's *when.* Planning can reduce the impact of these inevitable glitches and ensure that your business can continue to run smoothly. Backup systems come in many forms: copies of the data and software that reside on your computer's hard drive; alternative plans to implement when your system goes down; and support services such as on-site tech support or data recovery firms that can offer crucial help when you need it.

Don't Try to Know It All

The nature of technology, like nature itself, is continually changing and evolving. Therefore, you must approach your education in this area as an ongoing project. Get help when you need it. Crack the user manuals that came with your software, or buy a well-written, user-friendly guidebook and study it. Consider joining a network of computer users in your area. And check out the offerings at your local community colleges. They regularly host classes on specific operating systems and software applications at very reasonable fees.

And keep in mind that you don't have to know everything about how a technology works to make it work for you. After all, if we had to know the details of automobile engines in order to drive cars, not very many of us would be climbing behind the wheel. Don't let the complexity of technology distract you from your goals. Technologies are nothing more than tools; use them, don't let them intimidate you.

These are exciting times for entrepreneurs. Each new technology development adds power and capabilities we can potentially adapt to boost our businesses. Recent improvements in voice recognition software, for example, enable computers to "take dictation," which is a significant breakthrough for individuals with limited typing skills. Wireless devices free us from desktops, enabling us to communicate anywhere. Our cars and briefcases are becoming stand-alone offices, not just extensions of our traditional ones.

All of these advances—and the many more in development—mean we'll be able to expand the operations within and outside our offices. They'll even free us to outsource a greater percentage of those business tasks that kept us from doing the things we prefer. Technology can give us the best of both worlds—enabling us to increase our business capabilities but in a streamlined format. It's pivotal to growing a twenty-first-century business.

Take Action

1. Once a quarter, take action to broaden your technological knowledge and productivity. Buy a user-friendly manual for that new software, then read it; take the software tutorial that's offered instead of clicking past it; enroll in a local community college weekend computer course.

2. Call your local computer retailer or consultant and locate a user group network in your area. Get on the mailing list and attend a meeting or two. Tap into their expertise.

3. Become an informed consumer. Before making a purchase, read some computer magazines and spend some time online, reading FAQs, product press releases, and the like. Then when you go to a store to buy the product, you'll know what you want and won't be swayed by packaging, pricing, or sales pitches.

Chapter 30

Manage Data Efficiently

Information is the oxygen that keeps a business breathing, no matter what a company's size or the type of product or service it sells. How well you manage your data—from your customer list to price sheets to those scribbled notes of future plans—has a direct impact on your current earning capabilities and your potential for growth.

This chapter is designed to help you evaluate your company data, determine what is important and why, and show you how to manage your data for best results.

Separate Value from Context

Data becomes valuable only by its context—in relation to what we consider to be important. For example, a list of a dozen names, addresses, and phone numbers chosen randomly from a phone book holds little significance for us. However, a list of 12 names and contact information for top-level prospects has great meaning, and thus value.

This is the central focus of the data management strategy: Determine what is valuable to you and your company, and establish systems that capture, organize, and evaluate that information on a regular basis.

Smart Strategy

If you can't find the information you want when you want it, it doesn't matter how valuable it is. Data is worthless if you can't access it when you need it.

Sounds easy enough, but because today's technologies churn out data with alarming speed, it's a major challenge, especially for small business owners working solo or with very small staffs. Think about it: Computer printers spit out paper by the ream, the Internet gives us access to more information than we can possibly digest, and print publications pile up in precarious stacks on our desks and floors. Faced with the prospect of sorting it all out, most people put blinders on, push a few more piles of paper into a corner, and vow they'll get to it someday.

Ignoring the situation is not the answer. The solution begins with making a mental shift about the role information plays in your business. Here are four insights I've learned over the years while waging the data war.

1. *If you can't find the information you want when you want it, it doesn't matter how valuable it is.* Data is worthless if you can't access it when you need it. What's called for is a sensible and practical storage and access system (notice I didn't say filing system). We'll talk more about this later in this chapter.

2. *Data from the Internet isn't inherently valuable.* Do you treat information that comes through that expensive computer on your desk as more valuable than a note you jotted on a scrap of paper? If so, rethink. Internet content is often no better or worse than information you gather by phone, by reading, or in person. Outdated files, old-version software, useless e-mails, and other data can clog your computer systems to almost a dead stop. Back up data onto removable disks if appropriate, and hit the delete key.

3. *If you're drowning in data to the detriment of other critical company operations, it's devaluing your business.* It doesn't matter how potentially valuable this data is. When the daily operations of your company are clogged by stacks of paper, dozens of saved voice mails, and overcrowded hard drives, the information is having a negative consequence on your business. Less is more—or, in this case, reduction is improvement.

4. *The shelf life of data today is shorter than that of a carton of milk.* This is the issue of data *currency*—both meanings of the word apply here: the notion of value and of being up to date. Today's global network that makes information almost instantaneously available 24 hours a day also ages information faster. To remain competitive, you must implement systems to access up-to-date data on a regular basis and institute methods to purge out-of-date information to make room for the new.

Managing information is not an easy task, and you can't approach it with a cavalier attitude. Unless you set up systems, you'll be like a sailor adrift in a rowboat against a raging sea of data that crashes into your office each day. Bailing is only a temporary solution. To prevent being swept under, you must set sail in a sturdier craft. That craft is control.

Control the Clutter

To streamline the flow of paper in your office and to give your company room to breathe and grow, you must take bold, proactive steps to control the clutter in your office. This is an ongoing task, one that many of us—maybe most of us—were never taught. There were no classes on how to manage the paper, information, and other *stuff* that would accumulate and threaten to overwhelm us. So as business owners, we must teach ourselves.

I've worked with a number of professional organizers over the past few years, and I've learned to ask three key questions when facing a pile of paper. The answers to these questions instantly clarify the action to take.

Don't let the simplicity of these questions fool you—they can be powerfully liberating. The first two are courtesy of Barbara Hemphill, a pioneer in the field of organizing and author of *Taming the Paper Tiger at Home* (Kiplinger Books, 1998) and *Taming the Paper Tiger at Work* (Kiplinger Books, 1998). The third was asked of me by professional organizer Sheila Delson when we were working together, and I found it particularly compelling.

1. When faced with keeping or tossing something, ask yourself, "What's the worst possible thing that would happen if I didn't keep this paper?" If you can live with the results, toss it—better yet, recycle it. As Hemphill points out, 80 percent of the paper we keep we never use. (Yes, the 80/20 rule at work again!)

2. If you decide to keep and file an item, ask yourself, "Where's the first place I would look for this if I needed to find it again?" File it there. What you want to create is not a filing system but an *access system,* one that will let you retrieve items quickly and easily.

3. Still hesitating about whether to get rid of something now or later? Here's Delson's pointed question: "If this is going to end up at the dump or recycling center someday, what's going to increase its value between now and then?" The day I was asked this question I sent eight bins of paper to the recycling center.

Now I ask myself these three questions every time I'm faced with evaluating information: sorting through the daily mail, reviewing data I've received over the Internet, gathering information during client meetings, or collecting literature at conferences or trade shows. It's the first line of defense in fending off paper and information overload.

Most of all, keep in mind that managing data is a *process,* not a goal. It's never-ending—which at first can be distressing, until you have systems in place and understand the process. What's important is not how much you keep or toss, it's having the right information accessible so you can run your business efficiently and profitably.

Take Action

1. Review your current filing system as an access system to determine how well it serves your needs. Check out Barbara Hemphill's Taming the Paper Tiger software as a way to streamline your paper management (details in the list of resources at the back of the book).

2. Schedule an annual office cleanout day. Prepare for it in advance—and keep the date!

3. Explore some new ideas about gaining control of the clutter in your life by reading books such as Julie Morgenstern's *Organizing from the Inside Out* (Owl Books, 1998).

Chapter 31

Learn to Say No

No. It's one of the smallest words in our language, but for many of us it's one of the most difficult to say. Many phrases that mean the same thing—"Can't do it," "Don't have the time," "All booked up"—also stick in our throats.

All of us entrepreneurs can probably recall a recent occasion when we wanted to turn down—or should have turned down—a request or an assignment. But because we didn't, we became involved in something that didn't interest us or that became a drain on our business. Ultimately, we ended up resenting the assignment and the person who called on us.

Smart Strategy

If you don't establish priorities, in effect you're abdicating the direction of your business to whoever can sweet-talk you out of your valuable time, energy, and talent.

Like its namesake, the no strategy is simple to understand but difficult to execute. It requires a healthy selfishness (yes, there is such a thing). In the business arena, it means being able to establish priorities. If you don't or can't do this, in effect you're abdicating the direction of your business to whoever can sweet-talk you out of your valuable time, energy, and talent.

Have No Fear

Why is it so difficult for solo entrepreneurs and small business owners to say no? I believe there are three reasons, all based in fear.

1. *Fear of missing out on an opportunity.* When faced with a
   new option (client, challenge, whatever), we succumb to the
   tiny voice inside our head that chatters, "What if this is *the*
   opportunity I've been waiting for?" Of course, this voice is so
   persistent and annoying, we generally don't take the time to
   hear our calm, cool, and collected voice say, "No, wait. Let
   me clearly review the situation and see if it truly holds the
   potential to bring the results I seek." Result: We're trapped by
   the fear of missing something we can't even define, much
   less evaluate.

2. *Fear of causing bad feelings.* I don't know a single entrepreneur who hasn't been on the receiving end of rejection. It's
   not a pleasant sensation, and some of us deeply internalize it.
   Instead of confronting this emotional hornet's nest, we protect ourselves by saying yes to anyone who wants us. Result:
   Our self-respect slips another notch; then we usually resent
   our involvement in the situation, which increases our anger
   toward the other person—and ourselves.

3. *Fear of passing up potential revenue.* Who among us entrepreneurs hasn't thought (usually in the middle of a sleepless
   night), "Will I ever work again?" To ward off that fear,
   instead of investing time in planning our company's future,
   we take on every job that comes along, even if it's sometimes
   below our current pricing levels, something that bores us, or
   something that has no future potential. Result: We tie up our
   time in steady, lower-revenue activities instead of focusing
   on taking the next leap of growth.

If we allow ourselves to be driven by these fears, they will stunt
our business development. We must take on one of the greatest challenges for a solo entrepreneur: Establishing a distinction between
oneself and the business. We need to act responsibly on behalf of the

business. To do that requires looking at the *opportunity cost* of each situation.

Calculate the Economics of Opportunities

In economic terms, opportunity cost is the amount of time, energy, or money given up when resources are used to create one result instead of another. Think of it as a measure of what could have been.

For example, let's say a town wants to buy four new police cars, and it has *x* dollars in its total budget. Purchasing the cars means that those funds can't be used for other community services, such as road maintenance or trash removal. The opportunity cost is the value of the other goods or services that must be given up to buy the cars. It's different from the dollar cost of the new cars; rather, it's a measure of the value of what the dollars *could have* purchased if they weren't used to buy cars. (I agree, it's a subtle distinction, but stay with me—this concept has important ramifications for entrepreneurs.)

All choices come with opportunity cost, but we often don't think about the full impact. Let's assume someone asks you to do a project, and it sounds great. But down the road, there are complications; the project drags on longer than you scheduled it for, and you're unable to take on other work because you're still hung up with the first project. The opportunity cost has just skyrocketed for you, and your business suffers.

For solo entrepreneurs and small business owners, opportunity cost often (maybe even usually) is tied to time, because it's a finite rescource. But in this era of strategic partnerships, opportunity cost may also be tied to relationships and access. For example, if you align yourself with Company X, and later Company Y wants to do work with you—but only if you give up your work with Company X—you'll need to rethink the total opportunity cost of working with each company.

To clarify: Opportunity cost is *not* the benefits (or opportunities) that you'll gain from working with a client at a reduced fee. You know the benefits I mean. You usually rationalize them this way: "Well, they don't have a big budget and can't afford to pay me much, but this will lead to great exposure and other work." This is not considering opportunity cost in the true economic sense.

You have to be clear-headed about the total value of what you'll be giving up when you say yes. Calculating opportunity cost means reassessing the value you place on all your activities—including a quiet evening spent reading a novel to decompress or a weekend hike in the woods with someone you love.

Say Goodbye to Guilt

As my business has developed, a few pointers have helped me comprehend the true cost of saying yes when I wanted to say no, and have led me to ways to make the latter word easier to say. I had a startling moment of clarity while listening to author and entrepreneur Brian Tracy explain that, as business owners, "Our dance cards are all filled up." Tracy, the author of over 50 audio programs and books on business topics and the laws of success, knows how easy it is to get trapped into overcommitment. But without the "no" there can be no movement forward. The calendar and To-Do lists are full. Tracy states: "To add something new means you must take something off. To pick something up, you must first put something down."

In short, you've got to learn to set guidelines and limits. For me, these range from the number of activities to which I can volunteer my time to the minimum amount a client project must be worth or the qualities that a new client must have before I'll agree to work with him or her. Sound strict? It is, to some extent. But it's also liberating, because I don't have to spend valuable time and waste my brain cells ruminating on the merit of each and every opportunity. If it meets my guidelines, it's a go. If it doesn't, I say no.

Your guidelines and limits will of course be different, but I do recommend you leave enough wiggle room to do a favor, to take on an idiosyncratic job, or just because you feel like it. Only you can define your priorities and values. The structure you institute is meant to give you control, not hamstring your entrepreneurial spirit. Establishing a system for saying no liberates you from guilt and the time-wasting process of lamenting decisions. It places your business priorities first—where they must be if you intend to grow your company.

Take Action

1. Decide how many low-paying jobs and favors you can afford to do over the course of a year, then break this down by the quarter. When you've meted out all of your favors for that quarter, start to say no.

2. If you haven't already, determine a floor for your typical client—the amount below which you will not go in terms of your fee structure, billable amount, or percentage of project revenue.

3. Know your business priorities. Write them down and post them where you can see them. The next time a request comes in, *before* you respond, glance at your priorities and quickly assess the new opportunity. It may not actually be an opportunity.

Chapter 32

Develop Your Intuition

One of nature's gifts to all humankind is intuition. Unfortunately, most humans have tuned out this capability in favor of listening to what logic has to say. Entrepreneurs, however, perhaps because they are less apt to follow restrictive business traditions, are more likely than other businesspeople to pay attention to their intuitive guides—although they may not recognize that that's what they're doing. Instead, they often refer to making decisions that are based on a hunch, a gut feeling, or an inner sense. But no matter what they call it, even in the face of data and logic, entrepreneurs frequently use additional factors they can't explain or defend rationally to make their choices: "I just know this is the way I should do it," is a common explanation.

Smart Strategy

By reviewing your recent business decisions, you can often gain insights into how you leverage your natural perceptive capabilities and how you can refine them.

This willingness to listen to another level of reasoning is a hallmark of entrepreneurial superstars. (Recall Chapter 15, "Listen Between the Lines." This is a deeper implementation of that strategy—specifically, that of listening to yourself.) For example, how did Fred Smith know that creating a fleet of purple airplanes in the early 1970s would turn into the phenomenally successful Federal Express? He credits it to "a strong hunch" that the timing was right for a hub-and-spoke overnight air courier system to shuttle important documents. Similarly, Limited Inc.'s CEO Leslie Wexner, whose extensive retail empire includes such diverse brands as Limited, Structure, Henri Bendel, Lane Bryant, Victoria's Secret, and Bath & Body Works, concedes that he "never ever conducts formal research to determine brands' personalities." Instead, Wexner explains, "I trust my intuition and my own emotional responses."

In many cases, it's intuition that leads entrepreneurs away from the security of working for others. It's an inner radar system, offering feedback and guidance different and separate from all the outward signs that may be pointing in another direction. By paying attention to this radar, we are able to take calculated, rather than foolhardy, risks. The goal of this chapter is to increase your awareness of this inner you and to show you how to turn your intuition into a strategic tool as you build your business.

Track Your Hunches

Developing your intuition begins with increasing your awareness of how you currently use—or ignore—this sense in your business. By reviewing your recent business decisions, you can often gain insights into how you leverage your natural perceptive capabilities and how you can refine them.

  - ✓ *People.* Think back to the last time you had strong feelings—either positive or negative—about someone you just met. Were you on target? If not, in what way were you wrong in your assessment? Were you aware of these hunches at the time? Did you pay attention to them? Did your awareness result in any positive or negative action?

  - ✓ *Situations.* What was the last major business decision you had to make? What steps did you go through in the process? How long did it take? How much did you rely on outside information, and how effectively did you tune in to your gut feelings? What ultimately was the deciding factor? What was the outcome?

  - ✓ *Opportunities.* Recall the last time you *felt* you were on the verge of a remarkable business opportunity. How did you respond? How did you evaluate the opportunity? Did you struggle internally between your logic and your intuition? Which won out? In retrospect, do you wish you'd done anything differently?

Use the answers to these questions as a mirror to reflect how you integrate your intuition into your decision-making process for your business. By tracking your past successes—and failures—you can identify whether you need to trust your internal radar more often.

Listen to the Quiet

A good way to chart your intuition is to write down your thoughts and feelings on a regular basis—keep a journal. Don't dismiss this practice as something only New Age pioneers and spiritual pilgrims use to achieve inner peace. It also holds great practical benefits for business owners.

In the course of a day, we usually have dozens of issues that demand our attention, often amid a noisy environment—ringing telephones, beeping fax machines, conversations, perhaps even the drone of radio or television. Competing (and too often losing) against that din is our inner commentary, what we *really* think about all that we're doing. We have to achieve silence before we set priorities and become focused on what's truly important and right for us and our business.

As you begin to set aside some time to be quiet, literally to hear yourself think, you'll be surprised at how quickly you can hear your intuition speak up. And when it does, listen, and then write down what you hear. I know entrepreneurs who write for as little as 10 or 15 minutes a day and report greater peace with their decision-making and an increased sense of order to the hectic pace of their workdays.

If you're resisting this strategy, wondering what to write about, the answer is anything at all. That's the point: to write whatever pops into your mind via your intuition. *What* you write doesn't matter as much as *that* you write. Putting pen to paper, doing what's called free-form writing, can often uncover ideas and inspirations and break down roadblocks.

Think of this process as clearing a workspace, giving you an uncluttered surface on which to create. Many entrepreneurs make this strategy part of their daily routines. Give it a try and see if it works for you.

Find the Magic in the Mundane

Another technique for tapping into your intuition to help you break old patterns and gain new insights is to turn to objects in your environment. First clarify the question you are trying to answer, then choose three random objects in your environment to focus on—let's say a rubber band, a file folder, and the running shoes you tossed in the corner.

Contemplate these three items for several minutes; really concentrate on them. What comes to mind? Perhaps the rubber band prompts you to stretch your thinking in a new direction; or it may surface your previously unacknowledged concerns about stretching your budget too thin. The file folder may point out that you need to put things in order for the solution to become clear. Those well-worn running shoes may lead you to realize you have to act fast if you're going to succeed in your endeavor. Then, after you've considered the items individually, ask how they might interact, and what meaning you can gain from their relationship.

This approach, which admittedly may sound far-fetched, can open your decision-making mind in an intriguing fashion. As intuition expert Nancy Rosanoff explains, "Intuition speaks to us in the language of metaphors and symbols and lets us tap into the nonanalytic part of our brain." Rosanoff, who often works with entrepreneurs and business executives in strengthening decision-making, strategic planning, and innovation skills, has witnessed the benefits this technique offers. "Your mind brings forth ideas that you wouldn't have considered if you were focusing only on a strict analysis of your challenge," she says.

Rosanoff also dismisses the notion that intuitive potential is stronger in women than men. "Contrary to popular opinion, both sexes are equally endowed with intuition," she explains. "Men and women just access it in different ways." The key to tapping these abilities is to not try too hard to find a solution, Rosanoff adds. Rather, give the process time to work, and allow answers to emerge.

Stay Tuned In

Once you begin to reacquaint yourself with your inner radar, you'll find that the signal grows stronger, because you know what to listen to and look for. Most of us, either with embarrassment or regret, can recall when we didn't trust our intuition—to our detriment. What's more difficult is to acknowledge the times we did follow a hunch that led to an exceptional outcome or opportunity.

The next time your business takes a successful leap forward, take a moment to reflect on how it came about. By giving credence to the guidance your intuition provides, you can more easily generate positive results on a regular basis.

Take Action

1. Choose a problem you are currently trying to solve in your business and use journal writing, object focusing, or another unconventional way to discover possible solutions. Quiet your mind, then let it wander freely. Just as quietly, observe the ideas that come to you.

2. Think back to the last time you had a brainstorm or major breakthrough in your business thinking. Where were you and what were you doing? Try to reconstruct that setting and explore why it may have prompted such an exciting revelation.

3. Take time to learn more about how intuition can work in your personal and professional life. Here are two books to get you started:

   Intuition Workout: A Practical Guide to Discovering Developing Your Inner Knowing, by Nancy Rosanoff (Aslan Publishing, 1991).
   Practical Intuition for Success, by Laura Day (HarperCollins, 1997).

MONEY
STRATEGIES

Chapter 33

Renew Your Relationship with Money

Money—it's a topic that is never far from the thoughts of any solo entrepreneur or small business owner. We celebrate when it comes in and lament when it goes out. It makes us feel successful and it can make us feel like failures. We juggle it, stretch it, float it—always hoping to do better with it. And no wonder: No entrepreneur can propel his or her company to the next level without a sound understanding of financial management.

But talking about money is never easy, because everyone has a different relationship with it. Often we aren't even aware how much our attitude toward money affects how well or how poorly we manage it, either professionally or personally.

As an entrepreneur, it's important to define your relationship with money, because it speaks volumes about the potential success of your business. All of us have strong views about money and how it should be handled, and these views directly impact our money *behavior,* including how we earn, spend, and save.

Smart Strategy

It's important to learn to adopt a realistic attitude about the money you have and to come to terms with your financial comfort zone. This knowledge base will enable you to stop worrying about other people's opinions and value systems. Taking a more objective view, you'll discover that you make better business decisions.

If you're uncomfortable or unhappy with your attitude toward money, take heart: You can change your money behaviors. You can learn tools and techniques to make you at ease dealing with money, and this comfort level will eventually translate into more sales and profits.

Adjust Your Attitude

First things first: Money is a medium of exchange—nothing more, nothing less. We use (spend) money to purchase goods and services, and we receive (earn) money by providing goods and services. If we have money left over after we pay our bills, we can save it, invest it, or spend it. If we don't have enough cash, we have to cut expenses, delay payments, or borrow to cover our obligations. In business, we use money as a way to measure our growth, productivity, and progress.

Think about the expression "I'm broke." It means different things to different people. For one person, it may mean having to borrow to pay bills and stay afloat. Another person may feel broke when the $10,000 safety cushion she had established in her checking account dwindles to $8,500. Yet another may say he's broke if he has enough in the bank to pay his current bills, but hasn't enough new business lined up to meet next month's financial obligations.

Security is another term interpreted individually. One person may feel secure when she has $100 left over after paying her monthly bills, whereas another may feel he has to have a cash cushion equivalent to a full year of business expenses.

I raise these discrepancies in terminology because it's important to learn to adopt a realistic attitude about the money you have and to come to terms with your financial comfort zone. This knowledge base will enable you to stop worrying about other people's opinions and value systems. It's also important to view money more dispassionately. Taking a more objective view, you'll discover that you make better business decisions.

Change Your Mentality

Think about the following statements:

> What if I don't have enough money to pay my bills?
> I am always anxious about getting paid.
> I'm not getting paid what I'm worth, but it's all I can charge.

These are examples of a *scarcity* mentality. If you're constantly worrying about how much money you make and how much you have, you're no doubt familiar with that mindset. But such thoughts are not related to your bank balance; rather, they reflect your attitude. People with a scarcity mentality never believe there is enough money to go around. They often have undercurrent feelings of being a victim or martyr when it comes to money matters.

In contrast, look at the statements of someone with a mentality of *abundance:*

I am grateful for the money I make and am open to receiving more.

I charge a sufficient fee for my services based on my expertise.

There are always new opportunities to make money.

Such an attitude welcomes competition and acknowledges that there are plenty of opportunities for everyone. Individuals who view their business universe as an expanding pie, one that can feed many hungry mouths, know that they will be compensated for creating an excellent product or for providing an essential service that fulfills a need in the marketplace.

Reject Your Inheritance

Many of our attitudes and beliefs toward money are inherited from our parents' behaviors and/or from previous business experiences. One entrepreneur I know was heavily influenced by his father, who grew up during the Great Depression and had to scrimp and scrape to feed his family. After going into business, this entrepreneur realized that his spartan attitude toward money was incongruent with his business vision. His scarcity perspective held him back until he learned to practice the concept of abundance. Once he realized that his attitude was really his father's, he was able to alter his behavior. He continued to exercise thrifty financial procedures, but also began to incorporate a prosperous outlook among his clients and co-workers. His business began to flourish.

Perhaps you've experienced the thrilling sensation that occurs after you stop agonizing about the potential negative outcome of one of your actions or decisions. That feeling of release, of freedom, comes from letting go of negative thinking. You can apply the letting-go strategy to your approach to money as well. When you stop worrying about whether you have enough, you'll be amazed at what appears in your mailbox. As you become more practiced at this, you'll develop an ease in regard to the money flowing in and out of your business. This doesn't mean you ignore the financial activities of your company. Instead, you understand and accept that earning and spending are mirror actions inherent in every company's growth.

Use Money as a Tool

When you become comfortable dealing with money, you can evolve from treating it as a medium of exchange to using it as a tool for success. We all know of entrepreneurs who manage their money well, and we realize that they have a distinct strategic advantage in growing their businesses. Here are some successful money habits to institute in your own money behavior:

- ✓ Know the balance in your business checking account at all times—without having to look it up.
- ✓ Pay yourself first, and save for the future.
- ✓ Invest wisely in your business. This includes hiring the best people and buying the equipment, products, and services that enhance your and their work.
- ✓ Know your financial limitations; hire money professionals to offset your deficiencies.
- ✓ Be aware of outstanding invoice dates, and make sure you are paid on time.
- ✓ Know how to effectively price your products and services.

Anyone can learn these and other techniques of money management. But you must begin by believing that money is your business ally, not a foe. Don't become a slave to money matters. And remember, managing money is a natural part of business.

Take Action

1. Determine whether you have a scarcity or abundance mentality. Identify—and implement—one change you can make in your behavior that can shift you in the direction of an abundance mindset.

2. If you don't know your bank balance, look it up. Then find a way to stay on top of it. If you need help reconciling your statement, get it.

3. Review the money habits of successful entrepreneurs or anyone else you admire. How do you stack up? Identify both your strengths and weaknesses with money, then move forward accordingly.

Chapter 34

Assemble Your Money Team

Having a winning team of money professionals behind you is akin to having a business management group on call for you and your company. Even if you have a solid working knowledge of money matters, the right financial professionals can amplify your knowledge manyfold. They are, after all, experts, just as you are an expert in your field. And we all know the difference between amateurs and experts. Let's look at who you want to draft for your team.

Pick the Players

There are five key players you need to consider. Depending on where you are in your business development, you may not need to hire all these people immediately; assess your situation and engage them as your needs arise. But don't wait until the last minute to hire these professionals—you'll inevitably jeopardize your judgment skills if you employ someone because you have to. Be proactive in hiring these people.

✓ *Accountant.* An accountant does far more than simply prepare your tax returns every year. I recommend you hire a certified public accountant (CPA). He or she can assist you with tax strategies that have a direct bottom-line impact on your business, such as whether to defer or accelerate income or expenses and the effect of investing in one retirement plan over another. A CPA can also assist you in selecting the appropriate financial software and establishing a financial reporting system, two important management tools. If your business is the source of a substantial portion of your personal net worth, a CPA can also offer advice that may reduce your current personal tax liability as well as your estate taxes later.

✓ *Bookkeeper.* You can either hire a bookkeeper (part-time or full-time, depending on your needs and the size of your business) or outsource the work by using a bookkeeping service or your accountant. Your bookkeeper will either set up your financial systems for you or help you to do so (which I discuss in the next chapter) and work with you to create methods to maintain them. Many entrepreneurs have good intentions about keeping track of their money, but fall prey to more pressing issues. Concentrate on what you do best, and let another professional do what he or she does best: maintain the books.

Smart Strategy

At the outset of your relationship with your money team, it's a good idea to establish what you expect of your team members and—just as important—what they can expect from you. Hiring a money team does not mean that you can relinquish responsibility for your financial management.

✓ *Banker.* Today, small business banking needs extend far beyond a business checking account. You should form a relationship with a banker *before* you need to. Familiarize this person with your business, and provide him or her with financial statements. At some point, your business will need money to grow, and if you already have a connection with a banker, your chances of getting what you need are multiplied. Remember, it's bankers who lend money, not banks. Build personal relationships with more than one individual at your bank (remember, this is an era of merger mania and job-hopping), and keep these financial professionals up to date on what's happening in your business.

✓ *Attorney.* A general business attorney is a key member of any business money team. Attorneys are not financial professionals per se, but they can advise you on a variety of issues that do have financial impact. These may include the legal structure of your company (for example, whether incorporation makes sense), contracts, letters of agreement with suppliers, and many others. An attorney can also recommend specialists in areas such as intellectual property or tax planning. When interviewing attorneys (see the next section of this chapter), find out if any follow a growing trend toward project pricing; it's often more attractive than being charged for every photocopy and phone call. Some business associations are also teaming up with attorneys to offer package plans for basic legal services at a flat fee.

✓ *Financial planner.* For many solo entrepreneurs and small business owners, there's a fine line between business and personal money matters. A good fee-based financial planner (who is not dependent on selling you stocks, insurance, or other financial products or services) can advise you on issues ranging from estate planning to investment options. He or she can provide objectivity and expertise, in addition to resources that will help you manage all your money concerns. Look for an individual who is a Certified Financial Planner (CFP), and ask for a copy of his or her ADV Part 2, a disclosure document planners must file with the SEC that states their education, compensation, potential conflicts of interest, and other details. Speak to several of the planner's clients whose financial objectives are similar to yours to see if the match may be a good one. Remember, this is a relationship built on trust, and more than performance returns you're looking for someone with experience and integrity.

Get to Know Your Teammates

One of the best ways to find competent members of a money team is by networking. Speak with other business owners or tap into your trade and professional associations for referrals. Find out who they use and what kind of services they provide. Once you have identified some candidates, meet with them and ask questions specific to your business needs. Interview several in each category before hiring one.

The following are some generic guidelines you should adapt to your specific business needs:

✓ Find out if the person works with other businesses that are similar in makeup to yours and, preferably, that serve the same market. You want to work with people who are familiar with your company size and type as well as your industry.

✓ Find out the payment method. Is it hourly or on retainer? Will you be charged if you call with a quick question?

✓ Ask for references, and call them! Find out specifically why others like working with the person, and what drawbacks there may be.

✓ Pay attention to your chemistry (or lack thereof) with the candidate. If your instincts give you negative signals, say thank you and move on.

✓ Establish how stable the candidate's place is within the firm. You don't want to spend months getting up to speed and have to change advisors. Or, if you do have to make such a change, is the professional's team deep enough so that someone else could take over your work quickly and seamlessly?

✓ Determine whether this person's network can feed your business. Choosing the right professionals can also bring you an important source of new business through referrals.

Remember, a lot is at stake here, and you must have a great deal of confidence in the professionals you choose to manage your money, so don't rush the selection process. With the right groundwork, you'll find professionals who can and will serve you well.

Work with Your Money Team

At the outset of your relationship with your money team it's a good idea to establish what you expect of your team members and—just as important—what they can expect from you. Hiring a money team does not mean that you can relinquish responsibility for your financial management. Don't expect anyone to read your mind and know what you want. You must be able to clearly state your objectives.

Always take an active approach to managing your money and your money team. And keep in mind that if you realize you have made a mistake in one of your choices, or if your business outgrows the capabilities of one of your team, you should waste no time in finding someone new. You may, in fact, find it necessary to hire several different people before you find the appropriate ones for your business. (All the more reason not to wait to find the right people under pressure.)

Once you're happy with your team, establish a regular review process. This should take place at least once a year if not more often. Regular reviews will enable both you and your money team to stay on top of your financial matters as well as the relationship. Use the reviews to give—and take—feedback and to reassess your financial needs.

Investing in a good accountant, bookkeeper, banker, attorney, and financial planner will yield many rewards as you grow your business. With a solid financial foundation, you'll be better prepared to respond to new opportunities.

Take Action

1. Inventory your professional financial relationships. Where do you need to make additions or changes?

2. Network with other business owners to learn how they use their money teams.

3. Establish an annual review process with each member of your money team.

Chapter 35

Institute Financial Success Systems

L ike the operational systems we discussed in Chapter 27, financial systems can free you to navigate the growth path for your business. It may seem like an oxymoron to keep saying that by imposing structures you can achieve greater freedom. In practice, however, you'll discover that by instituting systems—especially financial systems—you'll be able to focus your time and energy on doing what it is you do best, and not have to spend hours worrying, calculating, and juggling your income.

A powerful momentum begins when you start instituting financial systems in your business. At the first stage, you begin to feel more in control of your finances. The second stage is one of empowerment—you realize that if you can manage your money effectively, you can achieve anything. Finally, your money systems become second nature, and you enter a stage of freedom that comes from a clear mind that's energized, creative, and productive.

This chapter introduces the three primary financial systems that can make such a difference in your business: bookkeeping, invoicing, and general record keeping. No doubt you're familiar with these terms, but perhaps only in a peripheral way. Let's review them to ensure that you know the importance of establishing each in your business, no matter its size or the market it serves.

Keep Books

Bookkeeping is, simply, a method of keeping track of cash coming into and going out from your business. For most growing businesses, the bookkeeping system will revolve around the business checkbook. Cash inflow may come as cash, checks, or credit card payments from your customers, and all these need to be recorded so that you know who paid you what amount of money. Cash outflow comprises the bills you pay, including expenditures for supplies, salaries, rent, taxes, and so forth.

Remember what I said about the benefits of a good bookkeeper in Chapter 34? If you're at all uncomfortable with or reluctant about setting up a bookkeeping system, by all means hire someone to do it for you. Don't wait until you need to answer to Uncle Sam or find proof of purchase on that fax machine that keeps jamming to realize that all your receipts and miscellaneous papers are scattered throughout your office, briefcase, and jacket pockets, or stuffed into a bursting shoebox.

Smart Strategy

Many entrepreneurs are challenged—even intimidated—by the prospect of collecting what is owed to them. In spite of this discomfort or fear, however, you must be proactive in collecting your receivables. If you're not, you gain nothing and lose everything.

A competent bookkeeper will create either a manual or electronic system (or both) for you, depending on your preference. Have your bookkeeper work in concert with your CPA, since your CPA will likely have preferences about how the books are set up, and incorporating the CPA's methods in the beginning is much easier than changing later. Once established, the system enables the CPA to better guide your financial management and to communicate clearly with you and your bookkeeper. With just a little self-discipline and ultimately very little time, you'll be able to easily and accurately track incoming and outgoing dollars.

Let Your Computer Do the Counting

I urge you to take advantage of the power that technology offers for bookkeeping functions. For less than $150 you can buy remarkably sophisticated financial software. As mentioned earlier, discuss your choice with your bookkeeper or CPA; their experience with a particular product can streamline your research and setup time—and may reduce the fees you have to pay them.

Once you've set up your accounts systems, it's a seamless move to monitoring your financial activity on a regular basis. Many software programs will even generate invoices for you, and will serve the dual purpose of tracking cash inflow and outflow. Furthermore, using automated financial systems will enable you to generate all kinds of financial reports, such as an income statement or a summary of accounts receivable (money your clients owe you), accounts payable (money you owe), or your loan history—really, you can customize just about anything related to your business finances. (We'll explore how to maximize the value of these reports as a business management tool in the next chapter.)

Generate Clear Invoices

The purpose of an invoicing system is to enable you to manage receipts coming into the business. You should create an invoice form that explicitly describes *all* of your information, terms, and conditions, including:

✓ Service or product you provided

✓ Purchase order number or other authorization

✓ Date you provided the product or service

✓ Return policies

✓ Due dates

✓ Payment terms

✓ Late charges

✓ Any other terms relevant to your business and the market you serve

✓ Federal Identification Number (FEIN) or Social Security number, as appropriate

✓ Complete contact information for you and your company

By generating an invoice for every sale, you'll be able to match the incoming payment to each invoice. By making sure all the proper information is on your invoice, you'll increase your chances for prompt payment. Keep unpaid invoices filed chronologically—that is, according to due date. This will enable you or your bookkeeper to easily track who owes you what and when. Or, if you've decided on an electronic invoicing system, the software can do all this for you. (Of course, you or your bookkeeper will have to keep the data current, or the system will be worthless.)

Get What's Coming to You

Many entrepreneurs are challenged—even intimidated—by the prospect of collecting what is owed to them, partly because most don't like being confrontational and partly because they are afraid to find out they've been had. In spite of this discomfort or fear, however, you must be proactive in collecting your receivables. If you're not, you gain nothing and lose everything.

Certainly, nonexistent or sloppy bookkeeping practices will slow down the process and exacerbate the discomfort, simply because you can't remember and/or can't prove that a customer is in arrears. Even when you're well organized, collecting overdue accounts is not easy or pleasant.

Over the years I've had my share of collection experiences, and I've formulated some collection tips as a result:

✓ *Invoice promptly!* If your customers don't have the paperwork, they can't pay you. And the longer you wait to invoice, the more distant your client's memory of the product or service you provided will be.

✓ *Invoice clearly and completely.* As defined previously in this chapter, state all your terms and the circumstances of the business exchange. If your invoice is vague or does not state all the terms of the agreement, you'll have a more difficult time collecting, especially on an overdue account.

✓ *Know your customers' invoicing and payment policies.* Do they need more than one copy of the invoice? Must the invoices be original hard copies, or are faxed or e-mailed invoices acceptable? Should the invoice be included inside a shipment or be sent to a separate department? In many cases, if you don't enter the system properly, your invoice may be delayed—or never paid at all.

✓ *Accurately record each payment you receive to keep your accounts current.* It's unsettling to have to pursue an overdue account, but it is humiliating to ask for a payment you've already received. You'll come off as unprofessional and may jeopardize a good client relationship.

✓ *With large companies, call the accounts payable department a few days before a payment is due and politely ask if the invoice has been processed properly.* Invoices often have a way of getting lost along the payment route. And be aware that large company accounting departments frequently delay payments to small companies and independents to manipulate their cash flow. So if you wait until you're supposed to receive payment, you may be unpleasantly surprised to learn your invoice is on the bottom of some pile and you'll have to wait another payment cycle for your money.

✓ *Take action the* day *an account becomes past due.* Make a phone inquiry or fax a second notice with a polite reminder. A fax carries an immediacy and creates a visual image that often generates better response than transcribed notes from your phone call. But if you still don't get paid, phone the customer and request payment.

✓ *Stay proactive.* If you don't, your weak demeanor will make it easier for your client to put you off.

And I remind you that you have to be honest with yourself about what you feel comfortable with and capable of handling on your own. If you're uneasy calling on overdue accounts, make it part of your bookkeeper's responsibility. He or she will be able to handle the matter with greater detachment.

Manage Other Financial Paperwork

In addition to the general data management issues we discussed in Chapter 30, there are other financial records whose management you need to systematize. These will improve the security and stability of your business as well as help you meet the requirements of the IRS. You'll have others specific to your business and the market you serve, but here are some general guidelines:

✓ Keep copies of your business tax returns in a special file forever. Retain all tax-related documents for at least seven years.

✓ Maintain a file of capital equipment expenses (computers, manufacturing equipment, office equipment, and so forth) forever.

✓ Make and maintain copies of any legal documents (commercial leases, contracts, and so forth) in one place.

✓ On a regular basis, back up on floppy or removable disks any financial records you maintain on your computer. Remember, there are only two types of people: those who've lost data, and those who will. Don't learn the hard way. Also, make a duplicate backup disk and store it in your safe deposit box or other secure off-site location. Replace the stored disk with an updated version on a regular basis.

✓ Keep your invoice file up to date.

✓ Establish a central location for storing regular financial reports regarding your business, to chart your business growth over time.

✓ When it's time to purge financial records, use a shredder. Compact shredders that perch over standard office wastebaskets are about $100 and are a wise investment for maintaining business security.

Minimize Taxes

Good record keeping can also pay off by helping you cut your tax bill. Keeping hard-earned dollars out of the hands of Uncle Sam should be incentive enough to keep careful track of your expenses, so if you haven't begun to do so yet, keep in mind that if you're in the 28 percent tax bracket, every $30 of expenses you document results in almost $10 of savings. (Add almost $5 to that if you aren't incorporated, because you'll save another 15% in Social Security tax.) Think of this as cold, hard cash in your pocket, which can be put to use growing your business.

Judith E. Dacey, a CPA in Orlando, Florida, who is a recognized consultant on small business issues, says that haphazard financial records cause many small firms to lose out on claiming valuable tax advantages. Here are six areas Dacey says are often overlooked:

1. *Log your mileage.* Business travel costs are deductible based on mileage. For 1998, the rate was 32.5 cents per mile, and this generally increases each year. The easiest way to track this figure is to write down the odometer reading in your car at the start and end of each year (so you have a record of total annual miles), then use your trip odometer for each individual trip and record it in your calendar or datebook. Beginning in 1998, you can use this mileage tracking method for leased cars, too. Tracking mileage at a few cents per mile may not seem like much, but at the end of a year it can mean a substantial tax savings.

2. *Use per diems on meal allowances.* Instead of keeping individual receipts, get a copy of IRS Publication Number 1542 from your local IRS office or call (800) TAX-FORM, and calculate the daily per diem for meal allowance for the cities where you travel. New rules allow you to deduct three-fourths of a daily rate for the day you leave and the day you return (even if you leave at 11:59 P.M.). Since many small business owners economize on meals, this approach can generate greater deductions than actual receipts. Keep in mind that the IRS still discounts the deduction for business meals by 50 percent, no matter which way you calculate them.

3. *Convert contributions to advertising.* Contributions are only deductible as an itemized expense on an individual tax return, whereas advertising is a legitimate business expense. Therefore, when you're solicited by an organization for a charitable contribution or donation, approach it as an advertising expense. But note: To make this "legit," you must get an ad in a program, a mention at the microphone, a banner or sign, or

some other recognition by the organization. Only then does it become a deductible business expense.

4. *Employ your spouse to qualify for fully deductible health insurance.* If you're operating as a sole proprietor and employ your spouse, your company can provide (and deduct) health insurance for the employee/spouse and family (which includes you). This often brings greater tax benefits than the partial write-off currently available for health insurance for the self-employed.

5. *Incorporate.* This legal option is not for every business, but it can bring important tax advantages and other benefits. If you're up to date on your financial picture, your CPA and other financial advisors can crunch the numbers and see if incorporation makes sense. This is *not* just for the big guys: Your business may benefit even if your net income is $25,000. Incorporation also lessens the likelihood that your business will be audited by the IRS.

6. *Invest in your retirement.* Setting aside money for your future is not only good financial planning, it's also a smart tax strategy. Since contributions to programs such as a SEP-IRA or SIMPLE IRA lower your taxable income, they bring both current and future benefits. To maximize your earnings and savings, it's important to work with a financial planning professional who understands your business and future goals.

I hope you noticed that each of these tax savings strategies springs from good record keeping and that many of them are fairly simple to implement. As with any financial matter affecting your business, consult with your CPA or other financial professionals to see how these strategies may apply to your particular situation and how you can best put them to use.

Finally, keep in mind that the goal of financial record keeping is to give you factual information that will help you make informed business choices and decisions. Well-designed systems are intended to *support* your business management, not impose one more task for your To-Do list. Your goal is to implement accurate, up-to-date informational systems that are easy to access—and that free you to focus on larger business issues.

Take Action

1. Review your current financial systems. Identify where you need to make improvements or additions.

2. Review your invoicing system from the viewpoint of your clients. Is anything lacking that might delay the processing of your invoices?

3. If you find yourself wanting in any of the categories covered in this chapter, start interviewing bookkeepers. No one can do it all, so if financial systems are one of your weak spots, admit it, then take decisive action to correct it.

Chapter 36

Familiarize Yourself with Financial Reports

A ssuming you have formed the money team I suggested in Chapter 34, you may be wondering why I'm suggesting you also learn about financial reports. You may even be thinking, "Isn't that what I hired an accountant, a bookkeeper, and a financial planner for—so I wouldn't have to read or understand financial reports?" The reason for this strategy is to expand on the caution I included in Chapter 34, to never relinquish responsibility for your own financial matters. The more fluently you can speak the language of money, the more successful you'll be in your business. By learning the basics about financial statements, you'll put yourself in a superior competitive position.

And if you're using computerized accounting systems as I recommended, it is very easy to generate a number of informative and easy-to-follow financial reports. The menu-driven software will guide you through the steps to create whatever you need. If, however, you've opted to use a manual accounting system, your CPA or bookkeeper can work with you to create the financial statements I discuss in this chapter.

Come to Terms

Three basic reports are crucial to understanding and managing the financial activity in your business: an income statement, a balance sheet, and a statement of cash flow. Before we begin to discuss them, though, be aware that the financial reporting uses a lot of terminology you'll need to understand. Don't give up; reread the definitions a few times, until you're confident you understand the meaning of the information presented to you in financial statements. I've italicized the terms you need to know for easy identification.

Smart Strategy

The more fluently you speak the language of money, the more successful you'll be in your business.

State Your Income

Also known as a P&L, for profit and loss, an *income statement* summarizes your revenue and expenses. It shows how much product or service you sold and what it cost you to sell it. The net income is that familiar term *bottom line,* that is, how much money you keep in your business after paying all of your expenses and taxes.

On an income statement, *revenue,* or *net sales,* indicates the amount of money received by your company in exchange for selling products or services to your customers after you've factored in returns. The *cost of goods sold* includes all of the costs directly incurred in making the product or offering the service you sell; it is one of the first expense items deducted from revenues. The *gross profit* is what remains after you subtract the cost of goods sold from net sales.

Selling, general, and administrative expenses (often abbreviated as *SG&A*) is another major category on an income statement. It reflects all expenses related to marketing, sales, promotion, and advertising, as well as general office expenses and other overhead. As the president of a solo service business, for example, you are the primary revenue generator, so you would allocate some of your salary to cost of goods sold—the direct labor component—and the rest to executive salary under SG&A.

After subtracting SG&A from gross profit, you are left with *operating income,* the business income prior to income taxes. From this, you deduct income taxes (and if appropriate, self-employment taxes), leaving you with *net income,* or your bottom line.

Stay Balanced

The balance sheet reflects what your company owns (*assets*) and what it owes (*liabilities*) on a specific date. When you subtract your liabilities from your assets, you are left with *shareholder's equity,* or *net worth.* The balance sheet always follows this formula:

$$\text{assets} = \text{liabilities} + \text{shareholder's equity}$$

Another way to look at this equation is:

$$\text{shareholder's equity} = \text{assets} - \text{liabilities}$$

All assets and liabilities are either *short-term* (due in one year or less) or *long-term* (due in more than one year). *Current assets* and *current liabilities* represent the components of your day-to-day business activity. Current assets include *cash on deposit, accounts receivable* (amounts that customers owe you) and *inventory* (product that will either be sold or made into product to be sold). Think of it as a natural financial flow: When you sell a product, the item will move from inventory to accounts receivable; and when the customer pays you, it becomes cash.

Current liabilities include *accounts payable* (what you owe your vendors), *payroll* (what you owe your employees), *loans payable* (due in one year or less) and *taxes payable* (the portion due in one year or less).

As a general rule, long-term assets are tangibles such as buildings, equipment, office furniture, and fixtures; long-term liabilities are business obligations with a maturity in excess of a year. Finally, the *shareholder's equity* account shows the value of your *capital stock* and *retained earnings.* Capital stock is the shares held in your corporation; retained earnings represent the cumulative net income of your company.

Go with the Cash Flow

The *statement of cash flow* is one of the most important tools in managing your business because it charts the change in the cash account from one period to another. It begins with net income and makes adjustments from three categories: *operations* (increases or decreases in current assets and current liabilities), *investing activities* (typically, capital investments such as equipment), and *financing activities* (such as long-term borrowing and stock issuance). For example, if accounts receivable significantly rose or fell in a particular period, or if the company purchased a major piece of equipment, this would be reflected on the statement of cash flow.

Interpret the Figures

Once you have the reports, what do you do with them? Printing them for your records isn't enough. You must institute a process for monitoring your financial information in a way that is *meaningful* for you and your business.

When you first attempt this, the figures could be hieroglyphics for all they reveal. But as you become more knowledgeable and comfortable with the process, you'll learn to recognize which figures represent good news or danger.

Be aware that examining a single report won't be as meaningful as studying comparisons of weeks, months, or years. Over time, you'll discern fiscal patterns and trends that will serve as valuable indicators and management guides. Here are some things the reports can tell you and how you can use that information.

Examine the Income Statement

By monitoring the income statement, you'll be able to chart the progress of your business from month to month and year to year. In addition to comparing total revenue and expense figures, you can also review line items or categories on a percentage basis. To do this, you create a *common size statement,* converting the total dollar amounts of revenue and expenses each to 100 percent. This way, you can quickly see that Client A represents 11 percent of your total revenue and Client B only 3 percent. Similarly, you can determine the value of spending 18 percent on that new marketing program or decide whether you need to pare back the phone bill that's creating 8 percent of your total expenses. Fortunately, most computer financial software programs calculate these percentage figures automatically, and you can opt to include them in your income statement printouts.

How do you know what the proper percentages should be for your business? That's one of the most often-asked questions—perhaps because the answer is elusive. If your business is part of a common industry, such as dry cleaning or construction, statistical data is available from research organizations such as Robert Morris Associates; your CPA can often track down these figures for you. Smaller firms, however, must rely on sharing data among industry colleagues or informally with peers.

In my encounters with solo entrepreneurs and small business owners, two questions commonly emerge: What percentage profit should I be making? and How much should I spend on marketing as a percentage of my overall budget? The range of answers reveals the reason standard percentages are so difficult: Every small business is unique. Several dozen consultants, for example, told me their pretax profits (operating income) ranged from 12 percent to 65 percent; many small business advisors indicate that 15 percent is standard for small manufacturing companies. Your profit depends on many factors from both the expense and revenue sides, including overhead and staff expenses, as well as the revenue level of your client base (recall Chapter 25, "Upgrade Your Customer Base"). Similarly, my informal surveys about how much small business owners are investing in marketing expenses shows that it ranges from 2 percent to 80 percent, with the rule of thumb being 20 to 40 percent of the total budget targeted for marketing.

What's the answer? Keep accurate data and review your reports regularly so you can compare the percentages with your past successes and setbacks. And network with peers who are seeking the same information you are.

Analyze the Balance Sheet

Balance sheet analysis reveals a company's *assets, liquidity,* and *debt capacity.* A company with strong liquidity has current assets that can be readily converted into cash, and thus is able to easily pay its short-term debts. This is also called *working capital.* When you divide current assets by current liabilities, the resulting *current ratio* is a frequently used liquidity measure. As a general rule, this ratio should be 2.0 to 1 or higher, although many businesses operate safely with a ratio lower than this.

For example, let's say your current assets (such as cash, accounts receivable, and inventory) equal $100,000, and your current liabilities (such as accounts payable and income tax payable) equal $45,000. Dividing $100,000 by $45,000, your current ratio is 2.22 to 1, a favorable fiscal situation. If your ratio is too low, you may be in danger of not being able to cover your bills; if it's too high, you may not be making the best use of your money—putting it to work producing a profit.

A cousin to the current ratio is the *quick ratio,* often known as the acid test ratio. This calculation includes only assets that are cash or that can be converted to cash quickly (hence its name), and excludes assets such as inventory. Bankers generally like to see a quick ratio of at least 1.0 to 1, which means you have enough cash on hand and accounts receivable to cover your current debt at all times.

The balance sheet also measures a company's *debt capacity.* Lenders don't want to advance a business more money than it can be expected to pay back, and they use financial ratios as benchmarks to assist them in making lending decisions. A common ratio is total liabilities (debt) divided by shareholder's equity (shares and retained earnings). The higher this number, the riskier it is to the lender. When this ratio is very high, it's known as being *highly leveraged,* a situation that's profitable for small business owners (since you're using the bank's money instead of your own) but risky from a banker's perspective because you're out on a financial limb with heavy debt.

Monitor the Cash-Flow Statement

A cash-flow statement shows where cash was generated and where it was used during a specific period. Keep a close eye on this statement; it allows you to stay in touch with such financial factors as the rate of your sales cycle, the time period for collection of receivables, the speed of inventory turnover, the impact of an investment in capital equipment, and more.

Savvy business owners review their cash-flow statements monthly, if not weekly. Countless businesses on the growth path get into trouble when they have strong sales but no cash to cover immediate operating needs. Never mistake profits for cash; your company may have booming sales but still be headed for disaster if you don't have funds available to pay bills. Carefully monitoring your cash-flow report is one way to avoid this problem.

Expand Your Knowledge Base

Is your head spinning? Don't be discouraged. This thumbnail sketch is meant to encourage you to learn more about a topic that is essential to the well-being of all business owners. As with any important matter in your business, use this material as a way to prompt your thinking, then consult financial experts who know you, your business, and your industry best. Here are a few tips to launch your education in this admittedly complex area:

✓ Be resourceful; consult several other references. Check out another Working Solo book, *The Small Business Money Guide: How to Get It, Use It, Keep It.* It presents a full overview of financial matters in easy-to-understand language.

✓ Get in the habit of reading the financial pages in your newspaper, or better yet, *The Wall Street Journal,* to familiarize yourself with financial vocabulary and current market activities.

✓ Make sure your accounting software is capable of generating the reports necessary for your financial management processes.

✓ Set aside a regular time each week to review your company's financial status. Don't be afraid to ask your financial team for help. Over time you'll become more comfortable with the language of money and will better understand the impact of the flow of money in and out of your business.

Take Action

1. Create a process to review your company's financial reports on your own and with your CPA on a regular basis. Make it standard practice to review your financials *before* you make business decisions.

2. Take a basic accounting course at your community college to learn more about using these tools to your advantage.

3. Increase your understanding of money and financial management by surfing the Internet and visiting Web sites such as:

   American Express Small Business Web site, http://www. americanexpress.com/smallbusiness
   Dun & Bradstreet Information Services, http://www.dnb.com
   Quicken Small Business Web site, http://www.quicken.com/ small_business

Chapter 37

Build Your Credit

Developing a strong credit history is a strategy that will help you in many ways, from getting a business loan to buying equipment to obtaining trade credit from a supplier. Anyone can establish good credit and maintain it. In this chapter you'll learn some techniques to enhance your credit picture so that you'll have more options as you expand your business.

Credit is important for one key reason: Banks and other creditors want to know that you are responsible and pay your bills on time. Really, it's that simple. There is a common misconception that bankers do not want to part with the bank's money and will run circles around anyone trying to make them do so. Instead of taking that negative viewpoint, let's look at credit from the banker's perspective:

✓ The bank loans you money, which, remember, is another person's hard-earned money that the bank is holding on deposit. You should be grateful for the caution bankers exercise in making loans; after all, you want them to be just as careful with your deposits, don't you?

✓ In exchange for giving you the money, the banker has to trust you to pay it back. And the bank has to make money, too, which it does by charging you interest on the loan.

Let's face another fact: Small businesses are regarded as higher risk by banks, simply because they may not have a track record or a substantial financial foundation. Bankers are acutely aware of the number of startup businesses that fail, many within the first five years. Additionally, the number of personal bankruptcies has skyrocketed over the last few years, making banks even more conservative regarding small business lending.

Know the Score

You know that prior to agreeing to loan you money, the bank will evaluate you and your business. If you have a good credit history, you are much more likely to be granted a loan. But what you may not realize is that because many small businesses are owned and operated by one person, banks also tend to look at the small businessperson's *personal* credit, too. In recent years, a technique called *credit scoring* has become standard practice at many of the larger banks that have a high volume of credit applications to review. Credit scoring is, essentially, a first cut; those who don't make it past the preliminary evaluation are not likely to move to the next level of review and have a loan approved.

Smart Strategy

Even if your business is not yet at a stage where you want to borrow money, you should prepare for that day by beginning now to build a good credit history.

This is important to understand, because credit scoring considers your business *and* personal credit. The bank wants to see consistency in your payment history. Let's say Dave started an antique restoration and resale business and maintained a reasonably good history of paying his bills on time. When the business began to take off, he approached his bank for a line of credit to support his growing cash flow needs as he wanted to buy interesting antiques coming on the market. Although the bank was impressed by what Dave had achieved so far in his business, it turned him down for a business credit line because his personal credit was a mess. He had maxed out on 12 credit cards and had not paid the minimum monthly payment on a consistent basis.

It's even more unsettling to realize that Dave's late payments will remain on his credit report for seven years. To begin to improve his credit resume, Dave will have to start making timely payments on all of his credit cards and other personal obligations. After three or four years, an astute credit analyst will see that Dave is addressing his past irresponsible credit behavior and perhaps seriously consider granting him a loan.

I think you see my point: Even if your business is not yet at a stage where you want to borrow money, you should prepare for that day by beginning now to build a good credit history.

Seek Other Sources

Of course, there are many places besides banks to obtain money for your growing business—enough, in fact, to fill a book, which is what I did when I teamed up with Lisa Aldisert to create *The Small Business Money Guide: How to Get It, Use It, Keep It* (John Wiley & Sons), another of the Working Solo series. This guide gives you details on often-overlooked money sources, what your chances are to raise money, the type of presentation you'll have to make to lenders, and more. It offers in-depth coverage of money issues that can be only one part of my larger focus here on strategies for growing your business.

The money sources available to small businesses range from finance companies and leasing firms to "angels" and other private investors, as well as government programs and the traditional banks. It's important to do your homework and be clear about what the money truly costs you, not only in terms of interest charges, but also in light of the management control you may have to give up or the collateral you may have to provide.

What all these lenders and investors will look to first, however, is the strength of your credit history. That's why this strategy plays such an important role in your company's development.

Trade Up

One of the easiest places to begin building your credit history is establishing what's called *trade credit.* This is invoked when you buy products or supplies from a vendor and agree to pay the vendor at some later date. This payment date typically occurs between 10 and 30 days after purchase.

Initially, some vendors may request (or demand) payment on delivery until you have established your creditworthiness. Thereafter, you tell them you're interested in establishing trade credit. You will probably be asked to fill out an application, on which the vendor will request bank and other credit references. Once your company has been approved, you will be able to purchase on credit. A tip: The first few times you purchase using the credit option, pay the bill early. This will go a long way toward establishing a good business relationship, which you will later be able to leverage to establish credit with other vendors. Here are a few other credit-related tips:

✓ Don't overdraw your bank account.

✓ If you have employees, always pay them on time. Even if you are strapped for cash, find a way to make payroll.

✓ *Never* be late sending payroll taxes to the IRS. If you do, rest assured the penalties are severe. They will come to your office and take your equipment, inventory, assets, the chair you're sitting on and the paintings on your wall—and you may end up wearing a striped suit, behind bars.

✓ If you use personal credit cards for business, keep one or two solely for business use. Don't mix business and personal purchases.

✓ Once you have established trade credit with one vendor, do so with one or two others. When cash flow is tight, this will come in handy.

Keep in mind that building credit is an ongoing, upward cycle for every growing business. The financial limits increase, but the goals remain the same:

1. Have enough credit in place to fund your growth when you need it.
2. Don't overextend.
3. Make regular payments.

Entrepreneurs must master the art of juggling cash flow without jeopardizing personal and business credit. A good credit history will enable you to take your business to the next level a lot more quickly and easily.

Take Action

1. Identify one change to improve your credit picture. Make it.

2. Find out how your banker evaluates credit when extending a business loan, even if you don't need the money at this time.

3. Send for a copy of your credit report once a year. Review it for discrepancies, and if you find errors on the report, respond in writing to have the report adjusted. The three primary credit agencies are:

   Experian (formerly TRW), (800) 682-7654; http://www.experian.com

   Equifax, (800) 685-1111; http://www.equifax.com

   Trans Union, (800) 916-8800; http://www.transunion.com

Chapter 38

Price for Profit

It may seem like stating the obvious to say that the profitability of any business hinges on the proper pricing of its products or services, but many eager entrepreneurs miscalculate this key variable, often with disastrous results. The reason? Disguised under this apparently straightforward strategy is the requirement to perform a somewhat delicate balancing act: If you price your product or service too high, the result will be a low level of sales; if you price too low, though you may reap short-term sales, ultimately the business itself will not be profitable and may fail.

Determine Costs

There are two opposing views about how to establish proper pricing. The accountant types will calculate what the product or service cost to produce, mark this up according to industry guidelines, and establish the price. On the other side, the marketing enthusiasts will experiment selling the product or service at different price points and try to determine what the buyers will pay. Each approach has merit, but neither should be used alone. Let's take a look at each side.

Before you can establish pricing, you must analyze all the costs that go into producing your product or service. If, for example, you're manufacturing a widget, you need to include all of its component costs, from the smallest nut and bolt to the package it comes in. Then you must add the cost of direct labor, whether only yours or that of staff, necessary to make the product.

Don't Labor for Nothing

I know a jewelry designer who makes fine jewelry, using only gold, silver, and precious gems in his pieces. He complained, however, that though his sales were strong, his profits were meager. In evaluating his costs, we discovered that he neglected to include the cost of special tools and molds he used in the process of working the precious metals and gems. Moreover, he had not accounted for the labor component. So in essence, he was working for free. Clearly, he had to reprice to include both the component and design costs as well as the cost of his labor.

If you offer a service, this figure may be a little more elusive to pin down. Consider Melissa, a personal trainer. She knows how much her business has to make in a year to enable her to cover her costs and make a decent wage. Melissa calculates the number of hours she will be able to work and estimates a price—although she may need to adjust it according to what the market will bear (more about that in a little bit).

In determining pricing, don't overlook or underestimate direct product and labor costs, which includes anything and anyone involved in the actual production of your product or service. A surprising number of entrepreneurs forget to count themselves as a labor component when calculating this cost of sales—the jewelry designer mentioned earlier is hardly the exception to the rule. And don't overlook direct overhead, the expenses such as rent or utilities for the studio, workroom, or office where you perform your labors. For example, what if our personal trainer Melissa has to rent space at a gym to work with her clients? Those costs must be factored into her pricing.

After adding up the direct labor, product cost, and overhead, you'll have your *base cost of manufacturing.* To that you'll add a profit margin, which results in your *wholesale cost,* or the cost at which you will sell your product to a retailer or service to a client. If you're selling a product to a retailer, the retailer will also add a profit margin to the price, to come up with the *retail selling price.* For example, let's say you make handpainted silk scarves and your base cost of manufacturing is $7, which represents your materials, labor, and a prorated portion of your overhead. You add a profit of $3 and sell the scarf to a retailer at a wholesale cost of $10. The retailer puts it in the shop window where it sells to the customer for $20.

Know Market Value

Now that you know the factors to calculate, we've addressed half the equation. The question remains, "How do I know the right price to charge?" For the purpose of this discussion, let's call the determination of your actual costs the "science" of pricing, and the establishing of an additional profit margin the "art." Or you can think of the science as comprising the tools you need to paint your pricing picture—your brushes, paints, and canvas.

Smart Strategy

A figure of $1 million in sales doesn't say how profitable your business is. Your profitability is your net figure—what's left over after subtracting your cost of materials, research and development, sales and marketing, administration, salaries, and other expenses.

As in the development of all good artwork, let's start with some sketches made from real life. By this I mean that you should tap into your network to learn the range of prices charged by your competition. This information is invaluable. In my experience, entrepreneurs have a tendency to "price down." I think it's a function of working on their own and not being in close enough touch with their marketplace (which of course links back to the discussion in the networking chapter). And keep in mind that the price you charge is a reflection of your perceived expertise, another strategy we discussed in Chapter 14.

It's also important not to become discouraged if you miscalculate your pricing. You'll learn, believe me. One of my early experiences taught me a couple of lessons I'll never forget. I was asked to review a project on the spot and to estimate the cost for my editorial work. Nervously I quoted a price, and to my chagrin heard: "Oh, that's all? Somehow I thought it would be much more." I knew I had left money on the table. I tried to regroup by saying, "Oh, perhaps I didn't fully understand the scope of the project." But it was too late.

I had to do the project for the fee I quoted, and learned never to be so hasty in my estimates again. I also learned the golden phrase: "Let me get back to you."

As they grow their companies, many entrepreneurs wonder, "Can I *really* charge this much?" If you are confident you're offering a high-quality product or service and expertise, the answer is a resounding yes. On the other hand, if you're still working out the kinks, focus on improving your product or service first. As your experience and reputation grow, the market perception will change over time and you can adjust your pricing accordingly.

Nothing But Net

One of the most common ways entrepreneurs gauge their success is by measuring their overall business income. Experienced entrepreneurs realize, however, that this benchmark can be dangerously deceiving because it can lead a business owner into a false sense of security. Just because your company is generating higher revenues every year doesn't automatically mean that the business is humming along at a solid growth rate. In the long run, what matters is not how much money you *make* (gross), it's how much you *keep* (net).

Don't get caught up in the thrill of boasting a large level of revenue. A figure of $1 million in sales doesn't say how profitable your business is. Your profitability is your net figure—what's left over after subtracting your cost of materials, research and development, sales and marketing, administration, salaries, and other expenses.

After you've been in business for a few years, you'll see patterns developing in your revenue and expense figures. For example, salaries, marketing, or research and development might consistently add up to a certain percentage range of sales. When you can chart such patterns, you'll be able to use them to forecast your expenses. In other words, for every additional $100 in sales, you may need to incur a certain level of expense. Understanding these relationships will be invaluable as your business grows, and it points out once again the importance of those financial reports we discussed in Chapter 36.

There's no getting around it. It will take time before you're knowledgeable about and comfortable with all of the nuances of pricing. And the global nature of today's marketplace means that a multitude of factors shift more frequently. As the leader of your firm, you must stay informed and flexible where pricing is concerned. Proper pricing means better chances of continuing profits for your company.

Take Action

1. Research your market to see what your competitors are charging and what you think the market will bear. Where do your prices fall in the range?

2. Identify where you can be flexible in your pricing. For example, by subcontracting some of the labor, you may be able to lower that cost component.

3. Expand your understanding about pricing by reading books such as:

   Price Wars, by Thomas J. Winninger (Prima Publishing, 1995).
   Priced to Sell: The Complete Guide to More Profitable Pricing, by Herman Holtz (Upstart Press, 1996).

Chapter 39

Manage Your Inventory

If your business creates and sells a tangible product, you're probably all too familiar with the challenge of inventory control. How you manage the excess or undersupply of your product can have a profound effect on your day-to-day business cash flow as well as your overall profits. This chapter offers a road map to help you navigate this often unpredictable terrain.

The inventory rule of thumb is, "Less is definitely more." Certainly, you need enough widgets in your warehouse to fill incoming orders. But if you have too many, the excess will wreak havoc with your company's financial picture as those widgets age, decay, depreciate, or become obsolete over time.

Use It or Lose It

To understand how and why inventory can have such a negative impact on your business, let's examine what really happens to your money when it's transformed into product. First, you purchase components or finished product from a vendor for resale. Whether or not you have current orders, you generally must pay the vendor within 30 days. The components or finished goods must be stored; depending on their size, this could be a cumbersome and expensive process. If your product fails to move as you anticipated, your investment can evaporate into worthlessness as weeks and months pass.

When you maintain inventory, you tie up your money not only in product, but in warehousing costs, insurance, and other fees. In addition, the inventory is counted as an asset on your company's balance sheet, and will remain there—possibly hurting you from a tax perspective—until it is sold or disposed of in another manner.

Smart Strategy

Inventory management demands discipline. You must understand all aspects of your business and how each part influences your overall profitability.

Most damaging, however, is that by putting your dollars into inventory, you rob your company of precious cash that could be put to use in other ways. This ties back to our discussion of opportunity cost in Chapter 31: Money invested in inventory means that it can't be put to work doing other good things for the company, such as supporting new product development or additional staff, or even generating interest in a money management account. Even worse, you could be jeopardizing the entire business by depleting the crucial cash flow needed for operations.

Time Everything

Think of managing inventory in a small business as visiting a Las Vegas casino, where your widgets are the chips. In addition to the luck factor—which every experienced business owner who sells product will admit is important—you must know the rules of the game and have a smart strategy for when to hold and when to fold. In the ideal situation, you bulk up when you know product demand will be high; when orders slow to a trickle, you maintain the minimum inventory necessary to fill those orders. To put yourself in this ideal situation requires that you closely examine your marketing efforts and account for the seasonality of product demand so that you can accurately predict peak and off-peak periods.

Without question, inventory management demands discipline. You must understand all aspects of your business and how each part influences your overall profitability. For example, marketing will drive demand, which may require hiring more staff to take and ship orders, which increases overhead and leads to a potentially higher debt burden. Throw in the variable of inventory and you can see the complexity of the equation.

Delve into Details

Above all, you must stay up to date on your company's financial details, so you have a true picture of what your inventory is costing you. Do your homework and find out what the average annual inventory turnover rate is for your industry. For example, a restaurant open year-round would turn nearly 365 times—fresh food every day of the year. At the other end of the scale, an independent housing developer may construct and sell four new homes a year, so his or her inventory (of one home) turns once a quarter. In many small companies, inventory turns at least three times a year, although some move at a much faster pace. A benchmark range is a three- to six-month supply of inventory, and higher turn rates are preferable since they mean less storage costs and better cash flow. Network and discover standards for your industry.

Another pitfall to watch out for is the enticement of a lower unit cost for a bigger run. Using such rationalizations as, "But if I buy only a little more, each one will cost me a lot less," has led to many overflowing warehouses—and the near ruin of the business owners. Fortunately, many manufacturers have adapted modern technologies to enable shorter runs, in response to demands for just-in-time inventory from larger corporations (that know too well the perils and expense of inventory).

When it's time to purchase product for your small business, conduct a competitive analysis and find companies that can offer you shorter runs at a good price. Here again, having your financial details in order will enable you to negotiate more aggressively and to calculate your needs more precisely.

Cut Your Losses

Unfortunately, no matter how adept you become at anticipating the ups and downs of your industry, probably one day, due to unforeseen fluctuations in the marketplace, you'll be faced with the harsh reality that the product sitting in your warehouse has become a drag on

your business, consuming dollars in warehousing and other costs—
not to mention the mental drain it is exacting on you.

When you reach this juncture, it's time to cut your losses and liquidate your inventory. It's also the time to brainstorm ways you might
be able to recoup some of your dollars. For example, you might:

✓ Sell off the product to a closeout distributor, which will in
turn sell it to discount outlets.

✓ Offer a deep discount to your current customers.

✓ Use the warehoused product as a free or discounted pre-
mium to encourage customers to purchase other products
you sell.

✓ Donate the product to charitable organizations for the income tax deduction.

The decision to liquidate has other fallout besides the hit you
take on overstock, so what you do with this excess inventory must be
considered carefully. You don't, for example, want to endanger other
current or future product offerings or sales by flooding the market
with discounted widgets in an out-of-date design, size, or color,
because you may deter customers from buying your new, improved
version at full price. That's losing on two fronts: by selling the older
version at discount and by impacting potential future revenue. You
must also be wary of job-lot or closeout buyers, particularly if you
have a recognized product or brand name to protect. Your widgets
could well end up in a discount store or other environment that
dilutes your overall marketing program.

It's a good idea, too, to make all liquidation decisions only after
consulting with your CPA and other financial advisors, because what
you do can have a significant impact on your tax situation. You may
not be able to get full sale price for your product, but with proper
planning you may at least be able to maximize your tax savings.

Though there's no way to be sure you'll never get stung by the
inventory bug, experience and careful tracking are your best guides.
Three pieces of advice to keep in mind: Be conservative, track your
numbers closely, and keep your business assets liquid. You want
your money in the right place, so it can be hard at work.

Take Action

1. Find out what the average annual inventory turnover rate is for your industry. And don't do this just once—make sure you have current information at all times.

2. Commit time to locating companies that are willing to offer you short runs competitively priced.

3. Liquidate with caution. Don't just get rid of the stuff to save on warehousing costs. The idea is to cut losses, not to accept a total writeoff.

EXPANSION
STRATEGIES

Chapter 40

Control Growth

Too often, small business owners trust in circumstance and/or serendipity to fuel their companies' growth—one project or product leads to another, until one day the entrepreneur wakes up with a company more complex than (or nothing like) anything he or she ever imagined—or wanted.

For some, the result of this growth can be a fascinating and exhilarating adventure; for others, it's a claustrophobic nightmare. They've created exactly what they were trying to get away from when they set out on their own—a big bureaucratic structure. This strategy addresses this issue, and shows how to execute effective plans to manage your company's growth.

Celebrate Your Capabilities and Accept Your Limitations

Every business owner has certain capabilities and limitations. As an entrepreneur, especially if you're working solo, you have to learn to maximize your capabilities yet not go so far as to tax them, thereby putting the firm and yourself at risk. As discussed earlier, you must come to terms with the practical limits of your growth. Even with the snazziest technology, a knock-'em-dead marketing program, and the most efficient use of strategic partnering (which we discuss in more detail in Chapter 42), there is only so much one person can do—and do well.

Even if you decide to hire help, you will still face limits—not to mention that you have added the always-challenging task of managing staff.

Look Inward

The challenge is to be honest with yourself about what you want your business to become, and to balance your company's growth against that goal. While you're looking inward, use the following questions as guides for your thinking:

✓ *What do you want your company to become?* Right now, as you're reading this, call to mind the vision I asked you to formulate in Chapter 6 and realistically assess how big your company must grow to accomplish your dream. Your response to this single issue can clarify all the other thinking you'll do when considering expansion. In my case, answering this question made me realize that after 18 years as an independent, my vision for Working Solo, Inc. had outgrown the capabilities of my one-person firm. I needed to hire an assistant.

✓ *What product or service are you planning to offer?* Whether you operate a solo consulting firm or produce a tangible product that requires several employees to produce, you must identify exactly what you plan to offer and what it will take to get that offering to market. Staying small *and* profitable means you'll have to make tough and smart decisions about creating quality products and services that can be delivered to customers efficiently so they'll provide valuable word of mouth and referrals. Again, know how to showcase your capabilities and particular expertise, so you can bring added value to your clients and generate profit margins big enough to sustain your growth.

Smart Strategy

The challenge is to know yourself well enough that you can extend your reach while retaining your grasp.

✓ *What's your growth time frame?* Do you want it to happen yesterday? Within a year? In five years? To ramp up quickly to take advantage of a short-term market opportunity, for example, you'll face additional challenges of staffing and cash flow. All the more reason to know what you are and are not capable of doing, admitting it, and getting help when and where you need it.

✓ *How do you want to fund your growth?* Don't assume you can bootstrap your growth. Rarely can a company, especially a small one, expand only on its own financing. Even without increases in staff or overhead, a solo business will encounter cash flow needs as it grows and takes on more demanding clients or greater numbers of customers. Are you prepared to turn to outside funding sources to fuel your growth? Do you know where to begin to do so? Is your personal credit, as well as your company's, strong enough to satisfy lenders?

✓ *Where do you want to work?* If you have a home-based setup and want to expand, think through how growth will impact how and where you work. Bringing on staff or contractors will change the dynamic of your business structure. Do you have enough space, or will you need to move? Can you afford to move before you grow? If you can't, have you calculated the psychological effects of sharing your private space until you can? Will you need additional wiring for phone or electricity? More computers or other equipment?

✓ *Why do you want to grow your business?* This is the tough one. Are you certain your overall vision segues smoothly from where you are now to where you want to be? What role do you want to play in your company's future?

Your honest answers to these questions will lead you to a decision that's right for you. Don't be swayed by the promise of prestige or make a change just because you're currently bored with the status quo. Be quite sure that bigger is better for you.

Set Your Tolerance Levels

Determining how well you tolerate change, risk, and debt is first cousin to coming to terms with your capabilities and limitations, and is an important step to take before deciding how large you want your business to become. Some individuals can accept—indeed, thrive on—the challenge of managing increased overhead and financial commitments, while others shudder at the thought.

Any level of growth requires a business owner to accept new depths of commitment. Only you can assess how far your comfort zone stretches before it snaps and you give way to unproductive stress.

Don't Forget the Net

No matter what size you grow your company, it's crucial to distinguish between your revenue and your profits. I've seen many successful solo entrepreneurs who, though making a good living from their businesses, felt compelled to grow their companies to a more substantial size. They added staff, office equipment, and other expensive overhead items. The result? The businesses were larger, but less profitable. The additional revenue was eaten up by the greater costs.

Growing a business presents many challenges. Some are predictable, but many more are unexpected. Without the proper planning and research, it can be like painting a floor without knowing where the door to the room is. Soon you find yourself backed into a corner, trapped and having to choose whether to wait for the paint to dry or to walk on the wet stuff and then painstakingly fix the mess. With preparation, you'll know where to start and can confidently paint your way to the door, free to move on to the next level of growth.

Take Action

1. Sit down and think about how big you'd ultimately like your business to be—1 year from now, 3 years from now, 5 years from now, 10 years from now. Factor in gross revenue, number of employees, number of locations, net income—the works.

2. Ask yourself how well you tolerate risk. Include all types: financial risk, the risk of making the wrong decision, the risk of taking time away from your family and friends, the risk of getting in over your head, and others. How can your answers help you chart your growth path?

3. Ask your mentor(s) and network colleagues to tell you honestly what they see as your capabilities and your limitations. Warning: Don't do this if you're not truly willing to listen objectively to what they have to say.

Chapter 41

Staff Up

W hen a company crosses the threshold to a new level of growth, it may be time for the business owner to build an on-site team. What marks that threshold? A mix of needs, financial stability, and projected growth—and the willingness of the entrepreneur to expand his or her thinking.

Hiring employees is a major step for a number of reasons, some business related, others personal. For starters, you must be very sure that your business is strong enough financially to carry the additional investment of salaried employees. Bringing on even a single employee will cause an explosion of paperwork and tax responsibilities. And consider that, while working solo, you can adjust your take-home pay based on the ebb and flow of your revenue, whereas employees expect—and deserve—a regular income. On the personal front, you'll have to confront issues of collaboration; if, for example, you resist input from others or insist on having things done your way, you'll have to recognize that no matter how good a fit your employee is, he or she will have another way of thinking and doing.

Fortunately, there are several ways to add staff to your company. We'll explore them here, along with methods of interviewing potential workers that help you discover if they're team material.

Wade into the Hiring Pool

Expanding a business to include others can be a challenge for many solo entrepreneurs. It forces us to shift into new work patterns: from doer of everything to trainer, delegator, and manager. If your background doesn't include management experience, and your business is still evolving, you should make this transition gradually. Consider which of the following five levels of staffing commitment you're willing—and can afford—to make.

Interns

One of the least expensive ways of staffing up is to hire an intern, who often works not for financial compensation but to earn college credit as part of school-sponsored programs. That said, working with interns poses a number of challenges. They will need to be trained; and they expect to be involved in an interesting work assignment relevant to their studies.

A good way to attract qualified student interns is to contact the business department at your local college or university. Ask about their work-study programs. Check out the possibility of your giving a short presentation to one of the classes involved in the program. With the permission of the professor, at the end of your talk mention that you sometimes need student interns to work in your company, and ask interested candidates to leave their names and contact information. Using this approach, you'll get a jump start on the screening process.

Projects that work best for interns are very specific and self-contained—and usually defined in part by the intern. You, on the other hand, will have to do some numbers crunching to make sure the time you have to spend teaching interns comes back in the help they provide.

Benefits: Enthusiastic help at little or no cost

Drawbacks: Untrained staff who may require time-consuming supervision

Freelancers and Other Independents

If you have a project or business task that requires a specific skill or experience, a freelancer or other independent may be the answer. The widespread growth in this employment category means that you'll be able to meet any business need you have.

This is also the talent pool from which you can draw to supplement your own talents or to make up for a particular limitation. Consider this source for help with designing and maintaining your Web site, for bookkeeping, correspondence, financial management, and a number of other areas. Be aware, however, that if you pay anyone more than $600 a year, current tax regulations stipulate that you must submit a 1099 form to report that person's earnings. So be sure to keep your records in order.

Benefits: A pool of specialized talent for individual projects

Drawbacks: May not be available when needed

Temporary Help

For short-term help or to meet ongoing needs without getting bogged down in employee paperwork, there's no better solution than hiring temporary employees. Courtesy of widespread corporate downsizing in recent years, the temp talent pool is deeper than ever.

Benefits: Prescreened, often high-quality workers available for flexible time periods; all paperwork is handled by the temp agency

Drawbacks: Higher labor costs that include payment of agency services; little loyalty; may not be available when needed

Part-Time Employees

Many entrepreneurs ease into staff expansion by hiring employees on a part-time basis. This arrangement raises your level of operational stability while enabling you to control costs and to test-run the benefits (and/or disadvantages) you can anticipate from hiring help.

Smart Strategy

The people you work with will have a direct impact on the success of your business and the quality of your life. Choose wisely.

One good source of part-time talent can be found among experienced businesswomen who have left full-time work to raise young children. This can be a win/win situation: You get someone with strong business experience and they get the flexibility they need to meet their personal commitments.

For this labor pool, you need to keep in mind that the IRS has strict guidelines about who qualifies as an independent contractor and who is categorized as an employee. If the hire has no other clients, works under your direct supervision, and works regular hours at your office, chances are the IRS will classify that person as an employee, and will expect you to pay the taxes mandated by that status. (For more details, check out the resources listed in the Take Action section at the end of this chapter.)

Benefits: Regular, often experienced, help without full-time financial commitment; higher degree of loyalty

Drawbacks: Potentially complex paperwork and expensive taxes; time-delimited work schedule

Full-time Employees

Even one full-time employee will change the nature of your business. Suddenly there's someone else in the office every day to handle ongoing tasks and execute plans. But along with this increased capability comes the responsibility for training and development, and the fiscal obligation for the employee's livelihood.

Entrepreneurs who have made the shift from a one-person venture to a company with full-time staff would be the first to admit that accepting the responsibilities for employees is daunting, particularly because taxes and benefits can increase employee costs by an additional 30 percent. But the advantages can be worth the investment, particularly since hiring help often is the most direct means for business owners to fulfill their company vision. The choice is yours.

Benefits: Regular, trained member of company; stability and high degree of loyalty

Drawbacks: Complex paperwork; expensive taxes and benefits; ongoing financial commitment

Manage Your Staff

Getting staff on board is only half the challenge. You must learn to work with employees effectively or you'll waste time and money. Here are five key insights gleaned from nearly two decades of staff experiences and feedback from entrepreneurial colleagues.

✓ *Choose wisely.* The people you choose to work with will have a direct impact on the success of your business and the quality of your life. Remember, attitude is paramount; skills can be taught. Don't discount the importance of finding enthusiastic and energetic self-starters who welcome the challenge of solving problems on their own.

✓ *Complement, don't clone.* It's a natural tendency to select staff based on their similarity to us in personality and capabilities. But you and your business will need individuals who can supplement your talent and skills while adding their own. Consider administering personality and capability assessment profiles to clarify strengths and weaknesses. (See the Take Action section for some firms that offer these tools.)

✓ *Learn to delegate.* Delegation is a learned skill, not an inborn trait. And it's not an easy skill for many entrepreneurs to master. You'll have to commit to becoming a better leader through delegation. It's tough, but worth it, because you'll be freeing up your time to do what you do best.

✓ *Invest in your staff.* And I don't mean just financially. Have a stake in your employees' professional and personal development. The time, energy, and other resources you expend to empower them with training and experience will be repaid to your business many times over and in many ways—that is, of course, *if* you've hired the right people in the first place.

✓ *Keep things in perspective.* Let's face it, no one, not even your closest friend or relative, will ever care as much about your business as you do. But you can encourage a deeper level of involvement from your staff members by remembering to take time to see things from their viewpoint and then investigating ways to connect that to your own business vision. And never underestimate the power of financial incentives, perhaps in the form of bonuses pegged to profits.

Above all, be patient with yourself and with your staff. You may have to go through some trial and error to find your ideal staffing solution, whether you decide to maintain your solo environment and work with other independents or build a company with multiple employees. Your choice must be congruent with your personal style and the goals you have for your company.

Take Action

1. Sit down with your accountant before you hire anyone and review the financial and paperwork implications of adding staff. Be clear about your legal and tax responsibilities if you hire independent contractors. Increase your understanding of this issue by reading *Hiring Independent Contractors: The Employer's Legal Guide,* by Stephen Fishman (Nolo Press, 1997).

2. Commit to learning more about how to train and motivate staff by reading books such as Nido Qubein's *Achieving Peak Performance* (Best Sellers Publishing, 1996).

3. Contact a career counseling professional or a firm that administers assessment profiles. Complete the assessment along with your staff to develop a snapshot of your personal strengths and weaknesses as well as those of the team. Two companies noted for their assessment profiles are:

   TTI Performance Systems, (800) 869-6908, http://www.ttidisc.com

   Kolbe Concepts, Inc., (602) 840-9778, http://www.koblecorp.com

Chapter 42

Expand Virtually

A big bonus of running a small business in the digital era is having the opportunity to grow your company in ways unimaginable only a few years ago. Using the power of e-mail and the Internet, entrepreneurs can form innovative collaborations and teams unlimited by geography or the burden and expense of adding staff.

With digital tools in hand (virtually, that is), savvy business owners are extending their capabilities and thus their market reach through the alignment of strategic relationships forged via electronic connections. For them, the world is not only a global marketplace but also a planetwide partnering pool.

If you're thinking about expanding your company but can't yet afford to or don't want to take on the commitment of an employee, consider working as part of a virtual team or creating strategic alliances. Using this strategy can give you the best of both worlds: Partners retain a level of independence while reaping the benefits of collaboration. Sound good? Read on.

Smart Strategy

Virtual partnerships work only when all parties understand and appreciate that their joint effort is more powerful than what they could achieve on their own.

Go Hollywood

By now you've heard the buzz phrase "virtual corporation," but probably within the context of Internet commerce. Actually, the concept has been in use in the film industry for years. When filmmaker Steven Spielberg, for example, sets out to create a movie, he gathers a project team of the most talented individuals he can find: actors, cinematographers, costume artists, set designers, special effects wizards, and so forth. Each brings his or her unique skills to the project, and the result is usually a megahit movie enjoyed by millions of people worldwide.

When the project is completed, the team disassembles and the individuals move on to their next commitment. Some may return and work with Spielberg on his next movie, others may not. In this type of virtual connection, the links last only as long as necessary; then the team dissolves and reforms in a different configuration.

Structure the Virtual

But perhaps for your purposes and market, you need a little more consistency and continuity in your collaborations. Well, virtual doesn't necessarily mean temporary. If you prefer a bit more structure behind your virtual partnerships, consider this implementation of the virtual partnership. Relaxation Resources, based in Santa Cruz, California, is a collaboration of nearly 50 independent practitioners in the field of human renewal, ranging from yoga teachers to massage therapists, stress management experts to acupuncturists, African drummers to theatre improv players. The company was launched by Shana Ross and Madelyn Keller in 1997 with the objective of working together yet separately. Each of the professionals retains his or her independent practice, but they also come together to work on larger projects for corporate clients in the nearby Silicon Valley and beyond. For example, a half-dozen Relaxation Resources associates may organize to present an hour-long program during lunch for several days to 25 members of a company conference.

The group's virtual connections enable members to accept clients and projects none could have tackled alone. "We're independent yet interrelated," explains co-founder Shana Ross, who likens her role to that of a circus ringmaster. "Each new client brings the chance for us to create a different combination of talent."

Members pay an annual fee, which goes toward the maintenance of their Web page (www.relaxationresources.com), a listing in all group materials, and the opportunity to participate in the organization's projects. Potential new members "audition" for the group to ensure a proper match both personally and professionally. Relaxation Resources also has written guidelines that define roles and professional behavior (for example, phone calls must be returned promptly, and members are expected to dress appropriately for corporate clients).

The group has found numerous personal benefits that come from their virtual business. "In this time of free agents, we still long for community," observes Shana Ross. "We appreciate the way this structure lets us come together in a way that's not competitive."

Go with the Flow

Forming virtual alliances is a fluid process. You pick and choose methods that work for you, and continually refine your approach as people come and go to accommodate the changes. But this strategy is not for everyone, particularly those who prefer the constancy of a formalized structure. If, however, you think this might be just the strategy you need to expand your business, I can offer the following guidelines gathered from years of working with virtual colleagues:

✓ *Institute clear communication practices.* For a virtual relationship—whether among colleagues, suppliers, or customers—to prosper, you must always be aware of how effectively you are communicating. Learn to use the telephone well, by which I mean improving your listening skills and leaving clear and concise voice mail messages. Master e-mail interactions; learn how to express enthusiasm and appreciation without the benefits of voice or body language. Never underestimate the need to communicate clearly with your partners.

✓ *On occasion, make the virtual real.* There is no substitute for actually meeting a person. It gives you the opportunity to "check each other out," to gauge your chemistry, read and interpret visual and verbal cues, and generally get a sense of your virtual partner's personality.

✓ *Clarify expectations.* Never assume you all agree. Especially with virtual collaborations where you can't supplement verbal or written interactions with face-to-face meetings, you must ensure that partners know precisely what's expected of them. Follow the example of the Relaxation Resources group: Write guidelines and establish a basic understanding among all virtual parties.

✓ *Set regular milestones.* Long-term projects involving virtual teams can be the most difficult to manage. To make sure everyone stays on track, it's important to establish intermediate target dates. Create realistic schedules, and don't forget to include some buffer time for the inevitable delays and slippage. The best strategy for on-time delivery of projects, however, is to hone your skills at choosing team members who respect schedules and are dependable.

✓ *Find the optimal communication vehicle.* Agree on a primary communications vehicle among team members, whether it's e-mail, fax, or phone. The goal is for everyone to feel comfortable with the method; if one of your partners is technophobic, don't insist on using e-mail, for example.

✓ *Express appreciation.* When a relationship is stretched by distance, it's more difficult to maintain a strong bond. So take time to say thanks to your virtual colleagues, suppliers, and customers.

✓ *Make the relationship win/win.* This point is last on the list for emphasis, not because it's the least important. Whether it's a strategic marketing alliance, a shared client, or other project that brings you together, it's important to establish parameters in your virtual relationships that are mutually beneficial. Virtual partnerships work only when all parties understand and appreciate that their joint effort is more powerful than what they could achieve on their own.

The beauty of virtual partnerships is that they give you the flexibility to form and reform their boundaries and substance. There are no hard-and-fast rules for creating these alliances. The digital world changes so quickly that new opportunities continually expand the possibilities. All this is good news for small business owners who stay nimble, with one eye always trained on future possibilities.

Take Action

1. Imagine a project you'd love to do but know you couldn't handle on your own. Who in the *world* might be able and willing to be on your dream team?

2. Investigate other virtual partnerships, especially those in your industry, to better determine if such an alliance might work for you. Network within your professional association—both online and in real time—to learn how your peers are creating virtual alliances.

3. Consider how you might expand your business if you could find individuals who are strong in capabilities you lack. What would those individuals be like, and what would they do? What could you do together?

Chapter 43

Check Your Status

In the 1980s, New York City's mayor, Ed Koch, became known for his media savvy. His oft-repeated question "How'm I doing?" became his trademark. It was a particularly effective, shortcut way of staying in touch with his public and in favor with his constituents.

Koch's verbal opinion poll is a strategy that can work for small business owners as well. You should be asking yourself that same question as you expand your business—in essence, conducting regular status checks in key business areas. This chapter identifies a dozen landmark areas that should be active on your radar screen at all times, so you can keep track of which may need attention. Read through them with a pen or pencil in hand and put a Y for Yes or N for No (or NA if Not Applicable to you) next to the boxes.

1. Revenue

❏ Can you state your revenues at any time (for example, year to date, this quarter, this month)?

❏ Do you know how they compare to a similar earlier period?

❏ If you calculate a percentage breakdown of where your revenues are coming from, do you find they are concentrated in a few areas or with a few clients? (If so, this could pose financial risk for your business.)

❏ If you analyze the patterns of revenue for your company, are there peaks and valleys? Can you say why?

❏ Have you run cash-flow projections for your business in anticipation of revenue fluctuations?

❏ Is your projected revenue stable? Do you have ongoing business?

2. Expenses

❏ Do you know how high your expenses are at any time (for example, year to date, this quarter, this month)? Can you compare them to a similar earlier period?

❏ If you calculate a percentage breakdown of your expenses, do you find they are concentrated in a few areas? Can you explain why? Can this be regulated, or are the costs fixed?

❏ If you analyze the expense patterns in your company, are there certain times of the year when expenses are high or low? If so, do you know the reason(s)?

❏ Have you calculated the return on investment (ROI) for the key projects or customers in your business? Do you know how much profit each project or customer brings to your business?

3. New Product (or Service) Development

❏ Do you have an ongoing plan to create new products or services? Is it systematized?

❏ Have you set aside a certain amount of time each week or month specifically for developing new revenue sources for your company?

❏ Do you have funds set aside or credit available for the development of new products or services?

❏ Have you identified companies that can help you develop prototypes or that can manufacture a product for you? Have you formed relationships that can help you deliver a new product or service?

❏ Have you conducted market research on your target market? Do you know the top three needs and wants of these customers?

4. Financial

❏ Do you know exactly how much money is flowing in and out of your business at all times?

❏ Are you aware how strong (or weak) your current cash position is?

❏ Have you been diligent about developing a good company (and personal) credit history?

❏ Do you have access to working capital, such as a credit line?

❏ Have you set up favorable credit terms with your suppliers?

❏ Do the employees at your bank know who you are? Do you keep one higher-level bank staff member apprised of your business dealings?

❏ Have you created a team of professional financial advisors for your business?

❏ Are your bookkeeping systems in order?

❏ Do you regularly run and review financial reports on your business?

❏ Have you established a retirement account; if so, are you funding it to its annual maximum? Have you set up additional retirement funding options?

❏ Do you have a financial reserve or other backup plan in case of disability? Have you investigated or invested in disability insurance? (I discuss this in further detail in Chapter 48, "Cope with Crisis.")

5. Marketing and Sales

❏ Is your customer database accurate and up to date?

❏ Do you contact your customers on a regular, scheduled basis?

❏ Have you calculated the lifetime value of your key customers? If so, have you taken steps to ensure their loyalty?

❏ Do you have a system in place to track all leads? Do you ask the question, "How did you hear about us?"

❏ Have you calculated the ROI for your marketing and sales efforts?

❏ Do you know how much it costs you to acquire a new customer?

❏ Can you state what percentage of your budget is devoted to marketing? Knowing that every business varies and that a range of 20 to 40 percent of revenue is common, have you networked with other professionals in your field to see how your marketing expenses compare?

❏ Do you regularly test-drive a new marketing approach?

6. Customer Service and Retention

❏ Can you identify the top 20 percent of your customer base? How much do you know about these people?

❏ Have you instituted programs to encourage customer loyalty?

❏ Do you have systems in place to handle customer complaints? Can they be used by someone with little training?

❏ Do you thank your customers?

❏ Do you have a system in place to reward current customers for sending you new business?

❏ Have you set a maximum response time for dealing with customer requests? Within 12 hours? 24 hours?

❏ Can your customers easily access information about your products and services, via a toll-free number, fax on demand, e-mail autoresponders, or Web sites?

❏ When you can't personally take customer calls, do you have an effective backup system in place to do so?

7. Technology

❏ Are your computer systems up to date, including software and hardware that maximize your productivity?

❏ Have you made a commitment to upgrade your own training as well as that of your staff?

❏ Have you instituted backup plans in the event of a systems failure? Do you have a technical support team on call?

❏ Have you established clear policies and systems for backing up your business data? Is at least one set of data stored off site?

❏ Are your phone systems adequate to handle your business needs? Have you utilized the full capabilities of your phone and messaging systems?

❏ Is your fax machine on a separate telephone line? Do you have a backup system or easy access to an outside fax service? Have you investigated the additional capabilities of your fax machine, such as sending broadcast faxes?

❏ Do you have Internet access and e-mail? Are you using at least 60 percent of the capabilities of your e-mail software? Do you have current Web browser software installed on your computer? Does your company have a simple Web page set up, if not a site?

❑ Have you set up systems to assess the value and timing of purchasing new technologies for your company? Have you identified sources for information to guide you in your decision-making process?

8. Operations

❑ Do you prioritize your To-Do list? Are you careful not to sacrifice revenue-generating tasks for superficial productivity?

❑ Do you have systems in place for managing information?

❑ Do you consistently and clearly track receivables and bills?

❑ Do you have a paper management strategy in place?

❑ Have you set up a dedicated office space? Is it designed for optimum performance?

❑ Do you learn from problems? How?

❑ Have you implemented a time management system? Is it portable? Is it compatible with your software programs?

9. Staff

❑ Is your relationship with independent contractors structured so that they retain their independent status and protect your business?

❑ Have you assessed the strengths and weaknesses of your business team?

❑ Is your staff results-oriented?

❑ Do you motivate and reward your staff? How?

❑ Have you fully compared the pluses and minuses of working with independent associates as opposed to hiring employees?

❑ Do you know where to find an intern should you need one?

❑ If you're planning to bring on an employee (full- or part-time), have you calculated the real costs of doing so?

10. Advisors

❏ Do you have financial advisors on call for bookkeeping, accounting, and financial planning?

❏ Do you have access to excellent legal advice? Are your attorneys qualified to help with all areas of your business? If not, do you have access to other professionals who are qualified to assist with the more specialized areas of your business?

❏ Are you satisfied with your relationship with your banker?

❏ Are the planning, design, and implementation of your advertising, publicity, and PR efforts all that they could be?

❏ Do you practice advisory etiquette, such as respecting advisors' time and making reasonable requests? Do you call them to share updates on your business as well as to ask for counsel?

❏ Do you consult with friends and family as a way of getting objective viewpoints on how you're doing?

❏ Have you set up systems to qualify the experience and credentials of prospective business advisors?

11. Professional Network

❏ Do you have a system for adding to your network of colleagues on an ongoing basis?

❏ Do you regularly stay in touch with your network? Do you initiate contact often enough to make your relationships reciprocal?

❏ Do you maintain detailed information on key individuals in your network? Do you update this information regularly?

❏ Do you regularly review your roster of contacts to ensure that it's composed of those most important to your changing business?

❏ Are you an active member of a trade association in your industry? Are your business interests represented by your involvement in the appropriate organizations?

❏ Are you in the habit of sharing news and success with your network?

12. Personal

❏ Are you always running on empty? Do you regularly postpone taking time off?

❏ Have you made a commitment to getting enough sleep every night? Do you know how much rest is enough for your needs? Are you factoring in the additional toll that stress takes?

❏ Do you have a regular program of exercise or sport activities? Do you monitor your overall fitness and choose healthy food?

❏ Are you investing in self-education as part of your overall plan for your business? Are you cultivating hobbies or other interests that are non-business related?

❏ Do you remember to nurture the important personal relationships in your life, not just those that have a business focus?

❏ Do you set aside time each week for meditation, reading, or prayer?

❏ Have you calculated the toll that burnout can take on your business? Have you calculated the gain that having energy in reserve can provide for your business?

There's no official rating system or scorecard here. The point is to analyze your business and personal caretaking systems. If you see a lot of Ns next to the boxes in these lists, it's time to sit down and reevaluate where you are and where you're going. The first important step is to be aware.

As you tackle the challenges of expanding your business, remember to check your status in these areas on a regular basis. Once you know what's working and what isn't, you'll be able to change those Ns to Ys and be much better prepared to chart a path to ongoing business success.

Chapter 44

Pace Yourself

A colleague of mine, Annelie Chapman, is a top-level competitive cyclist who used to race on the U.S. national team. Over lunch one day, we got to chatting about the similarities between our two careers, and how the lessons Annelie learned as a competitive cyclist are very appropriate for entrepreneurs. According to Annelie, there are two breeds of professional cyclists, pacers and sprinters. The distinction is made in part by genetics—body type and muscle development. But the other factor—what you do with what you're given at birth—is equally important. Either or both can determine champions.

Smart Strategy

Recognize that, as an entrepreneur, you need to be at different energy levels at various times in your life. You must appropriately align yourself with associates, colleagues, and friends to keep yourself on track.

Whereas pacers win races by setting a deliberate, steady pace, maintaining a constant speed and focus, unswayed by the gains others make at faster speeds, a sprinter's strategy is to explode in short bursts of very high energy at strategic times during the race.

Go the Distance

What occurred to me while listening to Annelie define these two types of athlete was that most entrepreneurs I know fall into the sprinter category, but not for short bursts that are strategically timed; rather, they try to maintain that pace *all* the time. Athletes know this is impossible, even dangerous to their "business tools"—their bodies. Yet most small business owners push themselves every day to perform at this peak pace. This strategy is about learning the power of both pacing and sprinting, and knowing when to use which.

On cycling teams the two types ride together, to create a synergy: Pacers keep sprinters from burning themselves out, so they'll have enough energy to finish the race, and sprinters push pacers to put forth a little more effort and increase their overall speed. The result is a balanced, winning team.

How can you put this sensible and successful strategy to work as you expand your business? First, determine which type of "racer" you are in this entrepreneurial journey. Are you the classic full-tilt sprinter trying to maintain a rapid pace all day, every day? Or are you a pacer who maintains a slower, steadier rate, but sometimes slows and needs a boost to get you moving faster when you really have to?

A successful implementation of this strategy is to recognize that, as an entrepreneur, you need to be at different energy levels at various times in your life. You must appropriately align yourself with associates, colleagues, and friends to keep you on track. If you're a sprinter headed for burnout, look to one of your pacer-type colleagues who can show you the benefits of structuring your work and setting a pace to prevent the exhausting energy drain caused by experiencing repeated cycles of peaks and valleys. If you're a pacer, get behind a faster-moving colleague now and then to get energized to finish a project or implement a new program.

Chart Your Own Course

Most small business owners, when asked who their competitors are, will spout names of individuals or companies that always seem to be turning up, vying for the same clientele, the same market niche.

Without question, it's important to know who is competing against you in the marketplace and how your companies compare. But it's a mistake to become so wrapped up in *reacting* to a competitor rather than charting your own course that you put yourself always in the position of follower, never leader. Remember: pacing *and* sprinting.

This is an issue I've raised before in the discussions of other strategies: the need to stay proactive. I can't stress the importance of this advice enough. If you are too often *reactive,* you become your own fiercest competitor. Instead, you must stay focused on your strengths and define what you bring to the marketplace that is unique. At the same time, you must have systems designed so you can deliver your unique capabilities repeatedly. When you have these elements in place, powerful results occur: You excel naturally, and the threat from external competition diminishes because no one can duplicate your one-of-a-kind offering. Let others imitate *you,* not the other way around.

Shifting your perspective in this way relates directly to expanding your business. Freed from the stress of always trying to catch or surpass your competitors, you begin to measure wisely—and more accurately—your company's progress on *your* terms.

Take Action

1. How do you run the entrepreneurial race? As either a pacer or sprinter? Does it work for you, or do you find you can't go the distance at your speed?

2. As you expand your business, consider implementing both pacer and sprinter strategies at appropriate times, either on your own or with the help of a colleague who has a contrasting style. In what ways would you benefit from adopting a contrasting business style?

3. Ask yourself whether you primarily chase or lead your competitors. If it's the former, it's time to refocus your energy and take a proactive stance.

Chapter 45

Be More than Your Business

The growth path of many solo businesses follows a similar trajectory. Led by a passion or skills in a particular area, entrepreneurs find some customers and juggle multiple tasks while getting a foothold in the market. Then they work long hours trying to keep it all going. Along the way, they may outsource activities such as bookkeeping, create virtual partnerships to extend capabilities, or hire freelance or part-time assistants. But as time goes on, more and more they see less and less distinction between themselves and their companies. Chances are they're hearing about it, too, from friends and family who are feeling (justifiably) neglected.

Simply, these business owners have reached the fork in the road. Exhausted, they finally have to accept:

✓ There are only so many hours in a day.
✓ They don't have the skill sets to take on every project that comes their way.
✓ Their cash flow must be adequate to support product or service development and delivery.
✓ They're sick of working nearly every waking hour.

That boundless and seemingly endless energy eventually gives way to the bone-weariness of the struggle.

Split the Difference

At this juncture, entrepreneurs must ask—and answer—two crucial questions. The first, which we discussed in Chapter 40 as we began this section on expansion strategies, is: "How big do I want this company to become?" The second is more personal and more difficult to answer, and so is often not addressed: "What is the distinction between me and my company?" Though most small business owners have some idea of what they want to accomplish with their ventures, even if it's just a vague notion of growth, too few take the time to clearly define what—if anything—separates them from their companies.

Smart Strategy

If a company and its owner are to flourish, there must be a balance between the self and the company. This can only come from the healthy distancing of yourself from your business.

This is particularly true in solo businesses, where the individual *is* the firm. In an effort to keep up, the boundary between the entrepreneur's life and his or her work often narrows until it merges entirely. This union can have negative—even disastrous—results for both the individual and the company, because all business has become personal and the personal has become nonexistent. Because the two spheres have become one and the same, the business owner has lost the perspective necessary to make wise decisions.

Perhaps you're still at that stage in your professional growth where the exhilaration of your new venture is necessarily the most important thing in your life. If so, as you read this you're probably saying, "But I *want* my personal and professional selves to intersect, to overlap!" Don't misunderstand. I know it's important to have meaningful work, and I know the thrill of pouring one's body, mind, and soul into a dream, to make a vision a reality. My point is, if a company and its owner are to flourish, it's equally important to maintain balance and perspective. This can only come from the healthy distancing of yourself from your business.

Shift Your Mindset

The separation begins with your mindset. You must delineate where your business responsibilities begin and end and what you need to leave at the office, not only to meet your personal obligations but to give your mind and body regeneration time. Here are 10 techniques to help you establish this distinction:

1. Treat yourself as an employee of your company—even if your firm consists only of you.

2. View your company as a separate entity of which you just happen to be president, owner, principal, or holder of another titled position. Introduce yourself as such.

3. Make every action in the name of the company (for example, signing correspondence, negotiating, and so forth).

4. If you describe yourself as a freelancer, depending on your profession, consider an alternate term—perhaps free agent or independent professional. In a number of industries, "freelancer" translates to "temporary and uncommitted," when what you are is solid and stable.

5. Pay yourself on a regular basis, not just when your clients pay you and you've written checks to cover all your outside obligations.

6. When you make decisions, first consider their long-range impact on the company before you evaluate your personal involvement and well-being.

7. Consider incorporating. This establishes your company as a separate legal entity, which may help you make the mental shift. But consult with your attorney and financial professionals beforehand to weigh the benefits and potential drawbacks of taking this important step.

8. As I've mentioned several times throughout the book, meet with your advisors on a regular basis.

9. Operate as a professional. Install a separate phone line and a dedicated fax line for your company (particularly if you're a home-based business). Set up a separate business checking account and maintain good financial records.

10. Establish—and try to keep—regular business hours. Abandon your thinking that taking time off is unproductive. If necessary, plan structured leisure activities so you won't be lured back to the office.

As you direct your company through growth and expansion, it helps to stop and assess your progress on a regular basis. Aldonna Ambler, a respected management consultant based in Hammonton, New Jersey, who guides entrepreneurial companies through fast-track growth, suggests that all small businesses hold regular staff meetings. Even one-person firms, she says, can do this by setting up two or more empty chairs. As various issues are raised, the individual entrepreneur moves from chair to chair and offers viewpoints from the various positions he or she fills in the company. Don't laugh. I know this exercise may sound straight out of a psychology class case study on multiple personalities, but I promise you it can yield remarkable results. Ambler explains: "The physical action of changing chairs forces you to consider things from various perspectives. It helps you uncover new ideas, and takes your thinking to higher levels." From my experience, it takes your business to higher levels, too. Try it, you'll like it.

Take Action

1. If you work alone, conduct a meeting with yourself—in all your guises. If you have trouble doing this, you probably have trouble separating yourself from your business, too.

2. Think whether friends and/or family have been saying lately that they never see you, or that you seem to be in another world when they talk to you. Be honest. These are sure signs of immersion in your business persona.

3. Review the ways your business and personal images and actions can and should be further separated.

MOMENTUM
STRATEGIES

Chapter 46

Maintain Your Focus

Entrepreneurs, in general, are great at beginnings. We love to launch projects, products, and programs and become energized by their potential. But as soon as those projects, products, and programs are under way, a lot of us get bored. Restless. Itching to start something new again.

The word *focus* puts some small business owners off, because they interpret it to mean discipline—the sit-down-for-as-long-as-it-takes-to-get-it-done syndrome. But focus isn't a form of discipline, or an evil twin of creativity. Focus allows you to follow through on your plan or project. Focused time can be—should be—very rewarding time. To focus means to shut out distractions and perform the work at hand. It's not about applying brute force to achieve results.

Focusing isn't about burning yourself out, either. The amount of time you can work effectively on a given task will vary from person to person and from day to day. For example, a film editor I know focuses for what she calls "informed periods of time," by which she means she monitors her attention span on a given project. When she notices her mind wandering, she stops, works on another project, or takes a break entirely from work. As she says, "I maintain my focus by letting go of it from time to time."

Harness Your Energy

The power of focus is apparent in the world around us. Nido Qubein, chairman of an international management consulting firm in High Point, North Carolina, and a respected entrepreneur and humanitarian, notes that the impact of focus can be seen in everyday life. He writes:

Steam rising from a boiling pot is unfocused, and fades into the atmosphere. Steam surging through a turbine is focused: It will generate electricity and propel locomotives. Light from an ordinary flame is unfocused and flickers impotently. A laser beam is highly focused light, and it will cut steel. Focus packs real power.

Qubein's examples clearly illustrate this impressive force. He observes further, "If you aren't focused and if your business isn't focused, your efforts are going to diffuse into nothing. To make a difference, you have to become focused."

Qubein understands this power and knows firsthand about making a difference. As a young man, he immigrated to America, learned the English language, and then went on to become the founder of several successful firms, author of more than a dozen books, and winner in 1997 of the Ellis Island Congressional Medal of Honor. His entrepreneurial secret? Focus. Harnessed energy.

Smart Strategy

Remember: Just because you can do something doesn't mean you should do it. Opportunity does not mean obligation.

Will your efforts be a flickering candle that will be extinguished by the slightest distraction that breezes through your day? Or will you harness your energies, with the direction of a laser beam, and be able to cut through the business challenges you face?

Your choice—and results—will be determined by how you view three different aspects of business growth: the notion of "overnight" success, the power of momentum, and the attraction of distraction. Let's take a look at each.

Calculate the Length of "Overnight"

After running my own business for 20 years, my definition of "overnight" success has extended to 15 years. When someone comments on what to them seems like my swift rise to success, I know they're not aware that I worked in the trenches for more than 15 years, paying my dues as I learned the art and craft of growing a business. But what about those individuals who do seem to spring from nowhere into instant success? Like me, probably, many of them have been laying the groundwork for years, behind the scenes, as it were. Remember, plans and ideas are in our minds long before we release them to the public in the form of our products or services.

And what of those few suddenly appearing, very bright stars? Many, as you know, become falling stars just as quickly because they did not lay the groundwork so essential to long-term success.

Tap the Power of Momentum

The first few years you spend developing your business demand phenomenal stores of energy and unflinching commitment. As your company grows, however, it requires a different, steadier energy—momentum. I call it the flywheel effect, reminiscent of the merry-go-rounds on school playgrounds. It takes a lot of huffing and puffing to get them going, but then you can jump on and ride for a while. And when the ride slows down, *as long as you're paying attention,* it takes less effort to speed it up again.

Momentum in your business is made up of your efforts, your reputation, your client base, your systems, and your expanding knowledge base. And it's often more than any one of these elements—it's the synergy that springs from all of them.

Be aware, if you change directions—or start over in a brand-new business—you'll likely lose the benefits of that momentum. So do your homework before you make such a move. I've seen the toll unplanned-for diversions can take. Savvy entrepreneurs understand momentum and gauge their business activities accordingly.

Resist the Attraction of Distraction

As I said at the beginning of this chapter, as an entrepreneur, you're probably attracted to the new—a new opportunity knocking at your door, a new idea buzzing in your head—and the new may look much more enticing than what you're currently struggling to achieve. The challenge is to assess these opportunities and ideas to discover what is compelling and *worthwhile* about each one. Are there parts you can incorporate into your current business? What are the trade-offs in doing so?

For example, let's say you're a gifted communicator who is at ease in front of an audience. One day, someone approaches you and says you should be on the road speaking to groups around the country. You evaluate your interest and assess your capabilities in light of what this person said, then define the commitment it would require in exchange for the return. In the end, you decide that your time is better spent serving your current clients from your local office, and that you'll reserve your speaking talent for client presentations or local service organizations.

As another example, let's assume you hear that one of your competitors has launched a very successful Web site, so you think of creating one, too. After all, you're very talented at design and a technology whiz to boot. But should you invest your company's time, energy, and resources? It depends on your business vision, what other work will have to be put on hold to realize the project, the state of your finances, and other factors. Remember: Just because you *can* do something doesn't mean you *should* do it. Opportunity does not mean obligation.

Master Dual Focus

When you learn to drive a car, you're taught how to be aware of everything happening around you—behind, alongside, and ahead. Similarly, as you grow your business, you must master this same skill: maintaining a dual focus, keeping your eyes on your long-term goals while navigating the day-to-day traffic surrounding you as you "drive" through your daily work. Here are two techniques to help you do this.

Write for the Long Term

For long-term focus, I recommend committing your goals to paper, then posting them where you can refer to them every day. (Recall our discussion in Chapter 7 about using Post-it Notes or 3 × 5 index cards and placing them in a strategic location.) Hang your goals on an office wall, stick them in your wallet, magnetize them to the refrigerator door, or pin them inside the medicine cabinet door. Just put them where they'll serve as motivation and a way to keep you on track. A warning: Your notes and cards can become "invisible" to you after a short time as they blend into your daily environment and you stop seeing them. Rotate them regularly so they retain their motivation power.

List for the Short Term

For short-term focus, you need to break the long-term goals down into manageable, doable bites. You might do this by plotting your focus objectives into quarterly, then weekly and even daily To-Do lists. (Remember the list of the Solo Seven in Chapter 28? That technique is part of your short-term focus toolbox as well.) The key is to eliminate the guesswork and strip out the opportunities for distractions. When you come into the office each morning, look at the list to focus your attention and jump in, rather than wasting the first hour struggling to ramp up.

The ability to initiate action and ideas is without question one of an entrepreneur's greatest strengths. But if we don't stay focused on our target, our energies become scattered, our thoughts become distracted, and eventually our results become diffused. Focus is the tool that keeps your entrepreneurial efforts on target and ready to generate maximum impact. As you build momentum for your business, learn to use it well.

Take Action

1. Think back to a project, product, or program that started off like gangbusters, then faded away. What made it lose steam? Is it worth reviving? What can you learn from that experience?

2. Decide where you'll keep a written list of your goals for easy and regular reference.

3. Locate an image that captures the essence of one of your goals, and display it where you can see it during your workday.

Chapter 47

Refine and Reinvent

Faster than dog years—or more than seven years to one human year: That's the rate at which today's business world is changing, estimates technology expert Richard Thieme, a business consultant, speaker, and author of the online digest *Islands in the Clickstream* (www.thiemeworks.com). "We're going through a looking-glass of transformation that, this side of the mirror, we can't fully grasp," Thieme observes. This powerful sea change means that, depending on how well you adapt your business to this fluid economic environment, you will either be swept away or ride the crest to success. The choice is yours.

This strategy is about turning what may seem to be overwhelming odds against small companies—against *your* small company— into odds in your favor. You don't have to lumber on the seas of commerce like the ungainly ocean liners of the corporate world; you can act as a swift-moving sailboat, responding to shifts in economic currents and the winds of customer demands.

But to succeed in this business climate, an entrepreneur must continually refine and occasionally reinvent his or her company. That maneuverability, coupled with a safety net of diversified income sources, will provide the balance (which I've been talking about throughout this book) that is so necessary to ongoing success.

Hone Your Skills

On the one hand, refining and reinventing may seem like contradictory terms: The first implies a concentrated, directed effort, the other flexibility and mobility. But in the same way ballet dancers and athletes strengthen and tighten their muscles to give them the *power* to be flexible and fluid in motion, so too you must hone your business fundamentals—your skills and talents (often called *core competencies*)—if you are to be maneuverable enough to respond successfully to economic shifts that impact your company.

Smart Strategy

Every business owner can achieve premier market positioning simply by focusing on building a business that showcases his or her true talents and capabilities.

Elevating your core competencies results in three important benefits:

✓ It positions you in the marketplace as a specialist, giving you a competitive advantage (recall our discussion in Chapter 14, "Become an Expert").

✓ It enables you to more selectively target clients who are willing to pay higher prices for your services or products (recall Chapter 25, "Upgrade Your Customer Base").

✓ It frees you to do what you enjoy and do best, and when you're happier and more fulfilled, your business will grow almost of its own accord (we'll cover this in more detail in just a bit).

A consulting colleague of mine, Dan Burrus, a noted technology futurist and author of *Technotrends,* says: "I only do what only I can do." There's so much power in that common-sense statement. By centering his business on that premise, Burrus has positioned himself as one of a kind in the area he knows and loves best. As a result, he stands completely apart from his competition, because no one can duplicate his unique talents and skills.

Every business owner can achieve premier market positioning simply by focusing on building a business that showcases his or her true talents and capabilities. That's what this book is about: Each of the strategies is geared in one way or another to helping you achieve this goal. As a review, let me lead you through some of the essential steps you need to take *as often as required* to refine and reinvent your business for success. This approach is similar in spirit to one that entrepreneurial coach Dan Sullivan, founder of The Strategic Coach, an entrepreneurial development program, calls "finding your unique ability." (My short summary below is a personal adaptation; for a more detailed approach from the concept's creator, check out Sullivan's audio program *How the Best Get Better,* listed in the Take Action steps.)

Pursue Your Passion

Begin by making a two-column list: On one side, put activities you're good at or enjoy doing, and on the other, activities you don't do well or don't enjoy. Now further divide the positive column into two more categories: items you can do well versus those that you can do well *and* that you love doing. There's a big difference between those two, and it's a distinction entrepreneurs don't make often enough. It's sometimes easier to continue doing something just because we're good at it and know we can fill that ever-empty coffer in the process. It takes a greater awareness—and a little more courage—to do what we love.

For example, first on my list of don't-do-well activities I'd place anything requiring spatial awareness. When it comes time to design a productive office layout, or pack product most efficiently in boxes, count me out. I also drive with multiple maps in my car, since I can easily get lost on the way to a client meeting—even if it's only a few miles away! On the other side, I'd list that I'm good at developing marketing strategies, speaking on entrepreneurial topics, and balancing my checkbook to the penny.

Further refining the list, I admit that while I *can* balance my checkbook accurately, and that it brings me some measure of satisfaction to do so, juggling numbers just doesn't interest me that much, whereas spinning out marketing strategies and speaking to entrepreneurs bring me great satisfaction; in fact, they rejuvenate me.

Everyone has unique talents, although most people don't spend enough time uncovering and developing theirs. Sullivan points out that once entrepreneurs tune in to their unique capabilities, they can reach higher levels of success because they'll be focusing on ways to further elevate those exceptional skills to the benefit of their businesses. Spend some time tuning in to your unique abilities and refine your business to reflect those talents. You'll be happier and your business will soar.

Create MIGs

The next step is to stabilize your evolving business. Any veteran entrepreneur will tell you that in business there definitely is safety in numbers. I call these numbers *multiple income generators* (MIGs).

Even though your small business will probably serve a particular niche, that shouldn't equate to narrowing your focus so far that if you lose one client you're essentially out of business. You must build multiple streams of revenue to minimize your dependency on any single revenue source, thereby reducing overall risk. Here are some tips to building MIGs:

✓ *Listen to your customers.* Are they making requests for additional products or services you might offer?

✓ *Broaden your reach.* Attend conventions and other events in your industry to learn about other customers you can serve, or about how competitors are more fully serving their clientele.

✓ *Stay in touch with key contacts.* If they're wise, soloists or small business owners can benefit from the fluctuating job market. Sometimes because they have to, but more often by choice, the nine-to-fivers are changing jobs more frequently than ever. When a contact of yours moves to another company, be sure he or she takes you along. Stay in touch; chances are high that the individual will do business with you again at his or her new company.

✓ *Ask for referrals.* Don't expect your clients to read your mind: If you'd like referrals, ask for them. If you're good, they'll be happy to oblige.

✓ *Say thank you.* I've said this a lot in this book, but that's because I don't believe you can say thank you enough. Get in the habit of following up after a sale or on the anniversary of your first project. This approach can go a long way toward encouraging repeat business.

Raise PIGs

In addition to accumulating MIGs, I recommend you also raise PIGs: *passive income generators*. This amusing acronym was introduced to me by entrepreneur Bill Brooks, the founder of a highly successful sales training firm in Greensboro, North Carolina. It represents a smart strategy for generating revenue through indirect means, and it's an effective solution for small business owners who want to break through the barrier of billing only for their time.

The purpose of PIGs is to free you from the vicious cycle. You know the one I mean:

Get job. $\rightarrow$ Do work. $\rightarrow$ Get paid. $\rightarrow$ Find next job.

The goal is to generate extra revenue for little or no extra time expenditure on your part. Let creativity reign. Here are some PIG-ish ideas:

- ✓ Create information resources—books, audio programs, training systems, templates—that complement your primary work. You create them once and reap the benefits repeatedly.

- ✓ Involve other people in selling your products and services; you create them and let others specialize in the distribution. If your product complements another business, the other company could become your extended sales force, earning a percentage of the sales it generates—a mutually beneficial arrangement.

- ✓ Serve as a clearinghouse for goods or services in a specialized niche. This is the flip side of the preceding idea. Position your business to act as a clearinghouse to a well-defined market for goods or services that can't be found elsewhere. You might create bundles of goods or services from other firms' individual offerings, or act as a reseller for another company.

- ✓ License or lease your products, services, content, goods, or property for use by others.

- ✓ Broker the products or services of others. Act as a general contractor on projects. Using your network of industry resources, act as the go-between and assemble a team of sub-contractors. Or leverage your knowledge of a particular industry—say, printing—and "chauffeur" work for clients successfully through the print production cycle. In exchange for your expertise, you make a commission on the printing.

✓ Form relationships that generate referral fees. Look for opportunities with the potential to generate referral fees for your business. The first place to look is to companies whose services you already rely on and believe in—and to which you find yourself referring colleagues anyway. Ask if the company would be interested in formalizing a referral policy or finder's fee with your business.

PIGs come in all shapes and sizes; to find those that work for you, you'll have to do a careful analysis of your marketplace and your current business. You also need to decide if it fits naturally with your ethics (think through conflict-of-interest issues carefully), expertise, and enthusiasm. Once you have the right PIGs in your backyard (so to speak), they can go to work for you, bringing an increased return on your investment of time and energy.

Take Action

1. Refine your understanding of your unique ability by listening to Dan Sullivan's audio program, *How the Best Get Better* (The Strategic Coach, 1996). What is it that only you can do?

2. Review your current products and/or services and brainstorm ways to create multiple streams of income. How can you re-invent a current product or service to generate additional revenue?

3. Of your products, service, or expertise, which might you put to work as PIGs for your business?

Chapter 48

Cope with Crisis

The typical entrepreneurial journey is a roller coaster ride of challenges. And while stomach-dropping dips are not always pleasant, we acknowledge they're part of the experience. Every so often, however, true hardship, even a catastrophe, can blindside the entrepreneur and threaten to ruin his or her business if not handled well. Ironically, it's the person in the middle of the tumult—the entrepreneur—who has to lend the stabilizing hand.

This, then, is a chapter to help you prepare yourself for such a crisis, which, if you're in business long enough, undoubtedly will one day raise its ugly head. Think of this strategy as an emergency preparedness test, like those you hear periodically on the radio: "This is only a test. If this had been a real emergency. . . ."

Consider the Chaos

Like an unseen danger lurking in the shadows, catastrophe strikes unexpectedly. It may come in the guise of fire, flood, or theft that wipes out your office and files. It could take the shape of an accident that keeps a key employee away for weeks or months. It may reveal itself in the loss of a major client, a complicated and expensive lawsuit, or another financial mishap that dries up your cash flow overnight. Perhaps most devastating, it might show up as something that prevents you, the business owner, from running your company. This may be an accident or illness that debilitates you or someone in your family. Or, like Baby Boomers all over America, you may be called on to care for your aging parents.

None of us likes to consider such alarming challenges, but by not doing so we put ourselves in even greater danger. If you're not prepared, the chaos can be devastating. But if you do the same kind of forward thinking to approach such a crisis that you do to plan the future of your company, you'll be able to cope and then move on more quickly. In short, do what positive people do to prepare for negative situations: Expect the best but prepare for the worst.

Smart Strategy

The most effective way to handle disruption is to strengthen your systems before *disaster hits. Well-designed operations become the stable backbone that supports your business during shaky times. As a bonus, they improve your overall efficiency when normalcy reigns.*

String a Safety Net

After 20 years in business and dealing with crises large and small, I've learned that the most effective way to handle disruption is to strengthen your systems *before* disaster hits. Well-designed operations become the stable backbone that supports your business during shaky times. As a bonus, they improve your overall efficiency when normalcy reigns (although there are those who would argue, and rightly so, that there is no such thing as normal in a small, growing company). With this attitude of preparedness in mind, I offer you some steps designed to augment the operations strategies covered in Section 4:

✓ *Prepare to autopilot.* Imagine a stranger walking into your office and being able to take control. Obviously this isn't totally feasible, but chances are you can establish systems—documented in writing—that would enable someone else to sustain your business in your absence. The bonus of taking this action: In crafting the documentation, you'll analyze your activities and discover new ways to do tasks more quickly, cheaply, and effectively.

✓ *Back up, back up, back up.* Make copies of all your valuable electronic data and paper documentation, store them off site, and update them regularly. Similarly, back up capabilities.

By this I mean you should have at least two people who know how to handle any office transaction or task.

✓ *Create a key contact list.* Who you gonna call? When crisis hits, you'll need to reach out to individuals and organizations for help. These may include, but not be limited to, the company's insurance representative, attorneys, financial advisors, and computer consultants, as well as personal medical professionals. Create a central list for emergency use and back this up as well. Distribute the list to one or two trusted friends, colleagues, or company advisors so they will have it should you be called away suddenly.

✓ *Cover your assets.* Make sure your business insurance is up to date and covers the *replacement* value, not just the purchase price, of your property. Check the policy to see if the business interruption coverage you have is adequate for your growing needs. If you're a mobile professional, make sure you and your equipment are covered while on the road. Talk to your insurance broker and attorney about asset protection coverage to protect your business against lawsuits. Also explore disability insurance; soloists and small business owners often find this coverage difficult to obtain because it is based on your average income level over several years, but more companies are offering policies (see the Take Action section of this chapter).

Be aware that loss may comprise more than tangible items such as files or office equipment. It also might include the following: intellectual property could be stolen; a staff member may leave; a valued independent contractor might return to corporate life; a key client could cancel a project; a line of credit might be revoked. The list, unfortunately, is endless. Expand your notion of business resources so you can be prepared for unexpected adversity.

Regain Your Bearings

In addition to keeping office operations going, it's important to keep *you* going during a crisis. Even though the burden of handling the crisis will fall primarily on you, the business owner, recognize the distinction between yourself and your business (as I discussed in detail in Chapter 45). To cope with this challenging period, here are some proactive steps to take:

✓ *Accept help.* This is not the time to be the Lone Ranger. When people offer their assistance in ways you can use, accept it. And don't be afraid to ask. Your colleagues and friends will feel good about helping, you'll learn something about yourself, and the business will recover more quickly.

✓ *Do nothing.* At least initially. Before rushing headlong into half-baked solutions, take a deep breath and analyze the situation. Get clear on how quickly you really need to act. Some crises need immediate attention; others benefit from a 24-hour cooling-off period.

✓ *Abandon the guilt.* Second-guessing everything you could have and should have done won't help the situation. Accept the current reality and deal with it, free from self-blame.

✓ *Take time for yourself.* Periods of crisis are physically and emotionally draining. Take time to pamper yourself and escape: Take a couple hours off for a massage, a round of golf, or an afternoon movie with a super-size box of popcorn. You'll return to the situation refreshed and with new perspective. And don't forget to eat well and get enough rest. As a close colleague once commented: "It all looks better after a good night's sleep."

✓ *Be patient.* Accept that it may take a while to resolve the situation; and, once things are resolved, it will take time to recover. Even after your business has resumed regular operations, memories may sting. Understand that with time the pain will be eased by your hard-earned wisdom.

Being in the middle of a crisis is never pleasant. But once you've come through one trial by fire, you and your company will both be stronger for it. Then one day, you'll be sharing war stories with colleagues, and someone will recount a recent disaster, and you'll lean over and say, "Oh, that's nothing. Let me tell you about the time . . ."

Take Action

1. Do you have crisis contingency plans to maintain office operations? Is there more than one person in your office or in your life who knows how things should run and where important documents, keys, codes, and other data are located?

2. When a crisis hits, who will you call? Update your Rolodex (paper or electronic) and create a master list of emergency contacts. Circulate the list to key staff and appropriate friends, colleagues, and advisors.

3. Review your business insurance policies. Check out the following small business insurance resources:

   Aon Enterprise Insurance Services Technical Center Hotline
      for small business customers, (888) 781-3272
   Quotesmith, (800) 431-1147; http://www.quotesmith.com

Chapter 49

Learn from Mistakes

T hink back to your last business success.

Now, recall your most recent failure. (Ouch.)

Which one came to mind quicker? Which taught you the most valuable and enduring lesson? I'm guessing the answer to both was: the failure. Painful and frustrating as it may be, in business as in life, failure is a memorable teacher.

I know I won't shock you when I say that every entrepreneur will fail to some degree, and perhaps quite often, along the road to growth and success. It's part of the journey. What's important, however, is how quickly you're able to recover, and how you integrate the experience into your business practices. The choice is yours: Fail with finesse, learn from it, and move on; or let failure defeat you.

Smart Strategy

Any mistake you turn into a learning experience becomes another incremental achievement that you can add to your business scoreboard.

Count Gains, Not Losses

To demonstrate that you're not alone in your stumbles, I'm going to share with you a dozen business mistakes I've made in the course of building my company over the last 20 years as well as the missteps made by some entrepreneurial colleagues. Through them we've learned, and I hope you will, too—if not from our mistakes, then from your own as you travel the rocky road of entrepreneurship.

1. *Didn't ask.* When we think we know it all, we're doomed. Ditto for being afraid to say "I don't know." In one of my first years in business, I had no clue about filing self-employment taxes. My not asking led to some penalties for not filing, but I now know it could have been a *lot* worse.

2. *Didn't listen.* When we ask for feedback, but don't really listen to the response, we're just paying lip service to our commitment to growth. Several colleagues and I warned another entrepreneur about a deadbeat client he was involved with who had stiffed us before. When he ignored our warnings, we knew he was the next to get taken. Unfortunately, he was.

3. *Dove in first, thought about it later.* When you launch into a project, do you sometimes feel you've just leaped off the high dive and halfway down you're wondering if there's still water in the pool? This is a blatant case of not paying attention. In the mid-1980s I started a project, ordered expensive marketing materials, and six months later the only thing left of the venture was $2,500 in printing bills to pay. In retrospect I realize that I should have evaluated the situation before I placed that expensive order.

4. *Tried to wing it.* Spontaneity can be an admirable quality, but it can backfire when a situation requires order and planning. I've learned the hard way—mostly in sleepless nights of worry and wasted time and money—that planning can shave half the time off a project and double the success rate.

5. *Cut off communications.* When people stop communicating, they start interpreting another party's thoughts and actions based solely on their own—a dangerous undertaking. Keep the dialog going, even if it means engaging in some heated discussions. A colleague, frustrated at the lack of communication between her and a major corporate client, chose to minimize any further discussions and just finish the project and move on. The client accepted the work, but my colleague has never heard from that client again. Through

the grapevine, however, she did learn that they had launched several major projects she would have loved to work on.

6. *Ignored my instincts.* If your instincts are telling you this is a three-alarm fire waiting to happen, listen to them. Assuming everything will be fine while you passively watch from the sidelines is a recipe for disaster. While I was working on a PR project, it became apparent that the clients and their ad agency did not see eye to eye. Even though I could tell things were tense and knew intuitively I should intervene, I stepped back to let them work things out. When things ignited, my work—and half my billable hours—went up in smoke.

7. *Moved too fast.* Some projects and processes can't be rushed. If you move too fast, you risk the chance of losing all you've gained. Trying to beat a deadline, one of my design colleague's clients rushed the prototype development of a new product. The designer tried to convince the company to take more time, since new processes and materials were only about 90 days away. The company refused, and a competitor came out six months later with a product that incorporated the new approach. Ultimately, the company lost its entire investment because of its impatience.

8. *Wasn't financially prepared.* Talent, skills, and organization will, for sure, take you a long way on the path to success, but if you don't have the financial stability (or a backup plan) to enable you to follow through, all your plans may come crumbling down quickly. I clearly remember the day several years ago when I needed to have more copies of one of my books printed, but the financial well was dry. I went to the bank for a credit line, but by the time it was approved, I had lost precious time in negotiating a major deal.

9. *Assumed.* From inside our own mental fishbowls, we forget the rest of the world doesn't necessarily see things the same way we do. People and companies have different standards

for quality, meeting deadlines, keeping commitments, and other important elements for success. When my company needed some packaging materials for an upcoming rush order a few years ago, I placed the request with a supplier who gave a date for delivery. When the materials didn't arrive, I called and learned they had been shipped two days late, which seemed perfectly normal for the customer service rep I was heatedly talking to on the phone. For me this difference in commitment standards resulted in the partial loss of the order; for the supplier, it resulted in the loss of a customer—me!

10. *Forced the fit.* Sometimes the chemistry just isn't right between people or companies. It's better to walk away than to endure countless hours of frustration and failure. In my early consulting years, I recall trying to complete a project for a manager who took over the work originally begun by a close colleague of mine. The new manager and I never hit it off, and the result was a painful experience for both of us, even though the project was finally completed. Today, I'd probably be up-front with the new manager and strategize a better mutual solution. Back then I was too timid to do so.

11. *Set unrealistic goals/deadlines.* You know how much you can do well in a given period of time, so don't let others dictate your workload or expect you to perform superhuman tasks. That is the quickest way to jeopardize your reputation. It's been a few years since I've pulled an all-nighter to finish a project, but in 20 years there have been many tight deadlines. I recall a project a few years ago that needed two more days of work; but the client refused, and it undermined all the work to date. I now ask—and try to schedule—appropriate timelines. And I always build in some buffer time for the inevitable snafus.

12. *Thought I knew better.* Every situation is unique, and when we forget this fact we can blind ourselves to potential problems. Wisdom is based, in part, on cumulative experience, but every encounter brings fresh opportunity for success—

or failure. My many stumbles have taught me that the quick-est way to disaster is to assume "been there, done that." This has been most obvious when I give presentations to groups; although my material may be 70 percent the same, I keep in mind that each audience has a different makeup. I over-looked this a couple years ago during one speech, and the sleepy and bored faces in the audience taught me never to do so again.

Do I regret these mistakes? In some ways yes; in other ways not at all, because they taught me to do better and thus raised my level of professionalism, thereby making me more successful. They also en-abled me to more deeply appreciate it when things go well!

Treat Success and Failure the Same

I suppose the ultimate lesson I've learned from my mistakes over the years is that success and failure must really be approached in much the same way—that is, as experiences to value and learn from, and as lessons that keep your efforts in perspective.

When you do experience failure, your process should be:

1. Fail quickly—by which I mean don't waste time obsessing about a bad situation.
2. Recover nimbly; bounce back as fast as you can.
3. Learn from the experience; really assimilate the lesson and add it to your knowledge base.
4. Accept that failure is a natural part of every business owner's growth.

Remember, failure is really only failure if you don't learn from it. Any mistake you turn into a learning experience becomes another incremental achievement that you can add to your business score-board. And as you'll read in the last chapter of this book, I believe that committing to a lifetime of learning is the only sure path to success.

Take Action

1. Think back to your last three business mistakes. Make a chart detailing what happened, then add what the experience taught you.

2. How long does it take you to recover from a mistake? What can you do to improve your rebound time? Learn to separate emotional reactions from your "take action" response to mistakes. Acknowledge the first, but get moving on the second.

3. If you find yourself making the same mistakes over and over, perhaps you need an objective view on things. Call your mentor(s) to get a second opinion on those recent business decisions and choices that resulted in bad feelings, poor-quality work, or low return on investment.

Chapter 50

Commit to Lifelong Learning

For more than a decade now I've been studying what makes entrepreneurs tick and which characteristics contribute to their success. Several common qualities continue to surface. In addition to having a clear vision of where they want to take themselves and their companies, entrepreneurs are invariably self-starters. They do not hit the snooze alarm on life. They know what they want and they find a way to make it happen. Two other entrepreneurial "DNA" success factors I see are an insatiable curiosity and its natural by-product, a commitment to lifelong learning. These ingredients combine in this last strategy to show how you can—really, *must*—create a lifelong journey of personal and professional development.

Smart Strategy

To structure your life and work to support a habit of self-education is to pave the path to all future growth.

You've heard this era called the Information Age. You've probably also heard that the fastest-growing segment of the job market is for so-called knowledge workers. Let's face it, information has become a form of currency in today's economy. So not only will you be better prepared to compete by continuing to educate yourself, my guess is you'll also be a lot happier doing so. After all, learning and growing are a lot more exciting than the alternative.

Learn to Love to Learn

When I say "learn to love to learn," I'm not just playing with words. I'm making a vital point: that learning should be something you approach with energy, enthusiasm, even joy, *every day*. It should not be another task—not even one of the Solo Seven I've asked you to list. Learning, ideally, should become almost innate, something you do as automatically and as easily as you breathe. What follows are some suggestions for instituting lifelong learning practices into your life.

Learn from Resources

Set aside specific amounts of time, energy, and/or funding to explore some of the innumerable opportunities knocking on the doors of today's solo entrepreneurs and small business owners. Don't let the good ones pass you by. Here are three areas worthy of your commitment:

✓ *Earmark 5 percent of your annual revenue for personal and professional development.* Figure out how you learn best—by reading, by listening, or by other means—and find ways to incorporate that process in your life. For example, attend a conference, listen to audiotapes while running errands or at the gym, or read at least two new books a month.

✓ *Focus on one new area.* Remember what I said in Chapter 46 about maintaining focus? It's particularly important when you're expanding your knowledge base—there's so much out there! Set up your learning program so that you derive maximum benefit. For most of us that means making a commitment to mastering one specific area at a time. Let's say you dedicate June to mastering that spreadsheet program you bought and never use, or choose tomorrow afternoon to really learn to make use of all those great capabilities that convinced you to buy that new printer. Or designate next quarter for learning how to create an effective e-mail newsletter. You get the idea.

✓ *Try something brand-new—just for the learning experience.*
Don't become so intent on keeping all the business balls in
the air that you become too timid to step outside your frame
of reference and take a risk. Doing so can bring unexpected
paybacks—and lead you straight into your future. For example, about 10 years ago I launched a small mail-order project
to sell a set of sample sheets of laser printer papers. At the
time, I knew little about mail order. I invested $5,000 in the
project, knowing that if nothing came of it I still would earn
what I called my MBA in direct mail. Ultimately, the project
brought me only a modest financial return, but what I
learned was significantly more valuable than the original
investment. Among other things, I discovered the challenges
of selling a $20 product by mail, the profit limitations of a
single-product company, and what to do when you land an
article in the Sunday *New York Times* and your phone rings
nonstop. Most of all, I learned what's needed to make mail
order work for my business, on my scale.

Learn from Others

Experienced independent professionals know that working solo is
not working alone: We have clients, suppliers, support services, and
the like. So the ROI we gain by learning from others is incalculable.
Here are three ways to extend and strengthen your connections with
the many individuals who make important contributions to your
work and your life.

✓ *Infect your staff with the learning bug.* One of the most
valuable benefits you can offer your staff is your enthusiasm
for lifelong learning. The time, energy, and dollars you
invest in employees—whether they're freelance, part-time,
or full-time—to expand their knowledge and skills helps you
and your business, too. Set aside time and budget for their
training.

✓ *Expand your network.* I'll come back to what I said in
Chapter 23 because it has such an impact on your success:

The strength of your business is directly related to the depth of your network of advisors, colleagues, and friends. Never stop reaching out and making new connections. Some entrepreneurs set specific targets for contacting potential new sources—say, two a week. Others make a point of accepting invitations to business networking events and then working the room. Find an approach that best fits your style, then use it.

✓ *Give as good as you get.* Often we learn the most about ourselves when we're learning about and helping others: We realize we're stronger than we thought; we acknowledge that we're talented and capable; we see how far we've come. So be generous in your support of others. You will be repaid many times over.

Learn from Yourself

Even though entrepreneurs often put their own welfare at the bottom of their To-Do lists, the commitment you make to learning how to become your best is perhaps the most important step you can make to ensure your ongoing business success. Consider implementing the following three approaches to honoring yourself.

✓ *Set aside 10 percent of every dollar you make for your future.* I promise you, you won't miss the money, and it's the best way to make sure you have a financial reserve for your later years. And do it as soon as the funds come into your business! If you have trouble committing to this, ask your banker or financial planner to set up an automatic deduction account for this purpose.

✓ *Silence the critic.* This the most valuable advice I can give you if you're hard on yourself—and that seems to be endemic among entrepreneurs. To put it bluntly: Lighten up. Keep in mind that finished is better than perfect. The world is not going to end because you didn't do everything just right. No, your high standards won't expire from lack of use. And you will be a much saner, happier—and probably more successful—person.

✓ *Take time for personal renewal.* Stop calling it slacking off. You've earned the time off. More to the point, you need it—to replenish your wellsprings of creativity and reserves of energy. Follow the example of the world's most successful entrepreneurs, such as Microsoft's Bill Gates, who take annual "think weeks" and head off to remote locations sans laptops, faxes, and cell phones. Accept the responsibility for caring for your company's most valuable asset—yourself.

Choose the Growth Path

To structure your life and work to support a habit of self-education is to pave the path to all future growth. Dedicate time and funds to learning—through business tools and resources; through your relationships with staff, colleagues, and others; and through time spent with yourself.

As an entrepreneur in this remarkable era of change and opportunity, it's up to you to make this commitment to lifelong personal and professional development. Simply put, when you stop learning, you stop growing.

Take Action

1. Brainstorm something you'd like to do just for the learning experience. Set aside a modest budget, put it on your calendar, and go for it!

2. Share your love of learning with a staff member or colleague by giving him or her a copy of your favorite book, audio program, or other resource—with a personal note inscribed by you.

3. Set aside a few days each year as your "think time," when you have no specific agenda but to reflect on what you've accomplished and where you want to take your business next. If possible, choose a site away from your regular office. Upon your return, turn your plans into concrete action steps with realistic deadlines attached.

As we come to the end of *Smart Strategies for Growing Your Business,* I encourage you to make this strategy of lifelong learning your jumping-off point to continue exploring and implementing all that we've covered in these pages. My hope is that this book will become a long-term business companion, one you turn to again and again as new challenges arise and as you reach new stages in your business development. So, until our paths cross again—in print, in person, or online—use and refine the strategies I've shared in these pages. Your business will be better for it.

Resources

Access to information is one of the important ingredients in keeping your business growing and profitable. In this section I've gathered some of the best small business resources in one handy place for easy reference. Here you'll find details on the books, audio programs, software, associations, Web sites, and other tools listed within the chapters as well as numerous other favorites I've found to be particularly valuable.

These are still only the tip of the iceberg, however. For the fullest collection of small business advice, check out another Working Solo book, the *Working Solo Sourcebook* (also published by John Wiley & Sons), which contains complete details on more than 1,200 valuable business resources.

Associations and Organizations

American Business Women's Association (ABWA), 9100 Ward Pkwy., P.O. Box 8728, Kansas City, MO 64114-0728. (816) 361-6621, phone; http://www.abwahq.org, Internet. Business information and career development resources for women.

National Association of Professional Organizers (NAPO), NAPO National Headquarters, 1033 La Posada Dr., Suite 220, Austin, TX 78752-3824. (512) 206-0151, phone; http://www.napo.org, Internet. National nonprofit association of professionals who offer organization, time management, and productivity services and products.

National Association for the Self-Employed (NASE), P.O. Box 612067, Dallas, TX 75261-2067. (800) 232-NASE, phone; http://selfemployed.nase.org/NASE/, Internet. A watchdog agency for the self-employed community.

National Federation of Independent Business (NFIB), 600 Maryland Ave. SW, Suite 700, Washington, DC 20024. (800) 634-2669, phone; http://www.nfib.org, Internet. Advocacy organization that protects the interests of small business.

National Small Business United (NSBU), 1155 15th St. NW, Suite 710, Washington, DC 20005. (202) 293-8830, phone; http://www.nsbu.org, Internet. Small business association representing over 65,000 small businesses.

National Speakers Association, 500 S. Priest Dr., Tempe, AZ 85281. 602/968-2552, phone; http://www.nsaspeaker.org, Internet. National organization of professional speakers.

Service Corp of Retired Executives (SCORE), a program partner of the U.S. Small Business Administration. (800) 634-0245, phone; http://www.score.org, Internet. Retired business executives provide small business counseling via e-mail and the SCORE Web site.

Toastmasters International, P.O. Box 9052, Mission Viejo, CA 92690-7052. (714) 858-8255, phone; http://www.toastmasters.org, Internet. National organization for increasing public speaking skills.

Audio and Video

How the Best Get Better, by Dan Sullivan. Toronto, Ontario, Canada: The Strategic Coach Inc., 1996. (800) 387-3206.

Insight. Monthly motivational and inspirational audio program. Niles, IL: Nightingale Conant. (800) 572-2770.

Guerrilla Selling in Action, by Orvel Ray Wilson. Boulder, CO: The Guerrilla Group. (800) 682-8385.

The Psychology of Selling: The Art of Closing Sales, by Brian Tracy. Solano Beach, CA: Brian Tracy International, 1995.

Books

99% Inspiration: Tips, Tales & Techniques for Liberating Your Business Creativity, by Bryan Mattimore. New York: Amacom, 1994.

101 Simple Things to Grow Your Business, by Dottie and Lilly Walters. Menlo Park, CA: Crisp Publications, 1996.

101 Tax Saving Ideas, by Randy Gardner and Julie Welch. Kansas City, MO: Wealth Builders Press, 1997.

101 Ways to Promote Yourself: Tricks of the Trade for Taking Charge of Your Own Success, by Raleigh Pinskey. New York: Avon Books, 1997.

201 Great Ideas for Your Small Business, by Jane Applegate. Princeton, NJ: Bloomberg Press, 1998.

301 Do-It-Yourself Marketing Ideas from America's Most Innovative Small

Companies, edited by Sam Decker. Boston, MA: Inc. Business Resources, 1997.

Achieving Peak Performance, by Nido Qubein. Minneapolis, MN: Best Sellers Publishing, 1996.

The Articulate Executive: Learn to Look, Act, and Sound Like a Leader, by Granville N. Toogood. New York: McGraw-Hill, 1996.

Blur: The Speed of Change in the Connected Economy, by Stan Davis and Christopher Meyer. Reading, MA: Addison-Wesley, 1998.

The Business Card Book: What Your Business Card Reveals About You . . . And How to Fix It, by Dr. Lynella Grant. Scottsdale, AZ: Off The Page Press, 1998.

Business Plans That Work for Your Small Business, edited by Susan M. Jacksack, J.D. Chicago, IL: CCH Incorporated, 1998.

The Cash-Flow Control Guide, by David H. Bangs, Jr. Chicago, IL: Dearborn Trade/Upstart, 1994.

Clicking: 16 Trends That Drive America, by Faith Popcorn and Lys Marigold. New York: HarperBusiness, 1998.

Connative Connection: Uncovering the Link Between Who You Are and How You Perform, by Kathy Kolbe. Reading, MA: Addison-Wesley, 1990.

Creating You & Co.: Learn to Think Like the CEO of Your Own Career, by William Bridges. Reading, MA: Addison-Wesley Publishing, 1997.

CyberWriting: How to Promote Your Product or Service Online (Without Being Flamed), by Joe Vitale. New York: Amacom, 1997.

Focus Your Business: Strategic Planning in Emerging Companies, by Steven C. Brandt. Friday Harbor, WA: Archipelago Publishing, 1997.

The Frugal Entrepreneur, by Terri Lonier. New Paltz, NY: Portico Press, 1996.

The Future and Its Enemies: The Growing Conflict Over Creativity, Enterprise, and Progress, by Virginia Postrel. New York, NY: The Free Press, 1998.

Guerrilla Marketing Handbook, by Jay Levinson and Seth Godin. New York: Houghton Mifflin, 1994.

Guerrilla Marketing for the Home-based Business, by Jay Levinson and Seth Godin. New York: Houghton Mifflin, 1995.

Guerrilla Marketing: Secrets for Making Big Profits from Your Small Business, by Jay Conrad Levinson. New York: Houghton Mifflin, 1993.

Guerrilla Marketing with Technology: Unleashing the Full Potential of Your Small Business, by Jay Conrad Levinson. Reading, MA: Addison-Wesley Publishing, 1997.

Guerrilla Selling: Unconventional Weapons and Tactics for Increasing Your Sales, by Jay Conrad Levinson, Bill Gallagher, and Orvel Ray Wilson. New York: Houghton Mifflin, 1992.

Guerrilla Trade Show Selling, by Jay Conrad Levinson, Mark S.A. Smith, and Orvel Ray Wilson. New York: John Wiley & Sons, 1997.

Hiring Independent Contractors: The Employer's Legal Guide, by Stephen Fishman. Berkeley, CA: Nolo Press, 1997.

Home Office Design, by Neal Zimmerman. New York: John Wiley & Sons, 1996.

Home Office: Home Design Work Book, by Sarah Gaventa, Alford Hall, and Monaghan Morris. New York: DK Publishing, 1998.

The Home Office Solution: How to Balance Your Professional and Personal Lives While Working at Home, by Alice Bredin and Kirsten M. Lagatree. New York: John Wiley & Sons, 1998.

How to Drive Your Competition Crazy, by Guy Kawasaki. New York: Hyperion/Warner Books, 1995.

How to Raise a Career and a Family Under One Roof, by Lisa M. Roberts. Moon Township, PA: Bookhaven Press, 1997.

How to Succeed in Business by Breaking All the Rules: A Plan for Entrepreneurs, by Dan S. Kennedy. New York: Dutton, 1997.

Intuition Workout: A Practical Guide to Discovering and Developing Your Inner Knowing, by Nancy Rosanoff. Fairfield, CT: Aslan Publishing, 1991.

The Joy of Working from Home, by Jeff Berner. San Francisco, CA: Berrett-Koehler Publishers, 1994.

Legal Guide for Starting and Running a Small Business, by Fred S. Steingold. Berkeley, CA: Nolo Press, 1997.

The Lessons of History, by Will and Ariel Durant. New York: Simon & Schuster, 1968.

Making a Living Without a Job, by Barbara J. Winter. New York: Bantam Doubleday Dell, 1993.

Managing by the Numbers: Financial Essentials for the Growing Business, by David H. Bangs, Jr. Chicago: Dearborn Trade/Upstart, 1994.

Marketing with Speeches and Seminars: Your Key to More Clients and Referrals, by Miriam Otte. Seattle, WA: Zest Press, 1998. (206) 523-0302.

Market Smarter, Not Harder: An Experiential Journey to Create a Customer-Driven Marketing Plan, by Pamela Larson Truax and Monique Reece Myron. Dubuque, IA: Kendall/Hunt Publishing Company, 1996.

The Master-Key to Riches, by Napoleon Hill. New York: Fawcett Books, 1965.

Maximum Achievement: Strategies and Skills That Will Unlock Your Hidden Powers to Succeed, by Brian Tracy. New York: Simon & Schuster, 1995.

Million Dollar Consulting: The Professional's Guide to Growing a Practice, by Alan Weiss. New York: McGraw-Hill, 1997.

Minding Her Own Business: The Self-Employed Woman's Guide to Taxes and Recordkeeping, by Jan Zobel. Oakland, CA: EastHill Press, 1998.

Money Smart Secrets for the Self-Employed: Make More and Keep More When You Work for Yourself, by Linda Stern. New York: Random House, 1997.

The One to One Future: Building Relationships One Customer at a Time, by Don Peppers and Martha Rogers. New York: Currency/Doubleday, 1997.

Online Marketing Handbook, by Daniel S. Janal. New York: Van Nostrand Reinhold, 1998.

Organizing from the Inside Out, by Julie Morgenstern. New York: Owl Books/Henry Holt, 1998.

Outrageous!: Unforgettable Service . . . Guilt-Free Selling, by T. Scott Gross. New York: Amacom, 1998.

Peak Your Profits: The Explosive Business Growth System, by Jeff Blackman. Franklin Lakes, NJ: Career Press, 1996.

The Perfect Business: How to Make a Million at Home, by Michael LeBoeuf. New York: Simon & Schuster, 1996.

Practical Intuition for Success, by Laura Day. New York: HarperCollins, 1997.

Priced to Sell: The Complete Guide to More Profitable Pricing, by Herman Holtz. Chicago, IL: Dearborn Trade/Upstart, 1996.

Price Wars: A Strategy Guide to Winning the Battle for the Customer, by Thomas J. Winninger. Prima Publishing, 1995.

The Profit Zone: How Strategic Business Design Will Lead You to Tomorrow's Profits, by Adrian J. Slywotzky and David J. Morrison. New York: Times Books, 1997.

Release 2.1: A Design for Living in the Digital Age, by Esther Dyson. New York: Broadway Books, 1998.

The Sales Bible, by Jeffrey H. Gitomer. New York: William Morrow & Company, 1994.

The Secrets of Savvy Networking: How to Make the Best Connections for Business and Personal Success, by Susan RoAne. New York: Warner Books, 1993.

Selling the Dream, by Guy Kawasaki. New York: Harper Business, 1992.

Selling for Dummies, by Tom Hopkins. Foster City, CA: IDG Books Worldwide, 1995.

The Small Business Money Guide: How to Get It, Use It, Keep It, by Terri Lonier and Lisa M. Aldisert. New York: John Wiley & Sons, Inc., 1999.

Solo Success: 100 Tips for Becoming a $100,000-a-Year Freelancer, by David Pearlstein. New York: Three Rivers Press, 1998.

Taming the Paper Tiger at Home, by Barbara Hemphill. Washington, DC: Kiplinger Books, 1998.

Taming the Paper Tiger at Work, by Barbara Hemphill. Washington, DC: Kiplinger Books, 1998.

Tax Savvy for Small Business: Year-Round Tax Advice for Small Businesses, by Frederick W. Daily. Berkeley, CA: Nolo Press, 1997.

Teaming Up: The Small Business Guide to Collaborating with Others to Boost Your Earnings and Expand Your Horizons, by Paul Edwards, Sarah Edwards, and Rick Benzel. New York: Penguin Putnam, 1997.

Technotrends: How to Use Technology to Go Beyond Your Competition, by Daniel Burrus with Roger Gittines. New York: HarperCollins, 1993.

The Future Ain't What It Used to Be: The 40 Cultural Trends Transforming Your Job, Your Life, Your World, by Mary Meehan, Larry Samuel, Vickie Abrahamson. New York: Penguin Putnam, 1998.

What Will Be: How the New World of Information Will Change Our Lives, by Michael Dertouzos. New York: HarperCollins, 1997.

Wishcraft: How to Get What You Really Want, by Barbara Sher with Annie Gottlieb. New York: Ballantine Books, 1986.

Working Solo, by Terri Lonier. New York: John Wiley & Sons, 1998.

Working Solo Sourcebook, by Terri Lonier. New York: John Wiley & Sons, 1998.

Your Money or Your Life: Transforming Your Relationship with Money and Achieving Financial Independence, by Joe Dominguez and Vicki Robin. New York: Penguin USA, 1993.

Zachronyms: Funny Words for Funny Times, by David Zach. Milwaukee, WI: Innovative Futures Press, 1998.

Periodicals

Bottom Line Business, Boardroom Inc., Box 2614, Greenwich, CT 06836-2614. Business news, stories, and information compiled in a handy digest format.

Business 2.0, Imagine Media Inc., 150 North Hill Dr., Brisbane, CA 94005. Reporting on trends and new business models fueled by technology and the Internet.

Classified Communications, Box 4242, Prescott, AZ 86302. (520) 778-6788. Small budget advertising strategies.

Entrepreneur, 2392 Morse Ave., Irvine, CA 92614, (714) 261-2325. (800) 274-6229, phone; http://www.entrepreneurmag.com, Internet. Information and news on and for the small business market.

Entrepreneur's Home Office, 2392 Morse Ave., Irvine, CA 92614. (714) 261-2325, (800) 274-6229, phone; http://www.entrepreneurmag.com, Internet. Information and news for SOHO business professionals.

Fast Company, 77 North Washington St., Boston, MA 02114-1927. (800) 688-1545, phone; http://www.fastcompany.com, Internet. Information and insights on the new leaders and rules of business.

Home Office Computing, 29160 Heathercliff Rd., Suite 200, Malibu, CA 90265. (800) 288-7812, phone; http://www.smalloffice.com, Internet. Information for the home office professional with a technology slant.

Inc., 38 Commercial Wharf, Boston, MA 02110. (800) 234-0999, phone; http://www.inc.com, Internet. Small business news and information.

Self-Employed Professional, Business Media Group, 462 Boston St., Topsfield, MA 01983-1232. (800) 874-4133. Articles and advice for the solo business owner.

Small Business Computing, 29160 Heathercliff Rd., Suite 200, Malibu, CA 90265. (800) 288-7812, phone; http://www.smalloffice.com, Internet. Small business information with highlights on technology.

Success, 733 Third Ave., New York, NY 10017. (212) 883-7100. Business magazine for the entrepreneurially minded.

Winning Ways, P.O. Box 390412, Minneapolis, MN 55439-0412. (612) 835-5647. Motivational newsletter for the self-employed.

Working at Home, 733 Third Ave., New York, NY 10017. (212) 883-7100. Magazine by the publishers of *Success,* for home-based entrepreneurs, telecommuters, and more.

Working Solo eNews, Our free monthly e-mail newsletter for solo entrepreneurs; subscribe at http://www.workingsolo.com or by sending an e-mail to solonews@workingsolo.com.

Software

Access database software (PC only). Microsoft Corp. (800) 426-9400, phone; http://www.microsoft.com, Internet.

Act!, contact management software (PC or Mac). Symantec. (800) 441-7234, phone; http://www.symantec.com, Internet.

FileMaker Pro database software (PC or Mac). FileMaker, Inc. (800) 438-3655, phone; http://www.filemaker.com, Internet.

Now Up-to-Date calendar software (Mac only). Now Software Inc., a division of Qualcomm, (800) 349-4188, phone; http://now.qualcomm.com, Internet.

Taming the Paper Tiger paper management software (PC only). Monticello Corporation, in conjunction with organizing consultant Barbara Hemphill, (800) 430-0794, phone; http://www.thepapertiger.com, Internet.

Web Sites

Sometimes the best way to begin your online research is through one of the popular Internet search engine sites, such as Yahoo (www.yahoo.com), Lycos (www.lycos.com), AltaVista (www.altavista.com), Infoseek (www.infoseek .com), or Excite (www.excite.com). If you prefer starting somewhere more specific, here are some sites that offer information on small business planning, marketing, management, and more.

1-800-My Logo. http://www.1800mylogo.com. Create and promote a corporate identity for your small business.

American Express Small Business. http://www.americanexpress.com/small-business. Small business financial news and information.

At Your Office. http://www.atyouroffice.com. Discount office supplies online.

Business at Home. http://www.gohome.com. Online magazine for owners of home-based businesses.

CCH Business Owner's Toolkit. http://www.toolkit.cch.com. Software and self-help tools for small business startup needs.

The Center for Entrepreneurial Leadership at the Kaufman Foundation. http://www.emkf.org. Supporters of entrepreneurial leadership in the profit and nonprofit sectors.

Costco Small Business Zone. http://www.pricecostco.com. Resources and information for small business owners.

Dun & Bradstreet Information Services. http://www.dnb.com. Financial, credit and collection information.

Entrepreneurial Edge Online. http://www.edgeonline.com. The Lowe Foundation's online small business magazine.

Free Agent Nation. http://www.freeagentnation.com. Information for independent entrepreneurs and free agents from business writer Daniel Pink.

Garage.com. http://www.garage.com. A matchmaking company and site linking inventive startups with venture capital funding.

Idea Cafe. http://www.ideacafe.com. A virtual watercooler for the SOHO set.

Intuit. http://www.quicken.com/small_business. Small business information from the makers of the popular financial software programs Quicken and Quick Books.

iPrint Inc. http://www.iprint.com. Design and order stationery and marketing specialties online.

Kinko's. http://www.kinkos.com. Connecting you to printing services globally.

LTBN (Let's Talk Business Network). http://www.ltbn.com. Online entrepreneurial community and host of weekly radio program for entrepreneurs.

Marketing 1 to 1. http://www.marketing1to1.com. Tips and strategies on creating personalized relationships with customers.

Microsoft Small Business. http://www.microsoft.com/smallbiz/. Small business guidance from the leading software company.

The Mining Company. http://entrepreneur.miningco.com, http://sbinformation.miningco.com. A site collective, with experts in topic areas (such as entrepreneurs and small business) searching the Web for information.

The Edward Lowe Foundation. http://www.lowe.org. A comprehensive online information toolbox for entrepreneurs.

The Sales Doctors. http://www.salesdoctors.com. Sales experts share strategies and techniques.

SBA Online (U.S. Small Business Administration). www.sba.gov. Central clearinghouse of information on federal programs for small business.

Women in Technology International (WITI). http://www.witi.com. Worldwide network of female leaders in science and technology.

Women's Work. http://www.wwork.com. An extensive business resource for women entrepreneurs.

Working Solo Online. http://www.workingsolo.com. Our site of news, information, and resources for solo entrepreneurs and small business owners.

Index

About the Author

TERRI LONIER is the nation's leading expert on solo entrepreneurs. As president of Working Solo, Inc., she advises clients including Microsoft, Hewlett-Packard, Visa, Apple Computer, Intuit, and Seagram's on how best to access and communicate with the rapidly growing small business and SOHO (small office/home office) audience. Her company hosts the SOHO Summit, an annual gathering of top-level executives from organizations creating the programs, policies, and products for this dynamic market.

Ms. Lonier's highly acclaimed Working Solo resources—including books, audio tapes, Web site (www.workingsolo.com), monthly e-mail newsletter, and seminars—offer information and inspiration to thousands of solo entrepreneurs worldwide. (For details, send an e-mail to info@workingsolo.com, or call (800) 222-7656.)

A successful entrepreneur since 1978, Ms. Lonier is an in-demand business speaker on entrepreneurial topics and a frequent media guest. Her work has been featured in *The New York Times, The Wall Street Journal, Inc., Fast Company, Business Week, Fortune,* and other leading business publications as well as on CNBC, CNN/fn, and radio programs nationwide. She was honored as the keynote speaker at the First International Conference of Women in Business in Tokyo.

Ms. Lonier lives in New Paltz, New York, with her husband, Robert Sedestrom.